Contents

Introduction 5

Household Spending Trends 2000 to 2005 7
1. Household Spending Trends, 2000 to 2005 8

Spending by Age, 2005 10
2. Average Spending by Age of Householder, 2005 11
3. Indexed Spending by Age of Householder, 2005 13

Spending by Income, 2005 15
4. Average Spending by Household Income, 2005 16
5. Indexed Spending by Household Income, 2005 18

Spending by High-Income Consumer Units, 2005 20
6. Average Spending by High-Income Consumer Units, 2005 21
7. Indexed Spending by High-Income Consumer Units, 2005 23

Spending by Age and Income, 2004–05 25
8. Under Age 25: Average Spending by Income, 2004–05 26
9. Under Age 25: Indexed Spending by Income, 2004–05 28
10. Aged 25 to 34: Average Spending by Income, 2004–05 30
11. Aged 25 to 34: Indexed Spending by Income, 2004–05 32
12. Aged 35 to 44: Average Spending by Income, 2004–05 34
13. Aged 35 to 44: Indexed Spending by Income, 2004–05 36
14. Aged 45 to 54: Average Spending by Income, 2004–05 38
15. Aged 45 to 54: Indexed Spending by Income, 2004–05 40
16. Aged 55 to 64: Average Spending by Income, 2004–05 42
17. Aged 55 to 64: Indexed Spending by Income, 2004–05 44
18. Aged 65 or Older: Average Spending by Income, 2004–05 46
19. Aged 65 or Older: Indexed Spending by Income, 2004–05 48

Spending by Household Type, 2005 50
20. Average Spending by Household Type, 2005 51
21. Indexed Spending by Household Type, 2005 53

Spending by Household Type and Age, 2004–05 55
22. Average Spending of Single-Person Consumer Units
    Headed by Women, by Age, 2004–05 56
23. Indexed Spending of Single-Person Consumer Units
    Headed by Women, by Age, 2004–05 58
24. Average Spending of Single-Person Consumer Units
    Headed by Men, by Age, 2004–05 60
25. Indexed Spending of Single-Person Consumer Units
    Headed by Men, by Age, 2004–05 62

Spending by Region, 2005 64
26. Average Spending by Region, 2005 65
27. Indexed Spending by Region, 2005 67

Spending by Region and Income, 2004–05 69
28. Average Spending in the Northeast by Income, 2004–05 70
29. Indexed Spending in the Northeast by Income, 2004–05 72
30. Average Spending in the Midwest by Income, 2004–05 74
31. Indexed Spending in the Midwest by Income, 2004–05 76
32. Average Spending in the South by Income, 2004–05 78
33. Indexed Spending in the South by Income, 2004–05 80
34. Average Spending in the West by Income, 2004–05 82
35. Indexed Spending in the West by Income, 2004–05 84

Spending by Metropolitan Area, 2004–05 86
36. Average Spending in Selected Northeastern Metros, 2004–05 87
37. Indexed Spending in Selected Northeastern Metros, 2004–05 88
38. Average Spending in Selected Midwestern Metros, 2004–05 89
39. Indexed Spending in Selected Midwestern Metros, 2004–05 90
40. Average Spending in Selected Southern Metros, 2004–05 91
41. Indexed Spending in Selected Southern Metros, 2004–05 92
42. Average Spending in Selected Western Metros, 2004–05 93
43. Indexed Spending in Selected Western Metros, 2004–05 94

Spending by Race and Hispanic Origin, 2005 95
44. Average Spending by Race and Hispanic Origin of Householder, 2005 96
45. Indexed Spending by Race and Hispanic Origin of Householder, 2005 98

Spending by Education, 2005 100
46. Average Spending by Education of Householder, 2005 101
47. Indexed Spending by Education of Householder, 2005 103

Spending by Household Size, 2005 105
48. Average Spending by Size of Household, 2005 106
49. Indexed Spending by Size of Household, 2005 108

Spending by Homeowners and Renters, 2005 110
50. Average Spending by Homeowners and Renters, 2005 111
51. Indexed Spending by Homeowners and Renters, 2005 113

Spending by Number of Earners, 2005 115
52. Average Spending by Number of Earners in Household, 2005 116
53. Indexed Spending by Number of Earners in Household, 2005 118

Spending by Occupation, 2005 120
54. Average Spending by Occupation of Householder, 2005 121
55. Indexed Spending by Occupation of Householder, 2005 123

Appendix: About the Consumer Expenditure Survey 125

Glossary 127

Introduction

Welcome to the 3rd edition of *Who's Buying: Executive Summary of Household Spending*. This report presents a broad overview of household spending in the year 2005. With this report in hand, students and researchers can gain important insights into consumer spending patterns and how those patterns differ by age, race, household type, region, and other significant demographic characteristics.

Consumer spending is the result of a complex mix of wants and needs, hopes and fears. This mix determines the success of individual businesses and the health of our economy. Knowing how consumers spend their dollars is the key to understanding where our economy is headed. *Who's Buying: Executive Summary of Household Spending* is for those who want to know the big picture of who does what with their money.

Who's Buying: Executive Summary of Household Spending is based on data collected by the Bureau of Labor Statistics' Consumer Expenditure Survey, an ongoing, nationwide survey of household spending. This report presents the average spending figures collected and published by the Bureau of Labor Statistics (BLS). It also presents indexed spending figures, showing at a glance which households spend the most on products and services. This report analyzes spending for the following demographic segments: age of householder, household income, high-income households, age by income, household type, region, region by income, metropolitan area, race and Hispanic origin of householder, educational attainment of householder, household size, housing tenure, earners in the household, and occupation of householder.

The Bureau of Labor Statistics' Consumer Expenditure Survey is a complete accounting of household expenditures, including everything from big-ticket items such as homes and cars, to small purchases like laundry detergent and videos. The survey does not include expenditures by government, business, or institutions. The lag time between data collection and publication is about two years. The data in this book are from the 2005 Consumer Expenditure Survey, unless otherwise noted. For more about the Consumer Expenditure survey, see the appendix at the end of this report.

The data in *Who's Buying: Executive Summary of Household Spending* reveal how American households allocate their spending. The starting point for all calculations is the average household spending data collected by the Consumer Expenditure Survey. These are shown in the average spending tables. The indexed spending tables were produced by New Strategist's statisticians and are based on the average figures. The indexed spending tables reveal whether households in a given segment spend more or less than the average for all households (or for all households in that segment), and by how much. These two types of tables are described below.

• **Average Spending Tables** The average spending tables show the average annual spending of households on each major product and service category in 2005. The Consumer Expenditure Survey produces average spending data for all households in a segment; i.e., all households with a householder aged 25 to 34, not just for those who purchased an item. When reviewing the spending data, it is important to remember that by including both purchasers and nonpurchasers in the calculation, the average is diluted—especially for infrequently purchased items. For universally purchased items, such as food, the average spending figures give a fairly accurate account of actual spending. But for infrequently purchased items, such as new cars and trucks, the average spending figures are less revealing than the indexes.

Average spending figures are useful for determining the market potential of a product or service in a local area. By multiplying the average amount households in Dallas spend on women's clothing, for example, businesses can estimate the size of the women's clothing market in Dallas. The Dallas media could show those figures to potential advertisers as evidence of the local demand for women's clothes.

Note that because of sampling errors, average values can vary—especially for infrequently purchased items. To examine the standard errors, visit: http://www.bls.gov/cex/csxstnderror.htm.

• **Indexed Spending Tables** The indexed spending tables compare the spending of each household segment with that of the average household. To compute the indexes, New Strategist's statisticians divide the average amount each household segment spends on a particular category by how much the average household spends on the category, multiplying the resulting figure by 100.

An index of 100 is the average for all households. An index of 125 means the spending of a household segment is 25 percent above average (100 plus 25). An index of 75 indicates spending that is 25 percent below the average for all households (100 minus 25). Indexed spending figures identify the best customers for a product or service category. Households with an index of 177 for furniture, for example, are a strong market for that product. They spend 77 percent more than the average household on furniture. Those with an index below 100 are either a weak or an underserved market.

Spending indexes reveal the household segments with a high propensity to buy a particular product or service. Householders aged 55 to 64, for example, spend 33 percent more than the average household on reading material. This is a higher index than that of any other age group, making householders aged 55 to 64 the best customers of these products. Married couples with children at home spend 55 percent more than the average household on cereal, making them the best customers of this category. Researchers can use the indexed spending tables to target their best customers.

Note that because of sampling errors, small differences in index values usually are not significant. But the broader patterns revealed by indexes can guide researchers to the best customers.

For more information

To find out more about the Consumer Expenditure Survey, contact the CEX specialists at the Bureau of Labor Statistics at (202) 691-6900, or visit the Consumer Expenditure Survey home page at http://www.bls.gov/cex/. The CEX web site includes news releases, technical documentation, and current and historical summary-level CEX data.

For a comprehensive look at detailed household spending data for all products and services, see the 12th edition of *Household Spending: Who Spends How Much on What*. Each of Strategist's books is available in hardcopy or as pdf downloads by visiting http://www.newstrategist.com or by calling 1-800-848-0842.

Household Spending Trends 2000 to 2005

Between 2000 and 2005, spending by the average household rose by a substantial 8 percent, after adjusting for inflation. In 2005, the average household spent $46,409, according to the Bureau of Labor Statistics' Consumer Expenditure Survey.

Spending surged on a number of items between 2000 and 2005. Not surprisingly, one of the biggest gainers was gasoline. The average household spent 38 percent more on gasoline in 2005 than in 2000, after adjusting for inflation. The average household spent $1,361 on out-of-pocket health insurance costs, 22 percent more than in 2000. Spending on property taxes was up 19 percent, and spending on natural gas increased by 36 percent. As college costs soared, average household spending on education rose by a substantial 31 percent. Households boosted their spending on a handful of discretionary categories. Spending on entertainment was up 13 percent, primarily due to a 26 percent increase in spending on the category audio and visual equipment and services. Behind this gain is the growing popularity of high-priced HDTVs. Spending on food away from home (primarily restaurant meals) climbed 9 percent.

The average household cut its spending on a number of products and services between 2000 and 2005. Apparel spending fell 10 percent, after adjusting for inflation. Spending on household personal services (a category dominated by day care) fell 13 percent because fewer households have day care expenses now that the small generation X dominates families with preschoolers. The category "other lodging," which includes hotels and motels on trips, fell 7 percent as households cut back on travel spending. Average household spending on public transportation (a category dominated by airfares) was also down 7 percent. Spending on gifts for people in other households fell by a substantial 11 percent between 2000 and 2005.

■ Household spending has recovered from the recession of 2001 and the sluggish economy that followed, but nondiscretionary items—such as gasoline, health insurance, and property taxes—are experiencing some of the biggest spending gains.

Households are spending less on some items, more on others.

(percent change in spending by the average household on selected products and services, 2000 to 2005; in 2005 dollars)

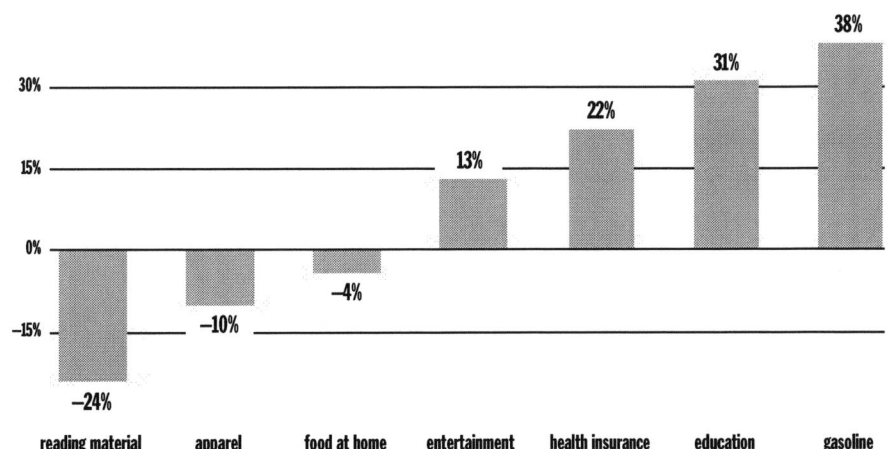

Table 1. Household Spending Trends, 2000 to 2005

(average annual spending of consumer units, 2000 and 2005; percent change, 2000–05; in 2005 dollars)

	2005	2000	percent change 2000–05
Number of consumer units (in 000s)	117,356	109,367	7.3%
Average annual spending of CUs	$46,409	$43,127	7.6
FOOD	5,931	5,847	1.4
Food at home	3,297	3,425	–3.7
Cereals and bakery products	445	514	–13.4
Cereals and cereal products	143	177	–19.2
Bakery products	302	337	–10.4
Meats, poultry, fish, and eggs	764	901	–15.2
Beef	228	270	–15.6
Pork	153	189	–19.0
Other meats	103	114	–9.6
Poultry	134	164	–18.3
Fish and seafood	113	125	–9.6
Eggs	33	39	–15.4
Dairy products	378	368	2.7
Fresh milk and cream	146	148	–1.4
Other dairy products	232	219	5.9
Fruits and vegetables	552	591	–6.6
Fresh fruits	182	185	–1.6
Fresh vegetables	175	180	–2.8
Processed fruits	106	130	–18.5
Processed vegetables	89	95	–6.3
Other food at home	1,158	1,051	10.2
Sugar and other sweets	119	133	–10.5
Fats and oils	85	94	–9.6
Miscellaneous foods	609	495	23.0
Nonalcoholic beverages	303	283	7.1
Food prepared by consumer unit on trips	41	45	–8.9
Food away from home	2,634	2,422	8.8
ALCOHOLIC BEVERAGES	426	422	0.9
HOUSING	15,167	13,964	8.6
Shelter	8,805	8,064	9.2
Owned dwellings	5,958	5,217	14.2
Mortgage interest and charges	3,317	2,991	10.9
Property taxes	1,541	1,291	19.4
Maintenance, repair, insurance, other expenses	1,101	935	17.8
Rented dwellings	2,345	2,306	1.7
Other lodging	502	542	–7.4
Utilities, fuels, and public services	3,183	2,821	12.8
Natural gas	473	348	35.9
Electricity	1,155	1,033	11.8
Fuel oil and other fuels	142	110	29.1
Telephone	1,048	994	5.4
Water and other public services	366	336	8.9
Household services	801	775	3.4
Personal services	322	370	–13.0
Other household services	479	406	18.0
Housekeeping supplies	611	546	11.9
Laundry and cleaning supplies	134	148	–9.5
Other household products	320	256	25.0
Postage and stationery	157	143	9.8
Household furnishings and equipment	1,767	1,756	0.6
Household textiles	132	120	10.0
Furniture	467	443	5.4
Floor coverings	56	50	12.0

	2005	2000	percent change 2000–05
Major appliances	$223	$214	4.2%
Small appliances and miscellaneous housewares	105	99	6.1
Miscellaneous household equipment	782	829	–5.7
APPAREL AND RELATED SERVICES	**1,886**	**2,104**	**–10.4**
Men and boys	**440**	**499**	**–11.8**
Men, aged 16 or older	349	390	–10.5
Boys, aged 2 to 15	91	109	–16.5
Women and girls	**754**	**822**	**–8.3**
Women, aged 16 or older	633	688	–8.0
Girls, aged 2 to 15	121	134	–9.7
Children under age 2	**82**	**93**	**–11.8**
Footwear	**320**	**389**	**–17.7**
Other apparel products and services	**290**	**302**	**–4.0**
TRANSPORTATION	**8,344**	**8,408**	**–0.8**
Vehicle purchases	**3,544**	**3,875**	**–8.5**
Cars and trucks, new	1,931	1,819	6.2
Cars and trucks, used	1,531	2,006	–23.7
Other vehicles	82	49	67.3
Gasoline and motor oil	**2,013**	**1,463**	**37.6**
Other vehicle expenses	**2,339**	**2,586**	**–9.6**
Vehicle finance charges	297	372	–20.2
Maintenance and repairs	671	707	–5.1
Vehicle insurance	913	882	3.5
Vehicle rentals, leases, licenses, other charges	458	625	–26.7
Public transportation	**448**	**484**	**–7.4**
HEALTH CARE	**2,664**	**2,342**	**13.7**
Health insurance	1,361	1,114	22.2
Medical services	677	644	5.1
Drugs	521	472	10.4
Medical supplies	105	112	–6.3
ENTERTAINMENT	**2,388**	**2,112**	**13.1**
Fees and admissions	588	584	0.7
Audio and visual equipment and services	888	705	26.0
Pets, toys, hobbies, and playground equipment	420	379	10.8
Other entertainment products and services	492	445	10.6
PERSONAL CARE PRODUCTS, SERVICES	**541**	**639**	**–15.3**
READING	**126**	**166**	**–24.1**
EDUCATION	**940**	**716**	**31.3**
TOBACCO PRODUCTS, SMOKING SUPPLIES	**319**	**362**	**–11.9**
MISCELLANEOUS	**808**	**880**	**–8.2**
CASH CONTRIBUTIONS	**1,663**	**1,351**	**23.1**
PERSONAL INSURANCE AND PENSIONS	**5,204**	**3,814**	**36.4**
Life and other personal insurance	381	452	–15.7
Pensions and Social Security*	4,823	3,362	43.5
PERSONAL TAXES	**2,408**	**3,533**	**–31.8**
Federal income taxes	1,696	2,731	–37.9
State and local income taxes	534	637	–16.2
Other taxes	177	166	6.6
GIFTS FOR PEOPLE IN OTHER HOUSEHOLDS	**1,091**	**1,228**	**–11.2**

* Spending on pensions and Social Security in 2005 is not comparable with 2000 because of changes in methodology.

Note: Spending by category will not add to total spending because gift spending is also included in the preceding product and service categories and personal taxes are not included in the total.

Source: Bureau of Labor Statistics, 2000 and 2005 Consumer Expenditure Surveys, Internet site http://www.bls.gov/cex/; calculations by New Strategist

Spending by Age, 2005

The average household spent $46,409 in 2005, but some spent more while others spent less. Because spending rises with income, affluent householders spend the most. Householders aged 45 to 54 are in their peak earning years, which explains why they spent 20 percent more than the average household in 2005, the highest level of spending among all age groups. Householders aged 35 to 44 were in second place, with spending 19 percent above average.

Households headed by people under age 25 and aged 75 or older spend the least because their incomes are lowest. Householders under age 25 spend just 60 percent as much as the average household, while householders aged 75 or older spend 58 percent as much as the average.

Householders aged 45 to 54 spend the most overall, but other age groups spend more in some categories. Householders under age 25 spend much more than average on rented dwellings, for example. Householders aged 25 to 34 spend the most on vehicle finance charges and clothes for children under age 2. Householders aged 35 to 44 spend the most on clothes for children aged 2 to 16. Spending on, education, public transportation, and entertainment is highest in the 45-to-54 age group. Households headed by people aged 65 or older spend the most on health care, including the individual categories of health insurance and drugs.

With the early retirement trend coming to an end, look for the two-earner couples of the baby-boom generation to boost spending by householders aged 55 to 64 in the years ahead.

Table 2. Average spending by age of householder, 2005

(average annual spending of consumer units (CUs) by product and service category and age of consumer unit reference person, 2005)

	total consumer units	under 25	25 to 34	35 to 44	45 to 54	55 to 64	aged 65 or older total	65 to 74	75 or older
Number of consumer units (in 000s)	117,356	8,543	19,635	23,835	24,393	18,104	22,847	11,505	11,342
Average number of persons per CU	2.5	2.1	2.8	3.2	2.7	2.1	1.7	1.9	1.5
Average before-tax income of CU	$58,712	$27,494	$55,066	$72,699	$75,266	$64,156	$36,936	$45,202	$28,552
Average annual spending of CU	46,409	27,776	45,068	55,190	55,854	49,592	32,866	38,573	27,018
FOOD	5,931	3,933	5,639	7,359	6,980	6,202	4,163	4,899	3,388
Food at home	3,297	1,917	2,945	4,121	3,807	3,487	2,605	2,967	2,222
Cereals and bakery products	445	273	387	564	499	465	366	405	326
Cereals and cereal products	143	106	138	183	159	139	106	114	97
Bakery products	302	167	249	381	340	326	261	291	229
Meats, poultry, fish, and eggs	764	449	654	963	918	827	569	691	440
Beef	228	149	189	293	283	250	150	189	108
Pork	153	79	121	199	179	167	126	152	98
Other meats	103	59	95	133	117	107	79	92	65
Poultry	134	83	137	170	162	134	85	104	65
Fish and seafood	113	59	82	131	140	132	102	124	79
Eggs	33	21	30	38	37	36	28	30	25
Dairy products	378	214	348	479	433	377	308	344	269
Fresh milk and cream	146	90	139	191	159	139	119	128	109
Other dairy products	232	124	209	288	274	238	189	216	160
Fruits and vegetables	552	298	461	663	614	626	490	553	424
Fresh fruits	182	87	145	218	201	211	170	192	146
Fresh vegetables	175	90	144	202	202	214	147	172	122
Processed fruits	106	69	91	132	114	104	101	106	96
Processed vegetables	89	51	82	111	98	97	72	83	61
Other food at home	1,158	684	1,094	1,452	1,342	1,192	871	974	762
Sugar and other sweets	119	60	91	144	142	129	107	118	95
Fats and oils	85	43	76	99	99	94	71	79	64
Miscellaneous foods	609	381	613	777	688	594	449	488	408
Nonalcoholic beverages	303	186	281	389	366	317	203	238	167
Food prepared by consumer unit on trips	41	13	32	42	47	58	40	51	29
Food away from home	2,634	2,015	2,694	3,238	3,173	2,715	1,558	1,933	1,166
ALCOHOLIC BEVERAGES	426	401	478	511	458	454	248	325	167
HOUSING	15,167	8,940	15,516	18,482	17,258	15,769	11,058	12,474	9,612
Shelter	8,805	5,538	9,491	10,835	10,281	8,686	5,836	6,423	5,240
Owned dwellings	5,958	1,263	5,206	7,936	7,686	6,650	3,903	4,664	3,132
Mortgage interest and charges	3,317	835	3,535	5,169	4,493	3,076	1,060	1,570	542
Property taxes	1,541	287	1,027	1,760	1,940	1,883	1,524	1,659	1,387
Maintenance, repair, insurance, other expenses	1,101	140	645	1,006	1,253	1,692	1,320	1,435	1,204
Rented dwellings	2,345	4,085	4,043	2,473	1,826	1,290	1,492	1,140	1,850
Other lodging	502	190	241	427	770	747	440	619	258
Utilities, fuels, and public services	3,183	1,755	2,909	3,569	3,693	3,427	2,813	3,091	2,531
Natural gas	473	191	396	524	536	521	489	504	474
Electricity	1,155	645	1,047	1,290	1,332	1,255	1,029	1,151	905
Fuel oil and other fuels	142	36	65	137	172	172	195	199	192
Telephone services	1,048	744	1,099	1,208	1,229	1,077	733	845	619
Water and other public services	366	140	302	410	425	402	367	392	341
Household services	801	387	1,004	1,145	668	689	650	677	623
Personal services	322	237	651	666	132	71	113	95	130
Other household services	479	151	354	479	536	618	538	582	493
Housekeeping supplies	611	242	504	716	717	736	534	644	418
Laundry and cleaning supplies	134	63	127	161	154	150	106	122	89
Other household products	320	110	253	385	389	383	271	326	212
Postage and stationery	157	69	123	170	174	203	157	195	116

	total consumer units	under 25	25 to 34	35 to 44	45 to 54	55 to 64	aged 65 or older total	65 to 74	75 or older
Household furnishings and equipment	$1,767	$1,018	$1,608	$2,216	$1,899	$2,231	$1,225	$1,640	$800
Household textiles	132	58	136	155	159	153	91	114	66
Furniture	467	297	537	626	423	527	306	442	168
Floor coverings	56	17	41	55	91	83	28	34	21
Major appliances	223	95	184	247	239	298	204	217	192
Small appliances, miscellaneous housewares	105	68	89	100	124	140	95	120	68
Miscellaneous household equipment	782	483	621	1,033	863	1,031	503	713	285
APPAREL AND RELATED SERVICES	1,886	1,577	2,082	2,365	2,318	1,784	957	1,313	584
Men and boys	440	316	468	598	573	397	191	276	101
Men, aged 16 or older	349	279	353	405	478	359	169	241	94
Boys, aged 2 to 15	91	37	115	193	95	38	21	35	7
Women and girls	754	678	728	927	955	709	448	629	257
Women, aged 16 or older	633	636	587	671	821	650	423	593	244
Girls, aged 2 to 15	121	42	141	256	135	59	25	36	14
Children under age 2	82	97	172	106	52	58	22	31	13
Footwear	320	297	384	397	369	298	159	189	128
Other apparel products and services	290	189	330	336	368	323	137	188	85
TRANSPORTATION	8,344	5,987	8,798	9,945	9,795	8,908	5,171	6,568	3,754
Vehicle purchases	3,544	2,721	3,949	4,407	3,945	3,756	2,007	2,608	1,398
Cars and trucks, new	1,931	720	1,877	2,381	2,160	2,370	1,370	1,761	973
Cars and trucks, used	1,531	1,907	2,001	1,852	1,723	1,296	630	833	424
Other vehicles	82	95	71	175	62	90	7	13	–
Gasoline and motor oil	2,013	1,538	2,123	2,379	2,424	2,101	1,208	1,567	843
Other vehicle expenses	2,339	1,536	2,361	2,669	2,850	2,513	1,594	1,926	1,257
Vehicle finance charges	297	199	402	395	331	289	110	167	52
Maintenance and repairs	671	444	618	727	810	738	542	657	427
Vehicle insurance	913	626	888	1,008	1,159	944	658	737	577
Vehicle rentals, leases, licenses, other charges	458	267	452	539	550	542	284	366	201
Public transportation	448	191	366	490	576	537	362	467	256
HEALTH CARE	2,664	704	1,522	2,272	2,672	3,410	4,193	4,176	4,210
Health insurance	1,361	377	822	1,160	1,283	1,585	2,307	2,352	2,260
Medical services	677	197	399	665	771	979	769	733	805
Drugs	521	99	237	354	494	713	977	956	998
Medical supplies	105	31	63	93	124	134	140	134	146
ENTERTAINMENT	2,388	1,393	2,455	2,765	3,034	2,429	1,593	2,143	1,032
Fees and admissions	588	249	489	753	753	633	416	548	282
Audio and visual equipment and services	888	631	943	1,029	1,046	862	642	797	484
Pets, toys, hobbies, playground equipment	420	184	443	468	539	526	233	327	137
Other entertainment products and services	492	328	580	516	697	408	301	471	129
PERSONAL CARE PRODUCTS AND SERVICES	541	337	504	627	627	550	462	495	427
READING	126	49	89	121	143	167	143	154	132
EDUCATION	940	1,359	779	931	1,769	733	211	256	165
TOBACCO PRODUCTS AND SMOKING SUPPLIES	319	308	307	357	427	336	165	228	102
MISCELLANEOUS	808	263	697	791	949	981	839	1,037	635
CASH CONTRIBUTIONS	1,663	393	1,080	1,735	2,076	1,960	1,889	1,925	1,852
PERSONAL INSURANCE AND PENSIONS	5,204	2,133	5,123	6,929	7,348	5,909	1,775	2,580	959
Life and other personal insurance	381	45	219	397	474	541	403	449	357
Pensions and Social Security	4,823	2,088	4,903	6,532	6,874	5,368	1,372	2,132	601
PERSONAL TAXES	2,408	373	1,809	3,080	3,824	3,088	929	1,226	628
Federal income taxes	1,696	200	1,189	2,190	2,794	2,192	612	862	357
State and local income taxes	534	161	509	739	823	631	97	113	81
Other taxes	177	13	111	151	208	264	220	250	190
GIFTS FOR PEOPLE IN OTHER HOUSEHOLDS	1,091	367	482	903	1,855	1,595	878	1,071	676

Note: Spending by category will not add to total spending because gift spending is also included in the preceding product and service categories and personal taxes are not included in the total.
Source: Bureau of Labor Statistics, 2005 Consumer Expenditure Survey, Internet site http://www.bls.gov/cex/

Table 3. Indexed spending by age of householder, 2005

(indexed average annual spending of consumer units by product and service category and age of consumer unit reference person, 2005; index definition: an index of 100 is the average for all consumer units; an index of 132 means that spending by consumer units in that group is 32 percent above the average for all consumer units; an index of 68 indicates spending that is 32 percent below the average for all consumer units)

	total consumer units	under 25	25 to 34	35 to 44	45 to 54	55 to 64	aged 65 or older total	65 to 74	75 or older
Average spending of consumer units, total	$46,409	$27,776	$45,068	$55,190	$55,854	$49,592	$32,866	$38,573	$27,018
Average spending of consumer units, index	100	60	97	119	120	107	71	83	58
FOOD	**100**	**66**	**95**	**124**	**118**	**105**	**70**	**83**	**57**
Food at home	**100**	**58**	**89**	**125**	**115**	**106**	**79**	**90**	**67**
Cereals and bakery products	100	61	87	127	112	104	82	91	73
Cereals and cereal products	100	74	97	128	111	97	74	80	68
Bakery products	100	55	82	126	113	108	86	96	76
Meats, poultry, fish, and eggs	100	59	86	126	120	108	74	90	58
Beef	100	65	83	129	124	110	66	83	47
Pork	100	52	79	130	117	109	82	99	64
Other meats	100	57	92	129	114	104	77	89	63
Poultry	100	62	102	127	121	100	63	78	49
Fish and seafood	100	52	73	116	124	117	90	110	70
Eggs	100	64	91	115	112	109	85	91	76
Dairy products	100	57	92	127	115	100	81	91	71
Fresh milk and cream	100	62	95	131	109	95	82	88	75
Other dairy products	100	53	90	124	118	103	81	93	69
Fruits and vegetables	100	54	84	120	111	113	89	100	77
Fresh fruits	100	48	80	120	110	116	93	105	80
Fresh vegetables	100	51	82	115	115	122	84	98	70
Processed fruits	100	65	86	125	108	98	95	100	91
Processed vegetables	100	57	92	125	110	109	81	93	69
Other food at home	100	59	94	125	116	103	75	84	66
Sugar and other sweets	100	50	76	121	119	108	90	99	80
Fats and oils	100	51	89	116	116	111	84	93	75
Miscellaneous foods	100	63	101	128	113	98	74	80	67
Nonalcoholic beverages	100	61	93	128	121	105	67	79	55
Food prepared by consumer unit on trips	100	32	78	102	115	141	98	124	71
Food away from home	**100**	**76**	**102**	**123**	**120**	**103**	**59**	**73**	**44**
ALCOHOLIC BEVERAGES	**100**	**94**	**112**	**120**	**108**	**107**	**58**	**76**	**39**
HOUSING	**100**	**59**	**102**	**122**	**114**	**104**	**73**	**82**	**63**
Shelter	**100**	**63**	**108**	**123**	**117**	**99**	**66**	**73**	**60**
Owned dwellings	100	21	87	133	129	112	66	78	53
Mortgage interest and charges	100	25	107	156	135	93	32	47	16
Property taxes	100	19	67	114	126	122	99	108	90
Maintenance, repair, insurance, other expenses	100	13	59	91	114	154	120	130	109
Rented dwellings	100	174	172	105	78	55	64	49	79
Other lodging	100	38	48	85	153	149	88	123	51
Utilities, fuels, and public services	**100**	**55**	**91**	**112**	**116**	**108**	**88**	**97**	**80**
Natural gas	100	40	84	111	113	110	103	107	100
Electricity	100	56	91	112	115	109	89	100	78
Fuel oil and other fuels	100	25	46	96	121	121	137	140	135
Telephone services	100	71	105	115	117	103	70	81	59
Water and other public services	100	38	83	112	116	110	100	107	93
Household services	**100**	**48**	**125**	**143**	**83**	**86**	**81**	**85**	**78**
Personal services	100	74	202	207	41	22	35	30	40
Other household services	100	32	74	100	112	129	112	122	103
Housekeeping supplies	**100**	**40**	**82**	**117**	**117**	**120**	**87**	**105**	**68**
Laundry and cleaning supplies	100	47	95	120	115	112	79	91	66
Other household products	100	34	79	120	122	120	85	102	66
Postage and stationery	100	44	78	108	111	129	100	124	74

	total consumer units	under 25	25 to 34	35 to 44	45 to 54	55 to 64	aged 65 or older total	65 to 74	75 or older
Household furnishings and equipment	100	58	91	125	107	126	69	93	45
Household textiles	100	44	103	117	120	116	69	86	50
Furniture	100	64	115	134	91	113	66	95	36
Floor coverings	100	30	73	98	163	148	50	61	38
Major appliances	100	43	83	111	107	134	91	97	86
Small appliances, miscellaneous housewares	100	65	85	95	118	133	90	114	65
Miscellaneous household equipment	100	62	79	132	110	132	64	91	36
APPAREL AND RELATED SERVICES	100	84	110	125	123	95	51	70	31
Men and boys	100	72	106	136	130	90	43	63	23
Men, aged 16 or older	100	80	101	116	137	103	48	69	27
Boys, aged 2 to 15	100	41	126	212	104	42	23	38	8
Women and girls	100	90	97	123	127	94	59	83	34
Women, aged 16 or older	100	100	93	106	130	103	67	94	39
Girls, aged 2 to 15	100	35	117	212	112	49	21	30	12
Children under age 2	100	118	210	129	63	71	27	38	16
Footwear	100	93	120	124	115	93	50	59	40
Other apparel products and services	100	65	114	116	127	111	47	65	29
TRANSPORTATION	100	72	105	119	117	107	62	79	45
Vehicle purchases	100	77	111	124	111	106	57	74	39
Cars and trucks, new	100	37	97	123	112	123	71	91	50
Cars and trucks, used	100	125	131	121	113	85	41	54	28
Other vehicles	100	116	87	213	76	110	9	16	–
Gasoline and motor oil	100	76	105	118	120	104	60	78	42
Other vehicle expenses	100	66	101	114	122	107	68	82	54
Vehicle finance charges	100	67	135	133	111	97	37	56	18
Maintenance and repairs	100	66	92	108	121	110	81	98	64
Vehicle insurance	100	69	97	110	127	103	72	81	63
Vehicle rentals, leases, licenses, other charges	100	58	99	118	120	118	62	80	44
Public transportation	100	43	82	109	129	120	81	104	57
HEALTH CARE	100	26	57	85	100	128	157	157	158
Health insurance	100	28	60	85	94	116	170	173	166
Medical services	100	29	59	98	114	145	114	108	119
Drugs	100	19	45	68	95	137	188	183	192
Medical supplies	100	30	60	89	118	128	133	128	139
ENTERTAINMENT	100	58	103	116	127	102	67	90	43
Fees and admissions	100	42	83	128	128	108	71	93	48
Audio and visual equipment and services	100	71	106	116	118	97	72	90	55
Pets, toys, hobbies, playground equipment	100	44	105	111	128	125	55	78	33
Other entertainment products and services	100	67	118	105	142	83	61	96	26
PERSONAL CARE PRODUCTS AND SERVICES	100	62	93	116	116	102	85	91	79
READING	100	39	71	96	113	133	113	122	105
EDUCATION	100	145	83	99	188	78	22	27	18
TOBACCO PRODUCTS AND SMOKING SUPPLIES	100	97	96	112	134	105	52	71	32
MISCELLANEOUS	100	33	86	98	117	121	104	128	79
CASH CONTRIBUTIONS	100	24	65	104	125	118	114	116	111
PERSONAL INSURANCE AND PENSIONS	100	41	98	133	141	114	34	50	18
Life and other personal insurance	100	12	57	104	124	142	106	118	94
Pensions and Social Security	100	43	102	135	143	111	28	44	12
PERSONAL TAXES	100	15	75	128	159	128	39	51	26
Federal income taxes	100	12	70	129	165	129	36	51	21
State and local income taxes	100	30	95	138	154	118	18	21	15
Other taxes	100	7	63	85	118	149	124	141	107
GIFTS FOR PEOPLE IN OTHER HOUSEHOLDS	100	34	44	83	170	146	80	98	62

Source: Calculations by New Strategist based on the Bureau of Labor Statistics' 2005 Consumer Expenditure Survey

Spending by Income, 2005

The average household spent $46,409 in 2005. Not surprisingly, households with incomes of $70,000 or more spend the most, 75 percent more than the average household. The highest income group spends the most on almost every product and service category, with a few exceptions such as rented dwellings and tobacco.

Households with incomes below $40,000 spend less than the average household on most categories. One of the few exceptions is rent. Many households with incomes below $40,000 spend more money than they make. The income they report to government interviewers is less than their reported expenditures. These households make up the difference through borrowing, the use of savings, and unreported income.

Income makes a bigger difference in the purchasing of some products than others. Everyone has to buy food, but only those who can afford to do so will buy a new car. Households with incomes of $70,000 or more spend close to the average on such items as eggs, drugs, and tobacco. They spend well over twice what the average household spends on other lodging (a category that includes hotel and motel expenses as well as housing for children in college), mortgage interest, and fees and admissions to entertainment events.

Table 4. Average spending by household income, 2005

(average annual spending of consumer units (CUs) by product and service category and before-tax income of consumer unit, 2005)

	total consumer units	under $10,000	$10,000– $19,999	$20,000– $29,999	$30,000– $39,999	$40,000– $49,999	$50,000– $69,999	$70,000 or more
Number of consumer units (in 000s)	117,356	10,903	15,987	14,712	13,925	11,451	16,956	33,422
Average number of persons per CU	2.5	1.6	1.8	2.1	2.4	2.6	2.8	3.1
Average before-tax income of CU	$58,712	$4,931	$14,853	$24,920	$34,625	$44,659	$59,110	$126,761
Average annual spending of CU	46,409	17,580	21,052	28,361	34,223	40,265	49,029	81,115
FOOD	5,931	2,887	3,216	3,949	4,540	5,238	6,563	9,251
Food at home	3,297	1,833	2,129	2,531	2,630	2,964	3,652	4,706
Cereals and bakery products	445	251	301	332	361	399	489	632
Cereals and cereal products	143	83	99	107	120	125	155	202
Bakery products	302	168	202	225	242	274	333	430
Meats, poultry, fish, and eggs	764	459	493	611	604	669	882	1,060
Beef	228	119	148	170	178	193	284	317
Pork	153	99	105	141	127	137	181	195
Other meats	103	62	65	81	81	97	115	144
Poultry	134	89	90	107	106	117	151	185
Fish and seafood	113	66	59	84	81	94	118	178
Eggs	33	23	27	29	30	31	33	40
Dairy products	378	202	251	290	306	348	421	534
Fresh milk and cream	146	93	107	121	126	144	154	192
Other dairy products	232	110	144	168	179	204	267	342
Fruits and vegetables	552	295	368	434	419	495	573	808
Fresh fruits	182	97	118	136	134	156	188	274
Fresh vegetables	175	96	112	138	125	148	182	262
Processed fruits	106	55	76	82	86	101	106	152
Processed vegetables	89	48	62	77	74	90	97	119
Other food at home	1,158	625	716	863	940	1,052	1,286	1,672
Sugar and other sweets	119	64	81	90	90	98	140	169
Fats and oils	85	49	68	72	68	80	90	113
Miscellaneous foods	609	322	359	458	487	554	668	894
Nonalcoholic beverages	303	179	199	227	257	287	346	415
Food prepared by consumer unit on trips	41	11	10	17	37	33	41	82
Food away from home	2,634	1,054	1,087	1,418	1,910	2,274	2,912	4,544
ALCOHOLIC BEVERAGES	426	176	172	229	333	366	454	733
HOUSING	15,167	6,990	8,197	9,966	11,922	13,532	15,443	25,138
Shelter	8,805	4,275	4,719	5,698	6,787	7,771	8,956	14,723
Owned dwellings	5,958	1,475	1,836	2,533	3,607	4,702	6,320	12,126
Mortgage interest and charges	3,317	645	612	1,062	1,864	2,680	3,677	7,115
Property taxes	1,541	531	678	810	965	1,279	1,556	2,926
Maintenance, repair, insurance, other expenses	1,101	299	546	660	777	742	1,087	2,086
Rented dwellings	2,345	2,634	2,779	2,984	2,971	2,800	2,272	1,382
Other lodging	502	166	104	180	209	269	363	1,215
Utilities, fuels, and public services	3,183	1,699	2,181	2,633	2,874	3,163	3,423	4,404
Natural gas	473	240	337	394	401	447	499	676
Electricity	1,155	673	843	1,000	1,062	1,154	1,216	1,538
Fuel oil and other fuels	142	65	104	130	105	155	142	200
Telephone services	1,048	551	655	832	976	1,059	1,169	1,457
Water and other public services	366	169	241	277	330	348	397	534
Household services	801	217	305	420	502	605	751	1,611
Personal services	322	63	92	157	168	259	295	688
Other household services	479	154	212	263	335	346	456	924
Housekeeping supplies	611	257	347	393	460	546	667	963
Laundry and cleaning supplies	134	75	86	104	110	141	156	179
Other household products	320	122	184	181	234	268	345	526
Postage and stationery	157	60	77	107	115	137	166	258

	total consumer units	under $10,000	$10,000– $19,999	$20,000– $29,999	$30,000– $39,999	$40,000– $49,999	$50,000– $69,999	$70,000 or more
Household furnishings and equipment	$1,767	$542	$647	$822	$1,300	$1,447	$1,646	$3,436
Household textiles	132	27	58	87	117	122	152	214
Furniture	467	134	189	183	320	379	383	969
Floor coverings	56	16	17	26	17	40	48	127
Major appliances	223	52	90	122	130	175	232	436
Small appliances, miscellaneous housewares	105	31	60	57	70	70	102	195
Miscellaneous household equipment	782	282	233	347	647	660	728	1,495
APPAREL AND RELATED SERVICES	1,886	865	871	1,112	1,473	1,440	1,978	3,233
Men and boys	440	203	189	227	312	395	506	740
Men, aged 16 or older	349	159	154	165	227	321	387	602
Boys, aged 2 to 15	91	44	34	62	85	74	119	138
Women and girls	754	328	343	440	570	532	815	1,299
Women, aged 16 or older	633	290	300	360	486	429	695	1,081
Girls, aged 2 to 15	121	38	43	80	84	104	120	218
Children under age 2	82	33	43	72	85	66	79	126
Footwear	320	192	192	228	325	269	352	450
Other apparel products and services	290	108	105	143	181	177	227	618
TRANSPORTATION	8,344	2,491	3,037	5,644	6,185	7,820	9,840	14,296
Vehicle purchases	3,544	866	868	2,460	2,289	3,221	4,423	6,362
Cars and trucks, new	1,931	308	230	1,213	937	1,339	2,317	4,012
Cars and trucks, used	1,531	548	635	1,207	1,337	1,810	1,988	2,174
Other vehicles	82	9	5	39	16	73	118	176
Gasoline and motor oil	2,013	771	1,018	1,454	1,793	2,059	2,390	3,026
Other vehicle expenses	2,339	698	1,019	1,517	1,863	2,228	2,646	3,943
Vehicle finance charges	297	48	83	154	244	316	365	523
Maintenance and repairs	671	252	335	466	537	581	734	1,110
Vehicle insurance	913	279	456	681	772	949	1,092	1,398
Vehicle rentals, leases, licenses, other charges	458	118	145	216	309	383	455	912
Public transportation	448	156	133	213	240	311	381	964
HEALTH CARE	2,664	1,102	1,877	2,251	2,354	2,784	2,738	3,775
Health insurance	1,361	572	1,002	1,203	1,229	1,433	1,476	1,830
Medical services	677	234	348	460	517	708	638	1,151
Drugs	521	249	472	508	528	550	512	625
Medical supplies	105	47	55	79	80	92	113	169
ENTERTAINMENT	2,388	824	963	1,203	1,676	1,950	2,399	4,515
Fees and admissions	588	152	148	219	324	360	497	1,338
Audio and visual equipment and services	888	415	503	590	763	820	955	1,397
Pets, toys, hobbies, playground equipment	420	139	178	241	309	414	453	723
Other entertainment products and services	492	118	135	154	279	357	494	1,058
PERSONAL CARE PRODUCTS AND SERVICES	541	222	282	346	402	497	562	898
READING	126	42	68	79	94	111	127	221
EDUCATION	940	763	303	301	366	494	644	2,123
TOBACCO PRODUCTS AND SMOKING SUPPLIES	319	251	277	326	391	364	372	286
MISCELLANEOUS	808	235	391	412	693	688	985	1,357
CASH CONTRIBUTIONS	1,663	418	705	1,002	1,124	1,235	1,502	3,272
PERSONAL INSURANCE AND PENSIONS	5,204	316	689	1,542	2,671	3,745	5,420	12,016
Life and other personal insurance	381	82	140	168	208	274	340	817
Pensions and Social Security	4,823	234	549	1,374	2,463	3,471	5,080	11,199
PERSONAL TAXES	2,408	−32	49	311	645	1,140	2,083	6,588
Federal income taxes	1,696	−91	−65	85	316	684	1,397	4,904
State and local income taxes	534	3	29	119	232	295	487	1,364
Other taxes	177	55	85	107	97	161	199	319
GIFTS FOR PEOPLE IN OTHER HOUSEHOLDS	1,091	280	416	517	736	631	892	2,318

Note: Spending by category will not add to total spending because gift spending is also included in the preceding product and service categories and personal taxes are not included in the total.

Source: Bureau of Labor Statistics, 2005 Consumer Expenditure Survey, Internet site http://www.bls.gov/cex/; calculations by New Strategist

Table 5. Indexed spending by household income, 2005

(indexed average annual spending of consumer units by product and service category and before-tax income of consumer unit reference person, 2005; index definition: an index of 100 is the average for all consumer units; an index of 132 means that spending by consumer units in that group is 32 percent above the average for all consumer units; an index of 68 indicates spending that is 32 percent below the average for all consumer units)

	total consumer units	under $10,000	$10,000– $19,999	$20,000– $29,999	$30,000– $39,999	$40,000– $49,999	$50,000– $69,999	$70,000 or more
Average spending of consumer units, total	$46,409	17,580	21,052	$28,361	$34,223	$40,265	$49,029	$81,115
Average spending of consumer units, index	100	38	45	61	74	87	106	175
FOOD	100	49	54	67	77	88	111	156
Food at home	100	56	65	77	80	90	111	143
Cereals and bakery products	100	56	68	75	81	90	110	142
Cereals and cereal products	100	58	69	75	84	87	108	141
Bakery products	100	56	67	75	80	91	110	142
Meats, poultry, fish, and eggs	100	60	65	80	79	88	115	139
Beef	100	52	65	75	78	85	125	139
Pork	100	65	69	92	83	90	118	127
Other meats	100	60	63	79	79	94	112	140
Poultry	100	66	67	80	79	87	113	138
Fish and seafood	100	58	52	74	72	83	104	158
Eggs	100	68	82	88	91	94	100	121
Dairy products	100	53	66	77	81	92	111	141
Fresh milk and cream	100	63	73	83	86	99	105	132
Other dairy products	100	47	62	72	77	88	115	147
Fruits and vegetables	100	54	67	79	76	90	104	146
Fresh fruits	100	53	65	75	74	86	103	151
Fresh vegetables	100	55	64	79	71	85	104	150
Processed fruits	100	52	72	77	81	95	100	143
Processed vegetables	100	53	69	87	83	101	109	134
Other food at home	100	54	62	75	81	91	111	144
Sugar and other sweets	100	54	68	76	76	82	118	142
Fats and oils	100	57	80	85	80	94	106	133
Miscellaneous foods	100	53	59	75	80	91	110	147
Nonalcoholic beverages	100	59	66	75	85	95	114	137
Food prepared by consumer unit on trips	100	27	24	41	90	80	100	200
Food away from home	100	40	41	54	73	86	111	173
ALCOHOLIC BEVERAGES	100	41	40	54	78	86	107	172
HOUSING	100	46	54	66	79	89	102	166
Shelter	100	49	54	65	77	88	102	167
Owned dwellings	100	25	31	43	61	79	106	204
Mortgage interest and charges	100	19	18	32	56	81	111	215
Property taxes	100	34	44	53	63	83	101	190
Maintenance, repair, insurance, other expenses	100	27	50	60	71	67	99	189
Rented dwellings	100	112	118	127	127	119	97	59
Other lodging	100	33	21	36	42	54	72	242
Utilities, fuels, and public services	100	53	69	83	90	99	108	138
Natural gas	100	51	71	83	85	95	105	143
Electricity	100	58	73	87	92	100	105	133
Fuel oil and other fuels	100	46	73	92	74	109	100	141
Telephone services	100	53	63	79	93	101	112	139
Water and other public services	100	46	66	76	90	95	108	146
Household services	100	27	38	52	63	76	94	201
Personal services	100	20	29	49	52	80	92	214
Other household services	100	32	44	55	70	72	95	193
Housekeeping supplies	100	42	57	64	75	89	109	158
Laundry and cleaning supplies	100	56	64	78	82	105	116	134
Other household products	100	38	58	57	73	84	108	164
Postage and stationery	100	39	49	68	73	87	106	164

	total consumer units	under $10,000	$10,000– $19,999	$20,000– $29,999	$30,000– $39,999	$40,000– $49,999	$50,000– $69,999	$70,000 or more
Household furnishings and equipment	100	31	37	47	74	82	93	194
Household textiles	100	20	44	66	89	92	115	162
Furniture	100	29	40	39	69	81	82	207
Floor coverings	100	28	30	46	30	71	86	227
Major appliances	100	23	41	55	58	78	104	196
Small appliances, miscellaneous housewares	100	30	57	54	67	67	97	186
Miscellaneous household equipment	100	36	30	44	83	84	93	191
APPAREL AND RELATED SERVICES	100	46	46	59	78	76	105	171
Men and boys	100	46	43	52	71	90	115	168
Men, aged 16 or older	100	45	44	47	65	92	111	172
Boys, aged 2 to 15	100	49	38	68	93	81	131	152
Women and girls	100	44	46	58	76	71	108	172
Women, aged 16 or older	100	46	47	57	77	68	110	171
Girls, aged 2 to 15	100	32	36	66	69	86	99	180
Children under age 2	100	40	52	88	104	80	96	154
Footwear	100	60	60	71	102	84	110	141
Other apparel products and services	100	37	36	49	62	61	78	213
TRANSPORTATION	100	30	36	68	74	94	118	171
Vehicle purchases	100	24	24	69	65	91	125	180
Cars and trucks, new	100	16	12	63	49	69	120	208
Cars and trucks, used	100	36	41	79	87	118	130	142
Other vehicles	100	11	6	48	20	89	144	215
Gasoline and motor oil	100	38	51	72	89	102	119	150
Other vehicle expenses	100	30	44	65	80	95	113	169
Vehicle finance charges	100	16	28	52	82	106	123	176
Maintenance and repairs	100	38	50	69	80	87	109	165
Vehicle insurance	100	31	50	75	85	104	120	153
Vehicle rentals, leases, licenses, other charges	100	26	32	47	67	84	99	199
Public transportation	100	35	30	48	54	69	85	215
HEALTH CARE	100	41	70	84	88	105	103	142
Health insurance	100	42	74	88	90	105	108	134
Medical services	100	34	51	68	76	105	94	170
Drugs	100	48	91	98	101	106	98	120
Medical supplies	100	45	52	75	76	88	108	161
ENTERTAINMENT	100	35	40	50	70	82	100	189
Fees and admissions	100	26	25	37	55	61	85	228
Audio and visual equipment and services	100	47	57	66	86	92	108	157
Pets, toys, hobbies, playground equipment	100	33	42	57	74	99	108	172
Other entertainment products and services	100	24	27	31	57	73	100	215
PERSONAL CARE PRODUCTS AND SERVICES	100	41	52	64	74	92	104	166
READING	100	33	54	63	75	88	101	175
EDUCATION	100	81	32	32	39	53	69	226
TOBACCO PRODUCTS AND SMOKING SUPPLIES	100	79	87	102	123	114	117	90
MISCELLANEOUS	100	29	48	51	86	85	122	168
CASH CONTRIBUTIONS	100	25	42	60	68	74	90	197
PERSONAL INSURANCE AND PENSIONS	100	6	13	30	51	72	104	231
Life and other personal insurance	100	22	37	44	55	72	89	214
Pensions and Social Security	100	5	11	28	51	72	105	232
PERSONAL TAXES	100	–1	2	13	27	47	87	274
Federal income taxes	100	–5	–4	5	19	40	82	289
State and local income taxes	100	1	5	22	43	55	91	255
Other taxes	100	31	48	60	55	91	112	180
GIFTS FOR PEOPLE IN OTHER HOUSEHOLDS	100	26	38	47	67	58	82	212

Source: Calculations by New Strategist based on the Bureau of Labor Statistics' 2005 Consumer Expenditure Survey

Spending by High-Income Consumer Units, 2005

The higher the income, the greater the spending. Households with incomes of $100,000 or more spent an average of $99,128 in 2005, more than double the $46,409 spending of the average household. The Consumer Expenditure Survey examines the spending of households with incomes up to $150,000 or more. The highest-income households spent nearly $126,000 in 2005. Spending surges as income rises, in part because affluent households have more earners—and consequently more expenses—than the average household.

On many products and services, the most affluent households spend four or even five times as much as the average household. On other lodging (motels, hotels, vacation homes, college dorms), households with incomes of $150,000 or more spend more than five times as much as the average household. They spend more than four times the average on fees and admissions to entertainment events, public transportation, and education. The most affluent households spend less than average on only two items: rent and tobacco.

Table 6. Average spending by high-income consumer units, 2005

(average annual spending of consumer units (CUs) by product and service category and before-tax income of consumer unit, 2005)

					$100,000 or more			
	total consumer units	less than $70,000	$70,000–$79,999	$80,000–$99,999	total	$100,000–$119,999	$120,000–$149,999	$150,000 or more
Number of consumer units (in 000s)	117,356	83,934	6,725	9,448	17,248	6,065	4,719	6,464
Average number of persons per CU	2.5	2.2	3.0	3.1	3.2	3.2	3.2	3.2
Average before-tax income of CUs	$58,712	$31,616	$74,523	$88,931	$167,851	$108,670	$132,190	$249,411
Average annual spending of consumer units	46,409	32,444	57,697	65,280	99,128	78,351	88,974	125,934
FOOD	**5,931**	**4,535**	**7,421**	**8,060**	**10,702**	**9,349**	**10,171**	**12,324**
Food at home	3,297	2,698	4,043	4,244	5,261	4,940	5,152	5,630
Cereals and bakery products	445	366	548	578	700	686	699	712
Cereals and cereal products	143	118	185	182	220	216	226	219
Bakery products	302	248	363	395	480	470	473	494
Meats, poultry, fish, and eggs	764	639	894	998	1,168	1,131	1,153	1,213
Beef	228	190	262	297	352	388	337	331
Pork	153	135	174	191	207	200	217	205
Other meats	103	86	127	126	162	155	144	181
Poultry	134	113	155	189	196	180	203	206
Fish and seafood	113	86	142	154	208	171	208	243
Eggs	33	29	34	40	43	38	43	47
Dairy products	378	312	472	484	590	553	572	636
Fresh milk and cream	146	127	180	181	203	195	200	211
Other dairy products	232	186	292	302	387	358	372	425
Fruits and vegetables	552	443	661	704	932	785	941	1,058
Fresh fruits	182	142	218	231	325	263	337	371
Fresh vegetables	175	137	207	225	308	246	296	372
Processed fruits	106	87	127	137	171	158	171	183
Processed vegetables	89	76	109	111	129	118	137	132
Other food at home	1,158	940	1,467	1,481	1,871	1,785	1,787	2,011
Sugar and other sweets	119	97	140	154	191	199	168	201
Fats and oils	85	73	95	104	125	119	132	126
Miscellaneous foods	609	488	817	794	986	908	957	1,077
Nonalcoholic beverages	303	256	366	371	462	467	441	473
Food prepared by consumer unit on trips	41	25	51	58	107	92	90	134
Food away from home	2,634	1,836	3,378	3,816	5,442	4,409	5,020	6,693
ALCOHOLIC BEVERAGES	**426**	**297**	**514**	**610**	**896**	**665**	**718**	**1,235**
HOUSING	**15,167**	**11,172**	**17,849**	**20,505**	**30,563**	**23,641**	**27,393**	**39,358**
Shelter	**8,805**	**6,448**	**10,394**	**11,750**	**18,040**	**13,462**	**16,192**	**23,685**
Owned dwellings	5,958	3,502	7,919	9,507	15,202	11,027	13,969	20,019
Mortgage interest and charges	3,317	1,804	4,811	5,820	8,722	6,331	7,978	11,509
Property taxes	1,541	989	1,972	2,245	3,670	2,707	3,375	4,791
Maintenance, repair, insurance, other expenses	1,101	708	1,137	1,442	2,810	1,990	2,617	3,719
Rented dwellings	2,345	2,728	1,896	1,489	1,123	1,300	1,086	985
Other lodging	502	218	579	754	1,715	1,135	1,137	2,681
Utilities, fuels, and public services	**3,183**	**2,697**	**3,682**	**4,094**	**4,856**	**4,400**	**4,636**	**5,443**
Natural gas	473	393	509	567	801	674	772	941
Electricity	1,155	1,003	1,307	1,436	1,683	1,532	1,568	1,909
Fuel oil and other fuels	142	118	168	211	207	192	191	231
Telephone services	1,048	885	1,263	1,378	1,575	1,464	1,555	1,693
Water and other public services	366	299	434	502	590	538	549	669
Household services	**801**	**478**	**975**	**1,289**	**2,036**	**1,434**	**1,593**	**2,924**
Personal services	322	176	435	649	807	634	608	1,115
Other household services	479	302	540	640	1,229	800	985	1,809
Housekeeping supplies	**611**	**461**	**718**	**811**	**1,158**	**1,105**	**1,144**	**1,216**
Laundry and cleaning supplies	134	115	155	164	198	190	200	204
Other household products	320	232	390	392	664	660	639	686
Postage and stationery	157	115	173	256	296	254	305	326

	total consumer units	less than $70,000	$70,000–$79,999	$80,000–$99,999	$100,000 or more total	$100,000–$119,999	$120,000–$149,999	$150,000 or more
Household furnishings and equipment	$1,767	$1,088	$2,081	$2,561	$4,473	$3,240	$3,828	$6,090
Household textiles	132	98	173	200	239	190	164	340
Furniture	467	268	588	675	1,279	808	1,295	1,709
Floor coverings	56	28	49	66	191	85	124	338
Major appliances	223	138	243	317	580	472	449	774
Small appliances, miscellaneous housewares	105	68	153	171	226	170	193	302
Miscellaneous household equipment	782	489	875	1,132	1,958	1,515	1,603	2,627
APPAREL AND RELATED SERVICES	1,886	1,327	2,147	2,503	4,097	2,998	3,573	5,490
Men and boys	440	315	464	594	939	743	796	1,222
Men, aged 16 or older	349	242	360	470	779	591	672	1,031
Boys, aged 2 to 15	91	72	104	124	159	152	124	192
Women and girls	754	524	833	1,082	1,622	1,236	1,499	2,063
Women, aged 16 or older	633	443	675	880	1,371	1,014	1,309	1,738
Girls, aged 2 to 15	121	80	158	202	252	221	190	325
Children under age 2	82	64	117	122	132	141	119	134
Footwear	320	265	341	379	539	381	486	719
Other apparel products and services	290	159	393	325	865	496	673	1,352
TRANSPORTATION	8,344	5,973	10,761	12,137	16,859	15,108	15,685	19,357
Vehicle purchases	3,544	2,422	4,517	5,093	7,777	7,388	6,940	8,753
Cars and trucks, new	1,931	1,103	1,923	2,969	5,398	4,949	4,797	6,258
Cars and trucks, used	1,531	1,274	2,387	1,943	2,218	2,333	1,971	2,290
Other vehicles	82	45	207	181	161	107	172	204
Gasoline and motor oil	2,013	1,610	2,603	2,935	3,242	3,168	3,214	3,332
Other vehicle expenses	2,339	1,699	3,126	3,456	4,529	3,756	4,443	5,316
Vehicle finance charges	297	207	426	533	556	534	546	585
Maintenance and repairs	671	495	994	984	1,225	1,082	1,249	1,341
Vehicle insurance	913	721	1,154	1,300	1,546	1,372	1,562	1,699
Vehicle rentals, leases, licenses, other charges	458	276	552	639	1,202	769	1,086	1,692
Public transportation	448	242	515	654	1,311	796	1,087	1,956
HEALTH CARE	2,664	2,220	3,278	3,533	4,104	3,782	3,908	4,549
Health insurance	1,361	1,174	1,586	1,735	1,978	1,870	1,897	2,138
Medical services	677	488	1,023	1,001	1,284	1,122	1,195	1,501
Drugs	521	479	545	637	651	594	654	703
Medical supplies	105	79	125	160	191	197	162	207
ENTERTAINMENT	2,388	1,534	3,438	3,225	5,656	3,853	5,613	7,369
Fees and admissions	588	289	747	884	1,817	1,159	1,320	2,797
Audio and visual equipment and services	888	685	1,089	1,219	1,614	1,317	1,481	1,990
Pets, toys, hobbies, playground equipment	420	296	487	632	870	766	842	989
Other entertainment products and services	492	263	1,115	490	1,355	611	1,971	1,593
PERSONAL CARE PRODUCTS AND SERVICES	541	395	652	721	1,098	868	1,077	1,326
READING	126	89	150	177	274	224	232	351
EDUCATION	940	468	1,247	1,247	2,947	2,040	2,100	4,414
TOBACCO PRODUCTS AND SMOKING SUPPLIES	319	332	274	341	260	324	238	216
MISCELLANEOUS	808	589	1,013	1,107	1,627	1,334	1,379	2,081
CASH CONTRIBUTIONS	1,663	1,023	1,689	2,211	4,471	2,781	3,473	6,785
PERSONAL INSURANCE AND PENSIONS	5,204	2,492	7,265	8,904	15,573	11,384	13,414	21,079
Life and other personal insurance	381	208	422	582	1,100	628	740	1,805
Pensions and Social Security	4,823	2,284	6,843	8,322	14,473	10,756	12,675	19,274
PERSONAL TAXES	2,408	743	2,600	3,679	9,736	4,545	6,861	16,705
Federal income taxes	1,696	419	1,788	2,539	7,415	3,195	5,148	13,029
State and local income taxes	534	204	620	849	1,937	1,046	1,340	3,208
Other taxes	177	120	192	292	384	304	373	468
GIFTS FOR PEOPLE IN OTHER HOUSEHOLDS	1,091	597	1,506	1,647	3,007	2,152	2,126	4,449

Note: Spending by category will not add to total spending because gift spending is also included in the preceding product and service categories and personal taxes are not included in the total.

Source: Bureau of Labor Statistics, 2005 Consumer Expenditure Survey, Internet site http://www.bls.gov/cex/

Table 7. Indexed spending by high-income consumer units, 2005

(indexed average annual spending of consumer units by product and service category and before-tax income of consumer unit reference person, 2005; index definition: an index of 100 is the average for all consumer units; an index of 132 means that spending by consumer units in that group is 32 percent above the average for all consumer units; an index of 68 indicates spending that is 32 percent below the average for all consumer units)

	total consumer units	less than $70,000	$70,000–$79,999	$80,000–$99,999	$100,000 or more total	$100,000–$119,999	$120,000–$149,999	$150,000 or more
Average spending of consumer units, total	$46,409	$32,444	$57,697	$65,280	$99,128	$78,351	$88,974	$125,934
Average spending of consumer units, index	100	70	124	141	214	169	192	271
FOOD	100	76	125	136	180	158	171	208
Food at home	100	82	123	129	160	150	156	171
Cereals and bakery products	100	82	123	130	157	154	157	160
Cereals and cereal products	100	83	129	127	154	151	158	153
Bakery products	100	82	120	131	159	156	157	164
Meats, poultry, fish, and eggs	100	84	117	131	153	148	151	159
Beef	100	83	115	130	154	170	148	145
Pork	100	88	114	125	135	131	142	134
Other meats	100	83	123	122	157	150	140	176
Poultry	100	84	116	141	146	134	151	154
Fish and seafood	100	76	126	136	184	151	184	215
Eggs	100	88	103	121	130	115	130	142
Dairy products	100	83	125	128	156	146	151	168
Fresh milk and cream	100	87	123	124	139	134	137	145
Other dairy products	100	80	126	130	167	154	160	183
Fruits and vegetables	100	80	120	128	169	142	170	192
Fresh fruits	100	78	120	127	179	145	185	204
Fresh vegetables	100	78	118	129	176	141	169	213
Processed fruits	100	82	120	129	161	149	161	173
Processed vegetables	100	85	122	125	145	133	154	148
Other food at home	100	81	127	128	162	154	154	174
Sugar and other sweets	100	82	118	129	161	167	141	169
Fats and oils	100	86	112	122	147	140	155	148
Miscellaneous foods	100	80	134	130	162	149	157	177
Nonalcoholic beverages	100	84	121	122	152	154	146	156
Food prepared by consumer unit on trips	100	61	124	141	261	224	220	327
Food away from home	100	70	128	145	207	167	191	254
ALCOHOLIC BEVERAGES	100	70	121	143	210	156	169	290
HOUSING	100	74	118	135	202	156	181	259
Shelter	100	73	118	133	205	153	184	269
Owned dwellings	100	59	133	160	255	185	234	336
Mortgage interest and charges	100	54	145	175	263	191	241	347
Property taxes	100	64	128	146	238	176	219	311
Maintenance, repair, insurance, other expenses	100	64	103	131	255	181	238	338
Rented dwellings	100	116	81	63	48	55	46	42
Other lodging	100	43	115	150	342	226	226	534
Utilities, fuels, and public services	100	85	116	129	153	138	146	171
Natural gas	100	83	108	120	169	142	163	199
Electricity	100	87	113	124	146	133	136	165
Fuel oil and other fuels	100	83	118	149	146	135	135	163
Telephone services	100	84	121	131	150	140	148	162
Water and other public services	100	82	119	137	161	147	150	183
Household services	100	60	122	161	254	179	199	365
Personal services	100	55	135	202	251	197	189	346
Other household services	100	63	113	134	257	167	206	378
Housekeeping supplies	100	75	118	133	190	181	187	199
Laundry and cleaning supplies	100	86	116	122	148	142	149	152
Other household products	100	73	122	123	208	206	200	214
Postage and stationery	100	73	110	163	189	162	194	208

	total consumer units	less than $70,000	$70,000– $79,999	$80,000– $99,999	$100,000 or more total	$100,000– $119,999	$120,000– $149,999	$150,000 or more
Household furnishings and equipment	100	62	118	145	253	183	217	345
Household textiles	100	74	131	152	181	144	124	258
Furniture	100	57	126	145	274	173	277	366
Floor coverings	100	50	88	118	341	152	221	604
Major appliances	100	62	109	142	260	212	201	347
Small appliances, miscellaneous housewares	100	65	146	163	215	162	184	288
Miscellaneous household equipment	100	63	112	145	250	194	205	336
APPAREL AND RELATED SERVICES	100	70	114	133	217	159	189	291
Men and boys	100	72	105	135	213	169	181	278
Men, aged 16 or older	100	69	103	135	223	169	193	295
Boys, aged 2 to 15	100	79	114	136	175	167	136	211
Women and girls	100	69	110	144	215	164	199	274
Women, aged 16 or older	100	70	107	139	217	160	207	275
Girls, aged 2 to 15	100	66	131	167	208	183	157	269
Children under age 2	100	78	143	149	161	172	145	163
Footwear	100	83	107	118	168	119	152	225
Other apparel products and services	100	55	136	112	298	171	232	466
TRANSPORTATION	100	72	129	145	202	181	188	232
Vehicle purchases	100	68	127	144	219	208	196	247
Cars and trucks, new	100	57	100	154	280	256	248	324
Cars and trucks, used	100	83	156	127	145	152	129	150
Other vehicles	100	55	252	221	196	130	210	249
Gasoline and motor oil	100	80	129	146	161	157	160	166
Other vehicle expenses	100	73	134	148	194	161	190	227
Vehicle finance charges	100	70	143	179	187	180	184	197
Maintenance and repairs	100	74	148	147	183	161	186	200
Vehicle insurance	100	79	126	142	169	150	171	186
Vehicle rentals, leases, licenses, other charges	100	60	121	140	262	168	237	369
Public transportation	100	54	115	146	293	178	243	437
HEALTH CARE	100	83	123	133	154	142	147	171
Health insurance	100	86	117	127	145	137	139	157
Medical services	100	72	151	148	190	166	177	222
Drugs	100	92	105	122	125	114	126	135
Medical supplies	100	75	119	152	182	188	154	197
ENTERTAINMENT	100	64	144	135	237	161	235	309
Fees and admissions	100	49	127	150	309	197	224	476
Audio and visual equipment and services	100	77	123	137	182	148	167	224
Pets, toys, hobbies, playground equipment	100	70	116	150	207	182	200	235
Other entertainment products and services	100	53	227	100	275	124	401	324
PERSONAL CARE PRODUCTS AND SERVICES	100	73	121	133	203	160	199	245
READING	100	71	119	140	217	178	184	279
EDUCATION	100	50	133	133	314	217	223	470
TOBACCO PRODUCTS AND SMOKING SUPPLIES	100	104	86	107	82	102	75	68
MISCELLANEOUS	100	73	125	137	201	165	171	258
CASH CONTRIBUTIONS	100	62	102	133	269	167	209	408
PERSONAL INSURANCE AND PENSIONS	100	48	140	171	299	219	258	405
Life and other personal insurance	100	55	111	153	289	165	194	474
Pensions and Social Security	100	47	142	173	300	223	263	400
PERSONAL TAXES	100	31	108	153	404	189	285	694
Federal income taxes	100	25	105	150	437	188	304	768
State and local income taxes	100	38	116	159	363	196	251	601
Other taxes	100	68	108	165	217	172	211	264
GIFTS FOR PEOPLE IN OTHER HOUSEHOLDS	100	55	138	151	276	197	195	408

Source: Calculations by New Strategist based on the Bureau of Labor Statistics' 2005 Consumer Expenditure Survey

Spending by Age and Income, 2004–05

Within age groups, spending on most categories of products and services rises with income. There are some interesting exceptions, however. Among householders under age 25, those with incomes below $10,000 spend the most on education—$2,188 in 2004–05. These young adults are attending college. Their incomes will rise when their schooling is complete and they embark on a career.

Only 11 percent of householders aged 65 or older have incomes of $70,000 or more. The proportion is a much larger 31 percent among householders aged 55 to 64 and peaks at 40 percent among those aged 45 to 54. Thirty-seven percent of householders aged 35 to 44 have incomes of $70,000 or more.

Householders aged 45 to 54 with incomes of $70,000-plus spent the most in 2004–05, fully $83,207. Close behind are affluent householders aged 55 to 64, spending $81,501 in 2004–05. Householders aged 45 to 54 with incomes of $70,000 or more spent 94 percent as much eating out as they did on groceries in 2004–05. For the average household, the ratio is 80 percent. Affluent householders aged 45 to 54 spent fully $4,471 on entertainment in 2004–05 compared to the $2,388 spent by the average household during that time period. Affluent householders aged 65 or older spent nearly three times the average for their age group on alcoholic beverages.

Table 8. Under age 25: Average spending by income, 2004–05

(average annual spending of consumer units (CUs) headed by people under age 25 by product and service category and before-tax income of consumer unit, 2004–05)

	total consumer units under age 25	under $10,000	$10,000–$19,999	$20,000–$29,999	$30,000–$39,999	$40,000 or more
Number of consumer units (in 000s)	8,731	2,943	1,819	1,278	952	1,739
Average number of persons per CU	2.0	1.2	1.8	2.2	2.4	2.9
Average before-tax income of CU	$24,770	$4,656	$14,377	$24,637	$34,609	$64,395
Average annual spending of CU	26,102	13,525	20,812	26,881	32,048	48,051
FOOD	**3,814**	**2,209**	**3,150**	**3,447**	**4,749**	**6,308**
Food at home	**1,885**	**1,028**	**1,645**	**1,861**	**2,198**	**3,059**
Cereals and bakery products	269	153	229	254	349	426
Cereals and cereal products	102	58	82	93	140	168
Bakery products	167	95	146	162	209	258
Meats, poultry, fish, and eggs	465	227	388	426	541	835
Beef	149	71	107	130	189	281
Pork	87	48	84	87	92	137
Other meats	56	25	45	53	60	104
Poultry	92	49	82	85	107	155
Fish and seafood	58	21	46	50	67	119
Eggs	24	13	23	21	27	38
Dairy products	209	109	178	215	243	346
Fresh milk and cream	88	45	73	84	115	146
Other dairy products	121	64	106	131	128	200
Fruits and vegetables	292	162	248	315	310	472
Fresh fruits	90	48	76	95	100	146
Fresh vegetables	88	46	76	97	85	147
Processed fruits	67	39	60	67	68	107
Processed vegetables	48	28	36	55	57	73
Other food at home	650	377	602	651	755	981
Sugar and other sweets	57	39	59	44	61	86
Fats and oils	44	22	49	44	51	63
Miscellaneous foods	357	203	336	368	412	530
Nonalcoholic beverages	178	101	142	181	218	283
Food prepared by consumer unit on trips	14	11	16	14	14	18
Food away from home	**1,929**	**1,181**	**1,505**	**1,586**	**2,551**	**3,249**
ALCOHOLIC BEVERAGES	**453**	**299**	**403**	**422**	**487**	**692**
HOUSING	**8,261**	**4,051**	**6,684**	**9,150**	**11,012**	**14,765**
Shelter	**5,203**	**2,711**	**4,359**	**5,893**	**6,891**	**8,873**
Owned dwellings	1,135	125	429	557	1,396	3,865
Mortgage interest and charges	732	34	182	324	877	2,707
Property taxes	258	83	150	159	238	751
Maintenance, repair, insurance, other expenses	145	13	97	74	281	407
Rented dwellings	3,847	2,294	3,680	5,245	5,310	4,819
Other lodging	222	292	249	91	185	189
Utilities, fuels, and public services	**1,574**	**638**	**1,338**	**1,828**	**2,086**	**2,937**
Natural gas	161	41	107	201	205	366
Electricity	572	250	511	687	757	995
Fuel oil and other fuels	31	2	32	32	31	80
Telephone services	690	309	608	796	924	1,216
Water and other public services	119	37	79	112	169	280
Household services	**328**	**85**	**248**	**370**	**458**	**718**
Personal services	199	22	155	226	276	482
Other household services	129	63	93	144	182	237
Housekeeping supplies	**248**	**152**	**184**	**265**	**313**	**384**
Laundry and cleaning supplies	69	47	52	67	87	108
Other household products	112	72	85	108	131	182
Postage and stationery	67	33	46	90	95	94

	total consumer units under age 25	under $10,000	$10,000–$19,999	$20,000–$29,999	$30,000–$39,999	$40,000 or more
Household furnishings and equipment	$908	$464	$557	$794	$1,264	$1,852
Household textiles	57	34	25	52	52	130
Furniture	271	57	199	273	296	693
Floor coverings	12	4	5	42	6	15
Major appliances	86	22	46	57	167	208
Small appliances, miscellaneous housewares	64	34	43	51	86	128
Miscellaneous household equipment	419	313	240	319	658	678
APPAREL AND RELATED SERVICES	1,472	1,040	1,003	1,438	1,634	2,535
Men and boys	276	166	167	181	283	616
Men, aged 16 or older	247	159	149	140	224	569
Boys, aged 2 to 15	29	6	19	42	60	46
Women and girls	633	472	420	619	684	1,061
Women, aged 16 or older	597	460	396	562	642	1,000
Girls, aged 2 to 15	35	12	24	57	42	61
Children under age 2	100	60	89	119	100	155
Footwear	277	245	170	290	344	391
Other apparel products and services	186	97	157	230	222	312
TRANSPORTATION	5,376	1,865	4,216	6,436	6,578	11,085
Vehicle purchases	2,428	548	1,855	3,274	2,412	5,596
Cars and trucks, new	622	47	244	1,219	704	1,507
Cars and trucks, used	1,728	481	1,591	1,807	1,694	3,940
Other vehicles	78	19	47	248	14	149
Gasoline and motor oil	1,321	677	1,129	1,441	1,746	2,288
Other vehicle expenses	1,425	515	1,075	1,579	2,109	2,839
Vehicle finance charges	170	27	95	179	248	441
Maintenance and repairs	423	234	398	484	597	626
Vehicle insurance	577	127	403	742	868	1,242
Vehicle rentals, leases, licenses, other charges	254	127	179	174	396	530
Public transportation	202	125	156	141	311	362
HEALTH CARE	668	193	362	733	889	1,607
Health insurance	341	74	145	393	511	868
Medical services	187	46	125	225	180	467
Drugs	108	61	61	93	152	214
Medical supplies	31	12	31	21	46	58
ENTERTAINMENT	1,275	721	1,172	1,288	1,585	2,097
Fees and admissions	262	212	210	227	293	408
Audio and visual equipment and services	563	299	461	636	708	981
Pets, toys, hobbies, playground equipment	201	88	164	168	437	296
Other entertainment products and services	249	122	337	257	147	412
PERSONAL CARE PRODUCTS AND SERVICES	335	230	285	303	350	557
READING	50	36	44	47	58	76
EDUCATION	1,609	2,188	1,781	879	714	1,472
TOBACCO PRODUCTS AND SMOKING SUPPLIES	269	129	269	360	365	382
MISCELLANEOUS	279	195	252	243	306	470
CASH CONTRIBUTIONS	343	108	254	326	506	760
PERSONAL INSURANCE AND PENSIONS	1,900	261	937	1,809	2,817	5,246
Life and other personal insurance	37	3	26	35	66	94
Pensions and Social Security	1,862	258	911	1,774	2,751	5,152
PERSONAL TAXES	356	–23	–30	229	506	1,413
Federal income taxes	203	–32	–85	52	280	971
State and local income taxes	142	8	53	166	208	405
Other taxes	12	2	2	10	18	37
GIFTS FOR PEOPLE IN OTHER HOUSEHOLDS	409	229	384	388	445	682

Note: Spending by category will not add to total spending because gift spending is also included in the preceding product and service categories and personal taxes are not included in the total.
Source: Bureau of Labor Statistics, 2004 and 2005 Consumer Expenditure Surveys, Internet site http://www.bls.gov/cex/; calculations by New Strategist

Table 9. Under age 25: Indexed spending by income, 2004–05

(indexed average annual spending of consumer units headed by people under age 25 by product and service category and before-tax income of consumer unit, 2004–05; index definition: an index of 100 is the average for all consumer units; an index of 132 means that spending by consumer units in that group is 32 percent above the average for all consumer units; an index of 68 indicates spending that is 32 percent below the average for all consumer units)

	total consumer units under age 25	under $10,000	$10,000– $19,999	$20,000– $29,999	$30,000– $39,999	$40,000 or more
Average spending of consumer units, total	$26,102	$13,525	$20,812	$26,881	$32,048	$48,051
Average spending of consumer units, index	100	52	80	103	123	184
FOOD	100	58	83	90	125	165
Food at home	100	55	87	99	117	162
Cereals and bakery products	100	57	85	94	130	158
Cereals and cereal products	100	57	81	91	137	165
Bakery products	100	57	88	97	125	154
Meats, poultry, fish, and eggs	100	49	83	92	116	180
Beef	100	48	72	87	127	189
Pork	100	55	97	100	106	157
Other meats	100	45	81	95	107	186
Poultry	100	54	89	92	116	168
Fish and seafood	100	37	79	86	116	205
Eggs	100	54	97	88	113	158
Dairy products	100	52	85	103	116	166
Fresh milk and cream	100	51	83	95	131	166
Other dairy products	100	53	87	108	106	165
Fruits and vegetables	100	55	85	108	106	162
Fresh fruits	100	54	85	106	111	162
Fresh vegetables	100	53	86	110	97	167
Processed fruits	100	59	89	100	101	160
Processed vegetables	100	59	75	115	119	152
Other food at home	100	58	93	100	116	151
Sugar and other sweets	100	68	103	77	107	151
Fats and oils	100	49	111	100	116	143
Miscellaneous foods	100	57	94	103	115	148
Nonalcoholic beverages	100	57	80	102	122	159
Food prepared by consumer unit on trips	100	78	111	100	100	129
Food away from home	100	61	78	82	132	168
ALCOHOLIC BEVERAGES	100	66	89	93	108	153
HOUSING	100	49	81	111	133	179
Shelter	100	52	84	113	132	171
Owned dwellings	100	11	38	49	123	341
Mortgage interest and charges	100	5	25	44	120	370
Property taxes	100	32	58	62	92	291
Maintenance, repair, insurance, other expenses	100	9	67	51	194	281
Rented dwellings	100	60	96	136	138	125
Other lodging	100	132	112	41	83	85
Utilities, fuels, and public services	100	41	85	116	133	187
Natural gas	100	25	67	125	127	227
Electricity	100	44	89	120	132	174
Fuel oil and other fuels	100	6	103	103	100	258
Telephone services	100	45	88	115	134	176
Water and other public services	100	31	66	94	142	235
Household services	100	26	76	113	140	219
Personal services	100	11	78	114	139	242
Other household services	100	49	72	112	141	184
Housekeeping supplies	100	61	74	107	126	155
Laundry and cleaning supplies	100	69	76	97	126	157
Other household products	100	64	76	96	117	163
Postage and stationery	100	49	69	134	142	140

	total consumer units under age 25	under $10,000	$10,000– $19,999	$20,000– $29,999	$30,000– $39,999	$40,000 or more
Household furnishings and equipment	100	51	61	87	139	204
Household textiles	100	60	44	91	91	228
Furniture	100	21	73	101	109	256
Floor coverings	100	33	39	350	50	125
Major appliances	100	25	53	66	194	242
Small appliances, miscellaneous housewares	100	54	66	80	134	200
Miscellaneous household equipment	100	75	57	76	157	162
APPAREL AND RELATED SERVICES	100	71	68	98	111	172
Men and boys	100	60	61	66	103	223
Men, aged 16 or older	100	65	60	57	91	230
Boys, aged 2 to 15	100	22	65	145	207	159
Women and girls	100	75	66	98	108	168
Women, aged 16 or older	100	77	66	94	108	168
Girls, aged 2 to 15	100	34	70	163	120	174
Children under age 2	100	60	89	119	100	155
Footwear	100	88	61	105	124	141
Other apparel products and services	100	52	85	124	119	168
TRANSPORTATION	100	35	78	120	122	206
Vehicle purchases	100	23	76	135	99	230
Cars and trucks, new	100	8	39	196	113	242
Cars and trucks, used	100	28	92	105	98	228
Other vehicles	100	24	60	318	18	191
Gasoline and motor oil	100	51	85	109	132	173
Other vehicle expenses	100	36	75	111	148	199
Vehicle finance charges	100	16	56	105	146	259
Maintenance and repairs	100	55	94	114	141	148
Vehicle insurance	100	22	70	129	150	215
Vehicle rentals, leases, licenses, other charges	100	50	71	69	156	209
Public transportation	100	62	77	70	154	179
HEALTH CARE	100	29	54	110	133	241
Health insurance	100	22	42	115	150	255
Medical services	100	25	67	120	96	250
Drugs	100	56	56	86	141	198
Medical supplies	100	38	101	68	148	187
ENTERTAINMENT	100	57	92	101	124	164
Fees and admissions	100	81	80	87	112	156
Audio and visual equipment and services	100	53	82	113	126	174
Pets, toys, hobbies, playground equipment	100	44	81	84	217	147
Other entertainment products and services	100	49	135	103	59	165
PERSONAL CARE PRODUCTS AND SERVICES	100	69	85	90	104	166
READING	100	72	88	94	116	152
EDUCATION	100	136	111	55	44	91
TOBACCO PRODUCTS AND SMOKING SUPPLIES	100	48	100	134	136	142
MISCELLANEOUS	100	70	90	87	110	168
CASH CONTRIBUTIONS	100	31	74	95	148	222
PERSONAL INSURANCE AND PENSIONS	100	14	49	95	148	276
Life and other personal insurance	100	9	69	95	178	254
Pensions and Social Security	100	14	49	95	148	277
PERSONAL TAXES	100	-6	-8	64	142	397
Federal income taxes	100	-16	-42	26	138	478
State and local income taxes	100	6	38	117	146	285
Other taxes	100	17	13	83	150	308
GIFTS FOR PEOPLE IN OTHER HOUSEHOLDS	100	56	94	95	109	167

Note: "–" means sample is too small to make a reliable estimate.
Source: Calculations by New Strategist based on the Bureau of Labor Statistics' 2004 and 2005 Consumer Expenditure Surveys

Table 10. Aged 25 to 34: Average spending by income, 2004–05

(average annual spending of consumer units (CUs) headed by people aged 25 to 34 by product and service category and before-tax income of consumer unit, 2004–05)

	total consumer units aged 25 to 34	under $10,000	$10,000– $19,999	$20,000– $29,999	$30,000– $39,999	$40,000– $49,999	$50,000– $69,999	$70,000 or more
Number of consumer units (in 000s)	19,558	1,204	2,128	2,620	2,788	2,309	3,542	4,967
Average number of persons per CU	2.8	2.2	2.7	2.6	2.7	2.9	2.9	3.2
Average before-tax income of CU	$53,826	$4,817	$15,182	$25,056	$34,538	$44,296	$58,898	$109,085
Average annual spending of CU	43,900	18,894	23,732	28,304	35,314	38,631	48,236	70,540
FOOD	5,669	3,389	4,028	4,084	5,039	4,981	6,274	7,784
Food at home	3,049	2,318	2,686	2,595	2,898	2,603	3,194	3,736
Cereals and bakery products	410	347	360	344	404	359	421	490
Cereals and cereal products	145	134	125	130	144	128	146	170
Bakery products	264	213	234	214	261	231	275	319
Meats, poultry, fish, and eggs	732	681	655	650	732	627	702	880
Beef	219	225	193	188	232	179	202	265
Pork	141	132	139	145	130	140	139	151
Other meats	96	75	75	87	86	98	113	105
Poultry	146	117	130	124	152	110	134	189
Fish and seafood	97	99	83	75	94	69	84	134
Eggs	34	34	35	31	39	30	31	36
Dairy products	347	228	295	302	333	298	384	417
Fresh milk and cream	143	96	145	138	142	119	151	161
Other dairy products	204	132	149	164	191	179	234	255
Fruits and vegetables	491	334	464	423	479	409	488	610
Fresh fruits	156	98	149	139	145	128	154	199
Fresh vegetables	155	107	149	133	143	122	158	197
Processed fruits	100	65	85	83	111	86	98	123
Processed vegetables	80	65	83	68	80	73	78	92
Other food at home	1,069	728	913	876	950	910	1,199	1,340
Sugar and other sweets	102	73	87	80	94	79	114	131
Fats and oils	77	58	76	71	73	69	81	89
Miscellaneous foods	579	372	462	478	484	481	655	758
Nonalcoholic beverages	281	214	274	228	269	256	320	316
Food prepared by consumer unit on trips	29	12	13	19	30	24	29	47
Food away from home	2,621	1,070	1,341	1,489	2,141	2,377	3,080	4,048
ALCOHOLIC BEVERAGES	499	125	264	265	460	408	582	784
HOUSING	14,962	7,542	8,768	10,054	12,229	13,164	15,634	23,822
Shelter	9,138	4,906	5,351	6,249	7,538	7,956	9,565	14,456
Owned dwellings	4,984	1,073	807	1,468	2,674	3,700	5,648	10,995
Mortgage interest and charges	3,408	639	471	986	1,835	2,613	3,998	7,446
Property taxes	965	284	186	261	509	701	1,013	2,180
Maintenance, repair, insurance, other expenses	611	150	149	222	331	386	637	1,370
Rented dwellings	3,922	3,708	4,495	4,711	4,753	4,077	3,684	2,942
Other lodging	233	124	50	70	111	179	232	518
Utilities, fuels, and public services	2,799	1,701	2,028	2,314	2,479	2,749	3,051	3,674
Natural gas	380	216	253	276	312	359	405	559
Electricity	1,003	680	841	917	914	974	1,023	1,245
Fuel oil and other fuels	62	21	33	38	49	69	74	93
Telephone services	1,063	651	747	877	971	1,061	1,222	1,337
Water and other public services	290	132	154	206	233	287	327	439
Household services	957	279	368	512	572	760	933	1,935
Personal services	614	155	247	331	343	504	593	1,251
Other household services	343	125	120	181	228	255	340	684
Housekeeping supplies	501	242	361	301	408	438	546	750
Laundry and cleaning supplies	135	80	99	111	120	124	141	180
Other household products	238	113	175	126	200	203	288	343
Postage and stationery	128	47	87	64	88	112	118	227

	total consumer units aged 25 to 34	under $10,000	$10,000–$19,999	$20,000–$29,999	$30,000–$39,999	$40,000–$49,999	$50,000–$69,999	$70,000 or more
Household furnishings and equipment	$1,566	$415	$659	$679	$1,232	$1,262	$1,539	$3,008
Household textiles	120	23	76	105	99	96	127	183
Furniture	490	152	156	197	355	415	454	1,007
Floor coverings	38	5	9	12	13	35	25	98
Major appliances	184	29	106	52	158	131	172	370
Small appliances, miscellaneous housewares	96	23	61	66	103	73	80	157
Miscellaneous household equipment	638	184	252	247	505	512	680	1,192
APPAREL AND RELATED SERVICES	2,107	1,013	1,570	1,433	1,909	1,753	1,845	3,331
Men and boys	463	222	319	302	400	499	438	682
Men, aged 16 or older	345	105	202	177	285	396	320	558
Boys, aged 2 to 15	118	116	117	125	115	103	118	124
Women and girls	741	363	453	516	632	485	630	1,283
Women, aged 16 or older	611	261	318	408	521	372	486	1,131
Girls, aged 2 to 15	129	102	136	108	111	114	143	152
Children under age 2	177	69	158	170	146	125	165	260
Footwear	391	237	454	254	505	373	342	444
Other apparel products and services	335	121	185	191	227	272	271	662
TRANSPORTATION	8,640	2,958	4,236	5,940	7,492	7,635	10,874	12,845
Vehicle purchases	3,984	1,042	1,691	2,738	3,606	3,170	5,575	5,791
Cars and trucks, new	1,870	186	469	870	1,620	1,019	2,990	3,170
Cars and trucks, used	2,056	965	1,221	1,839	1,972	2,064	2,470	2,543
Other vehicles	57	–	2	29	14	87	116	78
Gasoline and motor oil	1,903	924	1,165	1,458	1,638	1,964	2,238	2,574
Other vehicle expenses	2,390	791	1,194	1,553	2,037	2,272	2,742	3,730
Vehicle finance charges	406	84	134	191	276	445	522	685
Maintenance and repairs	614	240	390	469	585	487	681	904
Vehicle insurance	917	322	503	668	872	943	1,092	1,260
Vehicle rentals, leases, licenses, other charges	453	146	167	225	305	397	447	881
Public transportation	364	201	185	190	211	228	320	750
HEALTH CARE	1,524	404	537	950	1,200	1,685	1,764	2,448
Health insurance	834	197	257	498	643	952	986	1,356
Medical services	402	86	133	257	329	416	481	646
Drugs	225	93	128	158	184	265	230	331
Medical supplies	63	28	19	38	43	51	67	114
ENTERTAINMENT	2,280	1,081	1,095	1,318	1,591	1,808	2,383	4,105
Fees and admissions	452	156	149	208	293	355	464	910
Audio and visual equipment and services	890	473	553	634	766	801	966	1,329
Pets, toys, hobbies, playground equipment	424	204	237	284	346	450	455	632
Other entertainment products and services	513	247	156	193	186	202	499	1,234
PERSONAL CARE PRODUCTS AND SERVICES	527	245	316	359	428	490	565	807
READING	92	49	49	52	71	83	95	154
EDUCATION	759	1,109	688	558	502	813	759	929
TOBACCO PRODUCTS AND SMOKING SUPPLIES	296	242	315	348	318	327	321	227
MISCELLANEOUS	650	201	389	411	484	686	725	1,014
CASH CONTRIBUTIONS	948	221	395	509	673	821	880	1,855
PERSONAL INSURANCE AND PENSIONS	4,946	317	1,085	2,023	2,919	3,978	5,535	10,432
Life and other personal insurance	227	45	60	87	120	174	236	496
Pensions and Social Security	4,719	273	1,025	1,937	2,799	3,803	5,299	9,936
PERSONAL TAXES	1,732	–309	–374	-82	761	1,188	2,009	4,685
Federal income taxes	1,140	–332	–422	-264	369	714	1,371	3,374
State and local income taxes	489	4	29	135	348	376	518	1,103
Other taxes	102	20	20	47	44	97	120	208
GIFTS FOR PEOPLE IN OTHER HOUSEHOLDS	593	208	407	435	506	510	521	968

Note: Spending by category will not add to total spending because gift spending is also included in the preceding product and service categories and personal taxes are not included in the total. "–" means value is less than 0.5.
Source: Bureau of Labor Statistics, 2004 and 2005 Consumer Expenditure Surveys, Internet site http://www.bls.gov/cex/; calculations by New Strategist

Table 11. Aged 25 to 34: Indexed spending by income, 2004–05

(indexed average annual spending of consumer units headed by people aged 25 to 34 by product and service category and before-tax income of consumer unit, 2004–05; index definition: an index of 100 is the average for all consumer units; an index of 132 means that spending by consumer units in that group is 32 percent above the average for all consumer units; an index of 68 indicates spending that is 32 percent below the average for all consumer units)

	total consumer units aged 25 to 34	under $10,000	$10,000– $19,999	$20,000– $29,999	$30,000– $39,999	$40,000– $49,999	$50,000– $69,999	$70,000 or more
Average spending of consumer units, total	$43,900	$18,894	$23,732	$28,304	$35,314	$38,631	$48,236	$70,540
Average spending of consumer units, index	100	43	54	64	80	88	110	161
FOOD	100	60	71	72	89	88	111	137
Food at home	100	76	88	85	95	85	105	123
Cereals and bakery products	100	85	88	84	99	88	103	120
Cereals and cereal products	100	93	86	90	99	88	101	117
Bakery products	100	81	89	81	99	88	104	121
Meats, poultry, fish, and eggs	100	93	89	89	100	86	96	120
Beef	100	103	88	86	106	82	92	121
Pork	100	93	98	103	92	99	99	107
Other meats	100	78	78	91	90	102	118	109
Poultry	100	80	89	85	104	75	92	129
Fish and seafood	100	102	86	77	97	71	87	138
Eggs	100	99	104	91	115	88	91	106
Dairy products	100	66	85	87	96	86	111	120
Fresh milk and cream	100	67	102	97	99	83	106	113
Other dairy products	100	65	73	80	94	88	115	125
Fruits and vegetables	100	68	95	86	98	83	99	124
Fresh fruits	100	63	95	89	93	82	99	128
Fresh vegetables	100	69	96	86	92	79	102	127
Processed fruits	100	65	85	83	111	86	98	123
Processed vegetables	100	81	103	85	100	91	98	115
Other food at home	100	68	85	82	89	85	112	125
Sugar and other sweets	100	72	85	78	92	77	112	128
Fats and oils	100	75	99	92	95	90	105	116
Miscellaneous foods	100	64	80	83	84	83	113	131
Nonalcoholic beverages	100	76	98	81	96	91	114	112
Food prepared by consumer unit on trips	100	40	46	66	103	83	100	162
Food away from home	100	41	51	57	82	91	118	154
ALCOHOLIC BEVERAGES	100	25	53	53	92	82	117	157
HOUSING	100	50	59	67	82	88	104	159
Shelter	100	54	59	68	82	87	105	158
Owned dwellings	100	22	16	29	54	74	113	221
Mortgage interest and charges	100	19	14	29	54	77	117	218
Property taxes	100	29	19	27	53	73	105	226
Maintenance, repair, insurance, other expenses	100	25	24	36	54	63	104	224
Rented dwellings	100	95	115	120	121	104	94	75
Other lodging	100	53	21	30	48	77	100	222
Utilities, fuels, and public services	100	61	72	83	89	98	109	131
Natural gas	100	57	67	73	82	94	107	147
Electricity	100	68	84	91	91	97	102	124
Fuel oil and other fuels	100	34	54	61	79	111	119	150
Telephone services	100	61	70	83	91	100	115	126
Water and other public services	100	46	53	71	80	99	113	151
Household services	100	29	38	54	60	79	97	202
Personal services	100	25	40	54	56	82	97	204
Other household services	100	36	35	53	66	74	99	199
Housekeeping supplies	100	48	72	60	81	87	109	150
Laundry and cleaning supplies	100	59	73	82	89	92	104	133
Other household products	100	48	73	53	84	85	121	144
Postage and stationery	100	37	68	50	69	88	92	177

	total consumer units aged 25 to 34	under $10,000	$10,000–$19,999	$20,000–$29,999	$30,000–$39,999	$40,000–$49,999	$50,000–$69,999	$70,000 or more
Household furnishings and equipment	100	26	42	43	79	81	98	192
Household textiles	100	19	63	88	83	80	106	153
Furniture	100	31	32	40	72	85	93	206
Floor coverings	100	13	23	32	34	92	66	258
Major appliances	100	15	58	28	86	71	93	201
Small appliances, miscellaneous housewares	100	24	63	69	107	76	83	164
Miscellaneous household equipment	100	29	40	39	79	80	107	187
APPAREL AND RELATED SERVICES	100	48	75	68	91	83	88	158
Men and boys	100	48	69	65	86	108	95	147
Men, aged 16 or older	100	30	59	51	83	115	93	162
Boys, aged 2 to 15	100	99	99	106	97	87	100	105
Women and girls	100	49	61	70	85	65	85	173
Women, aged 16 or older	100	43	52	67	85	61	80	185
Girls, aged 2 to 15	100	79	105	84	86	88	111	118
Children under age 2	100	39	89	96	82	71	93	147
Footwear	100	61	116	65	129	95	87	114
Other apparel products and services	100	36	55	57	68	81	81	198
TRANSPORTATION	100	34	49	69	87	88	126	149
Vehicle purchases	100	26	42	69	91	80	140	145
Cars and trucks, new	100	10	25	47	87	54	160	170
Cars and trucks, used	100	47	59	89	96	100	120	124
Other vehicles	100	–	4	51	25	153	204	137
Gasoline and motor oil	100	49	61	77	86	103	118	135
Other vehicle expenses	100	33	50	65	85	95	115	156
Vehicle finance charges	100	21	33	47	68	110	129	169
Maintenance and repairs	100	39	64	76	95	79	111	147
Vehicle insurance	100	35	55	73	95	103	119	137
Vehicle rentals, leases, licenses, other charges	100	32	37	50	67	88	99	194
Public transportation	100	55	51	52	58	63	88	206
HEALTH CARE	100	26	35	62	79	111	116	161
Health insurance	100	24	31	60	77	114	118	163
Medical services	100	21	33	64	82	103	120	161
Drugs	100	41	57	70	82	118	102	147
Medical supplies	100	45	31	60	68	81	106	181
ENTERTAINMENT	100	47	48	58	70	79	105	180
Fees and admissions	100	34	33	46	65	79	103	201
Audio and visual equipment and services	100	53	62	71	86	90	109	149
Pets, toys, hobbies, playground equipment	100	48	56	67	82	106	107	149
Other entertainment products and services	100	48	30	38	36	39	97	241
PERSONAL CARE PRODUCTS AND SERVICES	100	46	60	68	81	93	107	153
READING	100	54	53	57	77	90	103	167
EDUCATION	100	146	91	74	66	107	100	122
TOBACCO PRODUCTS AND SMOKING SUPPLIES	100	82	106	118	107	110	108	77
MISCELLANEOUS	100	31	60	63	74	106	112	156
CASH CONTRIBUTIONS	100	23	42	54	71	87	93	196
PERSONAL INSURANCE AND PENSIONS	100	6	22	41	59	80	112	211
Life and other personal insurance	100	20	26	38	53	77	104	219
Pensions and Social Security	100	6	22	41	59	81	112	211
PERSONAL TAXES	100	–18	–22	-5	44	69	116	270
Federal income taxes	100	–29	–37	–23	32	63	120	296
State and local income taxes	100	1	6	28	71	77	106	226
Other taxes	100	19	19	46	43	95	118	204
GIFTS FOR PEOPLE IN OTHER HOUSEHOLDS	100	35	69	73	85	86	88	163

Note: "–" means sample is too small to make a reliable estimate.
Source: Calculations by New Strategist based on the Bureau of Labor Statistics' 2004 and 2005 Consumer Expenditure Surveys

Table 12. Aged 35 to 44: Average spending by income, 2004–05

(average annual spending of consumer units (CUs) headed by people aged 35 to 44 by product and service category and before-tax income of consumer unit, 2004–05)

	total consumer units aged 35 to 44	under $10,000	$10,000–$19,999	$20,000–$29,999	$30,000–$39,999	$40,000–$49,999	$50,000–$69,999	$70,000 or more
Number of consumer units (in 000s)	23,936	1,275	1,770	2,270	2,717	2,523	4,472	8,909
Average number of persons per CU	3.2	2.3	2.6	2.9	3.0	3.1	3.3	3.6
Average before-tax income of CU	$69,242	$2,786	$15,041	$24,898	$34,748	$44,772	$59,454	$123,187
Average annual spending of CU	52,905	19,006	22,084	28,415	35,427	40,874	49,774	80,038
FOOD	**7,052**	**3,277**	**4,212**	**4,561**	**5,432**	**5,962**	**6,895**	**9,471**
Food at home	**4,008**	**2,244**	**2,970**	**2,907**	**3,212**	**3,564**	**3,935**	**5,051**
Cereals and bakery products	558	334	419	381	461	485	541	707
Cereals and cereal products	189	122	176	127	157	165	187	230
Bakery products	369	213	243	254	303	320	353	477
Meats, poultry, fish, and eggs	992	608	817	797	813	955	996	1,173
Beef	303	174	245	239	240	291	300	366
Pork	202	128	187	185	174	181	211	226
Other meats	129	76	98	97	107	112	129	160
Poultry	176	101	149	131	150	176	177	207
Fish and seafood	141	98	98	106	102	154	141	169
Eggs	41	32	42	39	39	42	39	44
Dairy products	459	273	331	304	385	390	449	587
Fresh milk and cream	184	130	155	140	161	172	180	218
Other dairy products	276	144	176	164	223	218	269	369
Fruits and vegetables	639	344	455	439	497	602	609	819
Fresh fruits	208	113	136	136	159	215	185	273
Fresh vegetables	201	105	144	140	152	177	207	255
Processed fruits	127	67	89	88	99	109	117	167
Processed vegetables	103	59	87	76	87	101	100	123
Other food at home	1,360	686	948	987	1,057	1,132	1,341	1,764
Sugar and other sweets	145	100	98	97	112	118	148	186
Fats and oils	98	59	82	74	82	94	99	117
Miscellaneous foods	710	323	515	515	552	552	670	945
Nonalcoholic beverages	364	200	248	291	288	334	383	444
Food prepared by consumer unit on trips	43	4	6	10	23	34	42	73
Food away from home	**3,044**	**1,033**	**1,242**	**1,654**	**2,220**	**2,398**	**2,959**	**4,420**
ALCOHOLIC BEVERAGES	**523**	**144**	**161**	**204**	**326**	**620**	**475**	**761**
HOUSING	**17,712**	**8,477**	**8,725**	**10,077**	**12,373**	**13,919**	**15,907**	**26,305**
Shelter	**10,417**	**5,406**	**5,339**	**5,969**	**7,104**	**8,237**	**9,395**	**15,418**
Owned dwellings	7,548	2,061	1,609	2,108	3,976	5,306	6,673	13,063
Mortgage interest and charges	4,944	1,204	1,019	1,295	2,694	3,546	4,411	8,539
Property taxes	1,660	486	404	515	803	1,045	1,449	2,910
Maintenance, repair, insurance, other expenses	944	370	185	297	479	716	812	1,615
Rented dwellings	2,465	3,218	3,664	3,795	2,994	2,793	2,442	1,536
Other lodging	405	127	67	66	133	138	280	819
Utilities, fuels, and public services	**3,442**	**2,043**	**2,331**	**2,620**	**2,929**	**3,156**	**3,472**	**4,295**
Natural gas	498	224	330	377	412	449	477	651
Electricity	1,254	875	961	1,020	1,101	1,150	1,248	1,506
Fuel oil and other fuels	118	72	53	43	87	142	116	160
Telephone services	1,179	691	752	931	990	1,083	1,224	1,458
Water and other public services	393	181	235	248	339	332	406	520
Household services	**1,073**	**241**	**225**	**319**	**425**	**535**	**756**	**2,062**
Personal services	620	96	101	153	202	242	385	1,271
Other household services	453	144	124	166	223	293	372	791
Housekeeping supplies	**697**	**250**	**318**	**380**	**550**	**494**	**670**	**1,003**
Laundry and cleaning supplies	166	83	113	139	137	149	187	194
Other household products	361	111	158	170	296	238	314	549
Postage and stationery	169	57	47	71	118	107	169	260

	total consumer units aged 35 to 44	under $10,000	$10,000– $19,999	$20,000– $29,999	$30,000– $39,999	$40,000– $49,999	$50,000– $69,999	$70,000 or more
Household furnishings and equipment	2,083	537	512	790	1,366	1,496	1,614	3,527
Household textiles	171	24	51	87	187	140	113	263
Furniture	585	198	137	198	213	337	441	1,085
Floor coverings	53	6	5	11	5	55	67	86
Major appliances	241	31	71	61	99	269	195	404
Small appliances, miscellaneous housewares	99	25	37	58	59	63	68	164
Miscellaneous household equipment	935	254	210	375	803	632	730	1,524
APPAREL AND RELATED SERVICES	2,253	882	1,292	1,552	1,767	1,408	2,106	3,232
Men and boys	565	182	332	361	430	381	548	806
Men, aged 16 or older	380	94	251	212	283	261	369	547
Boys, aged 2 to 15	185	88	81	149	147	119	179	259
Women and girls	864	324	444	569	639	506	841	1,254
Women, aged 16 or older	625	213	316	353	492	363	644	900
Girls, aged 2 to 15	239	111	129	216	148	143	198	354
Children under age 2	96	48	46	75	84	65	70	141
Footwear	407	196	334	409	433	295	413	467
Other apparel products and services	322	131	135	138	181	162	234	565
TRANSPORTATION	9,570	2,774	3,153	5,415	6,423	7,371	10,189	14,145
Vehicle purchases	4,295	963	848	2,350	2,567	2,856	4,794	6,636
Cars and trucks, new	2,276	511	92	662	1,280	969	2,714	3,879
Cars and trucks, used	1,893	740	801	1,688	1,281	1,798	1,892	2,540
Other vehicles	126	–	1	–	6	89	188	218
Gasoline and motor oil	2,125	855	1,136	1,480	1,759	1,974	2,249	2,761
Other vehicle expenses	2,685	791	1,052	1,436	1,912	2,255	2,808	3,892
Vehicle finance charges	415	51	107	179	297	377	456	616
Maintenance and repairs	706	341	341	442	509	556	716	993
Vehicle insurance	1,049	294	506	631	854	995	1,157	1,391
Vehicle rentals, leases, licenses, other charges	516	103	98	186	252	328	479	892
Public transportation	465	165	117	148	186	285	338	856
HEALTH CARE	2,277	622	890	1,345	1,657	2,031	2,293	3,272
Health insurance	1,184	285	471	672	899	1,117	1,307	1,629
Medical services	664	169	208	398	434	497	562	1,062
Drugs	337	136	185	240	262	355	330	438
Medical supplies	92	32	26	35	63	62	93	143
ENTERTAINMENT	2,638	703	832	1,134	1,623	1,929	2,399	4,272
Fees and admissions	711	135	110	190	294	452	536	1,335
Audio and visual equipment and services	975	436	491	556	715	872	1,015	1,341
Pets, toys, hobbies, playground equipment	465	82	140	262	347	355	438	707
Other entertainment products and services	488	51	93	126	267	250	411	888
PERSONAL CARE PRODUCTS AND SERVICES	644	244	299	375	444	496	568	965
READING	122	38	37	48	65	88	108	203
EDUCATION	857	268	263	255	311	442	641	1,601
TOBACCO PRODUCTS AND SMOKING SUPPLIES	354	379	382	398	456	419	394	263
MISCELLANEOUS	791	503	349	334	586	708	781	1,124
CASH CONTRIBUTIONS	1,503	237	414	656	884	1,188	1,263	2,516
PERSONAL INSURANCE AND PENSIONS	6,608	459	1,074	2,061	3,077	4,292	5,754	11,908
Life and other personal insurance	396	130	107	125	171	260	314	708
Pensions and Social Security	6,213	330	967	1,936	2,906	4,032	5,441	11,200
PERSONAL TAXES	2,669	–240	–295	–83	410	732	1,822	6,038
Federal income taxes	1,852	–263	–367	–270	101	354	1,145	4,451
State and local income taxes	663	–8	99	136	238	266	507	1,335
Other taxes	154	30	23	51	72	112	170	253
GIFTS FOR PEOPLE IN OTHER HOUSEHOLDS	1,005	388	351	402	1,005	508	983	1,513

Note: Spending by category will not add to total spending because gift spending is also included in the preceding product and service categories and personal taxes are not included in the total. "–" means sample is too small to make a reliable estimate.
Source: Bureau of Labor Statistics, 2004 and 2005 Consumer Expenditure Surveys, Internet site http://www.bls.gov/cex/; calculations by New Strategist

Table 13. Aged 35 to 44: Indexed spending by income, 2004–05

(indexed average annual spending of consumer units headed by people aged 35 to 44 by product and service category and before-tax income of consumer unit, 2004–05; index definition: an index of 100 is the average for all consumer units; an index of 132 means that spending by consumer units in that group is 32 percent above the average for all consumer units; an index of 68 indicates spending that is 32 percent below the average for all consumer units)

	total consumer units aged 35 to 44	under $10,000	$10,000– $19,999	$20,000– $29,999	$30,000– $39,999	$40,000– $49,999	$50,000– $69,999	$70,000 or more
Average spending of consumer units, total	$52,905	$19,006	$22,084	$28,415	$35,427	$40,874	$49,774	$80,038
Average spending of consumer units, index	100	36	42	54	67	77	94	151
FOOD	100	46	60	65	77	85	98	134
Food at home	100	56	74	73	80	89	98	126
Cereals and bakery products	100	60	75	68	83	87	97	127
Cereals and cereal products	100	64	93	67	83	87	99	122
Bakery products	100	58	66	69	82	87	96	129
Meats, poultry, fish, and eggs	100	61	82	80	82	96	100	118
Beef	100	57	81	79	79	96	99	121
Pork	100	63	92	92	86	90	104	112
Other meats	100	59	76	75	83	87	100	124
Poultry	100	58	85	74	85	100	101	118
Fish and seafood	100	69	70	75	72	109	100	120
Eggs	100	78	101	95	95	102	95	107
Dairy products	100	59	72	66	84	85	98	128
Fresh milk and cream	100	70	84	76	88	93	98	118
Other dairy products	100	52	64	59	81	79	97	134
Fruits and vegetables	100	54	71	69	78	94	95	128
Fresh fruits	100	55	65	65	76	103	89	131
Fresh vegetables	100	52	71	70	76	88	103	127
Processed fruits	100	53	70	69	78	86	92	131
Processed vegetables	100	57	84	74	84	98	97	119
Other food at home	100	50	70	73	78	83	99	130
Sugar and other sweets	100	69	67	67	77	81	102	128
Fats and oils	100	60	83	76	84	96	101	119
Miscellaneous foods	100	45	72	73	78	78	94	133
Nonalcoholic beverages	100	55	68	80	79	92	105	122
Food prepared by consumer unit on trips	100	10	14	23	53	79	98	170
Food away from home	100	34	41	54	73	79	97	145
ALCOHOLIC BEVERAGES	100	28	31	39	62	119	91	146
HOUSING	100	48	49	57	70	79	90	149
Shelter	100	52	51	57	68	79	90	148
Owned dwellings	100	27	21	28	53	70	88	173
Mortgage interest and charges	100	24	21	26	54	72	89	173
Property taxes	100	29	24	31	48	63	87	175
Maintenance, repair, insurance, other expenses	100	39	20	31	51	76	86	171
Rented dwellings	100	131	149	154	121	113	99	62
Other lodging	100	31	16	16	33	34	69	202
Utilities, fuels, and public services	100	59	68	76	85	92	101	125
Natural gas	100	45	66	76	83	90	96	131
Electricity	100	70	77	81	88	92	100	120
Fuel oil and other fuels	100	61	45	36	74	120	98	136
Telephone services	100	59	64	79	84	92	104	124
Water and other public services	100	46	60	63	86	84	103	132
Household services	100	22	21	30	40	50	70	192
Personal services	100	16	16	25	33	39	62	205
Other household services	100	32	27	37	49	65	82	175
Housekeeping supplies	100	36	46	55	79	71	96	144
Laundry and cleaning supplies	100	50	68	84	83	90	113	117
Other household products	100	31	44	47	82	66	87	152
Postage and stationery	100	34	28	42	70	63	100	154

	total consumer units aged 35 to 44	under $10,000	$10,000– $19,999	$20,000– $29,999	$30,000– $39,999	$40,000– $49,999	$50,000– $69,999	$70,000 or more
Household furnishings and equipment	100	26	25	38	66	72	77	169
Household textiles	100	14	30	51	109	82	66	154
Furniture	100	34	23	34	36	58	75	185
Floor coverings	100	12	10	21	9	104	126	162
Major appliances	100	13	29	25	41	112	81	168
Small appliances, miscellaneous housewares	100	25	38	59	60	64	69	166
Miscellaneous household equipment	100	27	22	40	86	68	78	163
APPAREL AND RELATED SERVICES	100	39	57	69	78	62	93	143
Men and boys	100	32	59	64	76	67	97	143
Men, aged 16 or older	100	25	66	56	74	69	97	144
Boys, aged 2 to 15	100	48	44	81	79	64	97	140
Women and girls	100	38	51	66	74	59	97	145
Women, aged 16 or older	100	34	51	56	79	58	103	144
Girls, aged 2 to 15	100	46	54	90	62	60	83	148
Children under age 2	100	50	48	78	88	68	73	147
Footwear	100	48	82	100	106	72	101	115
Other apparel products and services	100	41	42	43	56	50	73	175
TRANSPORTATION	100	29	33	57	67	77	106	148
Vehicle purchases	100	22	20	55	60	66	112	155
Cars and trucks, new	100	22	4	29	56	43	119	170
Cars and trucks, used	100	39	42	89	68	95	100	134
Other vehicles	100	–	1	–	5	71	149	173
Gasoline and motor oil	100	40	53	70	83	93	106	130
Other vehicle expenses	100	29	39	53	71	84	105	145
Vehicle finance charges	100	12	26	43	72	91	110	148
Maintenance and repairs	100	48	48	63	72	79	101	141
Vehicle insurance	100	28	48	60	81	95	110	133
Vehicle rentals, leases, licenses, other charges	100	20	19	36	49	64	93	173
Public transportation	100	36	25	32	40	61	73	184
HEALTH CARE	100	27	39	59	73	89	101	144
Health insurance	100	24	40	57	76	94	110	138
Medical services	100	25	31	60	65	75	85	160
Drugs	100	40	55	71	78	105	98	130
Medical supplies	100	35	28	38	68	67	101	155
ENTERTAINMENT	100	27	32	43	62	73	91	162
Fees and admissions	100	19	15	27	41	64	75	188
Audio and visual equipment and services	100	45	50	57	73	89	104	138
Pets, toys, hobbies, playground equipment	100	18	30	56	75	76	94	152
Other entertainment products and services	100	11	19	26	55	51	84	182
PERSONAL CARE PRODUCTS AND SERVICES	100	38	46	58	69	77	88	150
READING	100	31	30	39	53	72	89	166
EDUCATION	100	31	31	30	36	52	75	187
TOBACCO PRODUCTS AND SMOKING SUPPLIES	100	107	108	112	129	118	111	74
MISCELLANEOUS	100	64	44	42	74	90	99	142
CASH CONTRIBUTIONS	100	16	28	44	59	79	84	167
PERSONAL INSURANCE AND PENSIONS	100	7	16	31	47	65	87	180
Life and other personal insurance	100	33	27	32	43	66	79	179
Pensions and Social Security	100	5	16	31	47	65	88	180
PERSONAL TAXES	100	–9	–11	–3	15	27	68	226
Federal income taxes	100	–14	–20	–15	5	19	62	240
State and local income taxes	100	–1	15	21	36	40	76	201
Other taxes	100	20	15	33	47	73	110	164
GIFTS FOR PEOPLE IN OTHER HOUSEHOLDS	100	39	35	40	100	51	98	151

Note: "–" means sample is too small to make a reliable estimate.
Source: Calculations by New Strategist based on the Bureau of Labor Statistics' 2004 and 2005 Consumer Expenditure Surveys

Table 14. Aged 45 to 54: Average spending by income, 2004–05

(average annual spending of consumer units (CUs) headed by people aged 45 to 54 by product and service category and before-tax income of consumer unit, 2004–05)

	total consumer units aged 45 to 54	under $10,000	$10,000–$19,999	$20,000–$29,999	$30,000–$39,999	$40,000–$49,999	$50,000–$69,999	$70,000 or more
Number of consumer units (in 000s)	24,014	1,398	2,014	2,098	2,428	2,316	4,116	9,645
Average number of persons per CU	2.7	1.9	2.1	2.1	2.3	2.6	2.7	3.1
Average before-tax income of CU	$72,769	$4,023	$15,071	$25,117	$34,760	$44,799	$59,361	$127,143
Average annual spending of CU	54,359	20,225	21,836	27,751	33,566	38,288	48,217	83,207
FOOD	7,009	3,826	3,735	4,133	4,643	5,374	6,615	9,730
Food at home	3,944	2,622	2,594	2,746	2,965	3,155	3,914	5,027
Cereals and bakery products	523	353	343	352	376	423	526	667
Cereals and cereal products	170	135	118	122	129	137	168	210
Bakery products	353	218	224	229	247	286	358	457
Meats, poultry, fish, and eggs	1,014	740	705	759	784	824	1,064	1,233
Beef	310	196	232	211	236	247	360	371
Pork	200	167	135	166	174	171	206	234
Other meats	128	97	97	98	102	117	121	156
Poultry	179	142	114	129	127	130	189	224
Fish and seafood	153	98	89	117	103	121	147	201
Eggs	43	39	37	38	41	38	41	47
Dairy products	435	268	276	289	327	362	425	561
Fresh milk and cream	160	120	117	117	133	150	152	193
Other dairy products	275	149	158	172	194	212	273	368
Fruits and vegetables	643	389	429	426	482	491	605	848
Fresh fruits	215	117	134	143	154	152	192	294
Fresh vegetables	211	130	140	139	157	160	199	277
Processed fruits	120	71	82	77	99	98	117	153
Processed vegetables	98	71	73	67	72	81	96	124
Other food at home	1,329	871	841	920	996	1,054	1,293	1,717
Sugar and other sweets	152	90	98	104	100	97	153	204
Fats and oils	106	83	98	85	80	103	96	125
Miscellaneous foods	656	406	343	432	489	505	651	865
Nonalcoholic beverages	368	276	281	287	293	322	351	446
Food prepared by consumer unit on trips	48	15	22	13	34	26	42	77
Food away from home	3,066	1,204	1,141	1,388	1,678	2,219	2,702	4,704
ALCOHOLIC BEVERAGES	479	178	149	221	271	382	435	721
HOUSING	16,800	8,135	8,290	9,638	11,529	12,920	14,833	24,447
Shelter	9,889	4,915	4,643	5,622	6,572	7,388	8,557	14,636
Owned dwellings	7,420	1,637	1,850	2,767	3,708	4,943	6,616	12,305
Mortgage interest and charges	4,344	876	988	1,470	2,229	2,934	3,961	7,207
Property taxes	1,843	542	521	711	862	1,329	1,649	3,006
Maintenance, repair, insurance, other expenses	1,233	220	341	586	617	680	1,007	2,091
Rented dwellings	1,732	3,165	2,728	2,723	2,685	2,235	1,548	820
Other lodging	736	112	65	132	178	210	394	1,512
Utilities, fuels, and public services	3,554	2,117	2,219	2,617	2,842	3,234	3,491	4,529
Natural gas	505	319	276	373	372	443	495	661
Electricity	1,281	868	898	988	1,047	1,199	1,255	1,574
Fuel oil and other fuels	160	54	81	93	113	142	157	225
Telephone services	1,204	661	737	881	999	1,093	1,177	1,541
Water and other public services	404	215	228	283	311	357	407	527
Household services	680	184	197	283	334	347	566	1,154
Personal services	133	37	25	70	85	69	118	216
Other household services	547	147	172	212	248	278	448	938
Housekeeping supplies	736	393	445	362	509	606	669	1,023
Laundry and cleaning supplies	171	137	122	105	150	200	173	196
Other household products	387	175	262	181	254	243	331	568
Postage and stationery	178	82	62	76	106	163	165	258

	total consumer units aged 45 to 54	under $10,000	$10,000–$19,999	$20,000–$29,999	$30,000–$39,999	$40,000–$49,999	$50,000–$69,999	$70,000 or more
Household furnishings and equipment	$1,940	$526	$786	$754	$1,273	$1,345	$1,550	$3,105
Household textiles	170	56	123	54	96	112	146	261
Furniture	415	160	188	116	246	225	289	708
Floor coverings	76	8	9	19	14	43	61	143
Major appliances	238	57	43	131	102	185	266	362
Small appliances, miscellaneous housewares	125	38	68	53	99	44	98	200
Miscellaneous household equipment	915	208	355	381	716	735	691	1,431
APPAREL AND RELATED SERVICES	2,269	1,016	1,112	1,053	1,366	1,493	1,832	3,485
Men and boys	558	218	254	219	305	317	490	874
Men, aged 16 or older	467	165	187	157	234	251	410	752
Boys, aged 2 to 15	91	53	68	62	71	65	80	122
Women and girls	964	411	493	427	615	767	828	1,419
Women, aged 16 or older	831	375	443	384	534	643	717	1,215
Girls, aged 2 to 15	133	36	49	43	81	124	111	204
Children under age 2	53	26	30	40	31	36	43	76
Footwear	377	243	221	244	288	226	280	542
Other apparel products and services	318	118	115	124	126	147	192	574
TRANSPORTATION	9,612	3,030	3,471	5,284	6,097	7,023	9,256	14,444
Vehicle purchases	3,909	1,236	1,045	1,986	2,252	2,592	3,898	6,050
Cars and trucks, new	1,980	568	513	809	548	1,166	1,571	3,525
Cars and trucks, used	1,825	975	533	1,156	1,700	1,376	2,143	2,367
Other vehicles	104	30	–	21	3	50	185	158
Gasoline and motor oil	2,208	808	1,160	1,435	1,718	1,907	2,256	2,972
Other vehicle expenses	2,954	782	1,130	1,660	1,919	2,327	2,752	4,425
Vehicle finance charges	364	70	92	197	247	315	389	529
Maintenance and repairs	823	239	317	447	537	671	735	1,237
Vehicle insurance	1,219	380	544	783	875	1,061	1,198	1,711
Vehicle rentals, leases, licenses, other charges	548	92	176	233	259	280	429	948
Public transportation	541	205	135	203	209	197	350	996
HEALTH CARE	2,693	925	1,323	1,675	1,981	2,394	2,731	3,687
Health insurance	1,294	346	626	811	940	1,179	1,412	1,741
Medical services	792	258	375	383	523	627	729	1,179
Drugs	480	259	277	423	427	458	480	582
Medical supplies	128	61	46	58	90	130	110	184
ENTERTAINMENT	2,793	971	857	1,288	1,761	1,626	2,386	4,471
Fees and admissions	709	145	99	167	266	287	504	1,335
Audio and visual equipment and services	988	440	493	611	762	728	909	1,403
Pets, toys, hobbies, playground equipment	509	250	206	253	290	373	481	750
Other entertainment products and services	588	137	60	258	442	239	492	983
PERSONAL CARE PRODUCTS AND SERVICES	658	296	264	354	428	534	562	975
READING	146	40	41	69	83	106	132	232
EDUCATION	1,669	180	275	259	402	374	855	3,456
TOBACCO PRODUCTS AND SMOKING SUPPLIES	402	362	481	447	445	400	423	362
MISCELLANEOUS	865	411	417	494	668	510	975	1,194
CASH CONTRIBUTIONS	1,849	400	406	802	716	1,056	1,343	3,280
PERSONAL INSURANCE AND PENSIONS	7,116	455	1,017	2,034	3,177	4,094	5,838	12,723
Life and other personal insurance	492	89	114	170	242	312	417	837
Pensions and Social Security	6,625	366	903	1,864	2,936	3,781	5,421	11,886
PERSONAL TAXES	3,723	−20	−231	409	856	1,271	2,812	7,511
Federal income taxes	2,710	−60	−307	171	492	724	2,038	5,615
State and local income taxes	787	−3	27	166	265	394	535	1,529
Other taxes	226	43	50	72	98	152	239	367
GIFTS FOR PEOPLE IN OTHER HOUSEHOLDS	1,903	450	630	706	862	701	1,230	3,462

Note: Spending by category will not add to total spending because gift spending is also included in the preceding product and service categories and personal taxes are not included in the total. "–" means sample is too small to make a reliable estimate.
Source: Bureau of Labor Statistics, 2004 and 2005 Consumer Expenditure Surveys, Internet site http://www.bls.gov/cex/; calculations by New Strategist

Table 15. Aged 45 to 54: Indexed spending by income, 2004–05

(indexed average annual spending of consumer units headed by people aged 45 to 54 by product and service category and before-tax income of consumer unit, 2004–05; index definition: an index of 100 is the average for all consumer units; an index of 132 means that spending by consumer units in that group is 32 percent above the average for all consumer units; an index of 68 indicates spending that is 32 percent below the average for all consumer units)

	total consumer units aged 45 to 54	under $10,000	$10,000–$19,999	$20,000–$29,999	$30,000–$39,999	$40,000–$49,999	$50,000–$69,999	$70,000 or more
Average spending of consumer units, total	$54,359	$20,225	$21,836	$27,751	$33,566	$38,288	$48,217	$83,207
Average spending of consumer units, index	100	37	40	51	62	70	89	153
FOOD	**100**	**55**	**53**	**59**	**66**	**77**	**94**	**139**
Food at home	**100**	**66**	**66**	**70**	**75**	**80**	**99**	**127**
Cereals and bakery products	100	68	65	67	72	81	101	128
Cereals and cereal products	100	80	69	72	76	81	99	124
Bakery products	100	62	64	65	70	81	101	129
Meats, poultry, fish, and eggs	100	73	70	75	77	81	105	122
Beef	100	63	75	68	76	80	116	120
Pork	100	83	68	83	87	86	103	117
Other meats	100	76	76	77	80	91	95	122
Poultry	100	80	64	72	71	73	106	125
Fish and seafood	100	64	58	76	67	79	96	131
Eggs	100	91	87	88	95	88	95	109
Dairy products	100	62	63	66	75	83	98	129
Fresh milk and cream	100	75	73	73	83	94	95	121
Other dairy products	100	54	58	63	71	77	99	134
Fruits and vegetables	100	61	67	66	75	76	94	132
Fresh fruits	100	55	62	67	72	71	89	137
Fresh vegetables	100	61	66	66	74	76	94	131
Processed fruits	100	60	68	64	83	82	98	128
Processed vegetables	100	72	75	68	73	83	98	127
Other food at home	100	66	63	69	75	79	97	129
Sugar and other sweets	100	59	64	68	66	64	101	134
Fats and oils	100	78	93	80	75	97	91	118
Miscellaneous foods	100	62	52	66	75	77	99	132
Nonalcoholic beverages	100	75	76	78	80	88	95	121
Food prepared by consumer unit on trips	100	31	46	27	71	54	88	160
Food away from home	**100**	**39**	**37**	**45**	**55**	**72**	**88**	**153**
ALCOHOLIC BEVERAGES	**100**	**37**	**31**	**46**	**57**	**80**	**91**	**151**
HOUSING	**100**	**48**	**49**	**57**	**69**	**77**	**88**	**146**
Shelter	**100**	**50**	**47**	**57**	**66**	**75**	**87**	**148**
Owned dwellings	100	22	25	37	50	67	89	166
Mortgage interest and charges	100	20	23	34	51	68	91	166
Property taxes	100	29	28	39	47	72	89	163
Maintenance, repair, insurance, other expenses	100	18	28	48	50	55	82	170
Rented dwellings	100	183	157	157	155	129	89	47
Other lodging	100	15	9	18	24	29	54	205
Utilities, fuels, and public services	**100**	**60**	**62**	**74**	**80**	**91**	**98**	**127**
Natural gas	100	63	55	74	74	88	98	131
Electricity	100	68	70	77	82	94	98	123
Fuel oil and other fuels	100	33	51	58	71	89	98	141
Telephone services	100	55	61	73	83	91	98	128
Water and other public services	100	53	56	70	77	88	101	130
Household services	**100**	**27**	**29**	**42**	**49**	**51**	**83**	**170**
Personal services	100	28	19	53	64	52	89	162
Other household services	100	27	31	39	45	51	82	171
Housekeeping supplies	**100**	**53**	**61**	**49**	**69**	**82**	**91**	**139**
Laundry and cleaning supplies	100	80	71	61	88	117	101	115
Other household products	100	45	68	47	66	63	86	147
Postage and stationery	100	46	35	43	60	92	93	145

	total consumer units aged 45 to 54	under $10,000	$10,000– $19,999	$20,000– $29,999	$30,000– $39,999	$40,000– $49,999	$50,000– $69,999	$70,000 or more
Household furnishings and equipment	100	27	41	39	66	69	80	160
Household textiles	100	33	72	32	56	66	86	154
Furniture	100	38	45	28	59	54	70	171
Floor coverings	100	10	12	25	18	57	80	188
Major appliances	100	24	18	55	43	78	112	152
Small appliances, miscellaneous housewares	100	31	54	42	79	35	78	160
Miscellaneous household equipment	100	23	39	42	78	80	76	156
APPAREL AND RELATED SERVICES	100	45	49	46	60	66	81	154
Men and boys	100	39	46	39	55	57	88	157
Men, aged 16 or older	100	35	40	34	50	54	88	161
Boys, aged 2 to 15	100	58	74	68	78	71	88	134
Women and girls	100	43	51	44	64	80	86	147
Women, aged 16 or older	100	45	53	46	64	77	86	146
Girls, aged 2 to 15	100	27	37	32	61	93	83	153
Children under age 2	100	48	56	75	58	68	81	143
Footwear	100	64	59	65	76	60	74	144
Other apparel products and services	100	37	36	39	40	46	60	181
TRANSPORTATION	100	32	36	55	63	73	96	150
Vehicle purchases	100	32	27	51	58	66	100	155
Cars and trucks, new	100	29	26	41	28	59	79	178
Cars and trucks, used	100	53	29	63	93	75	117	130
Other vehicles	100	29	–	20	3	48	178	152
Gasoline and motor oil	100	37	53	65	78	86	102	135
Other vehicle expenses	100	26	38	56	65	79	93	150
Vehicle finance charges	100	19	25	54	68	87	107	145
Maintenance and repairs	100	29	39	54	65	82	89	150
Vehicle insurance	100	31	45	64	72	87	98	140
Vehicle rentals, leases, licenses, other charges	100	17	32	43	47	51	78	173
Public transportation	100	38	25	38	39	36	65	184
HEALTH CARE	100	34	49	62	74	89	101	137
Health insurance	100	27	48	63	73	91	109	135
Medical services	100	33	47	48	66	79	92	149
Drugs	100	54	58	88	89	95	100	121
Medical supplies	100	48	36	45	70	102	86	144
ENTERTAINMENT	100	35	31	46	63	58	85	160
Fees and admissions	100	20	14	24	38	40	71	188
Audio and visual equipment and services	100	45	50	62	77	74	92	142
Pets, toys, hobbies, playground equipment	100	49	40	50	57	73	94	147
Other entertainment products and services	100	23	10	44	75	41	84	167
PERSONAL CARE PRODUCTS AND SERVICES	100	45	40	54	65	81	85	148
READING	100	27	28	47	57	73	90	159
EDUCATION	100	11	16	16	24	22	51	207
TOBACCO PRODUCTS AND SMOKING SUPPLIES	100	90	120	111	111	100	105	90
MISCELLANEOUS	100	48	48	57	77	59	113	138
CASH CONTRIBUTIONS	100	22	22	43	39	57	73	177
PERSONAL INSURANCE AND PENSIONS	100	6	14	29	45	58	82	179
Life and other personal insurance	100	18	23	35	49	63	85	170
Pensions and Social Security	100	6	14	28	44	57	82	179
PERSONAL TAXES	100	–1	–6	11	23	34	76	202
Federal income taxes	100	–2	–11	6	18	27	75	207
State and local income taxes	100	0	3	21	34	50	68	194
Other taxes	100	19	22	32	43	67	106	162
GIFTS FOR PEOPLE IN OTHER HOUSEHOLDS	100	24	33	37	45	37	65	182

Note: "–" means sample is too small to make a reliable estimate.
Source: Calculations by New Strategist based on the Bureau of Labor Statistics' 2004 and 2005 Consumer Expenditure Surveys

Table 16. Aged 55 to 64: Average spending by income, 2004–05

(average annual spending of consumer units (CUs) headed by people aged 55 to 64 by product and service category and before-tax income of consumer unit, 2004–05)

	total consumer units aged 55 to 64	under $10,000	$10,000– $19,999	$20,000– $29,999	$30,000– $39,999	$40,000– $49,999	$50,000– $69,999	$70,000 or more
Number of consumer units (in 000s)	17,785	1,617	2,117	2,035	1,884	1,868	2,733	5,531
Average number of persons per CU	2.1	1.4	1.7	1.8	1.9	2.1	2.2	2.5
Average before-tax income of CU	$62,736	$5,687	$14,962	$24,750	$34,598	$44,703	$59,105	$129,155
Average annual spending of CU	48,544	18,463	22,741	29,838	34,258	39,634	48,865	81,501
FOOD	6,051	2,769	3,150	4,223	4,499	5,417	6,297	9,239
Food at home	3,431	1,874	2,039	2,741	2,881	3,161	3,746	4,703
Cereals and bakery products	451	274	268	363	395	424	511	593
Cereals and cereal products	138	89	83	109	125	121	151	184
Bakery products	313	185	186	255	270	302	359	409
Meats, poultry, fish, and eggs	860	458	507	779	751	789	933	1,144
Beef	254	122	158	214	227	208	278	348
Pork	185	105	107	193	175	191	219	215
Other meats	105	72	59	81	81	92	109	149
Poultry	145	80	89	147	122	152	161	179
Fish and seafood	131	49	64	107	100	109	124	206
Eggs	41	31	30	37	45	38	42	47
Dairy products	374	215	236	296	312	346	410	506
Fresh milk and cream	138	98	105	132	133	136	135	165
Other dairy products	237	116	131	164	179	210	275	342
Fruits and vegetables	607	319	376	455	489	565	634	860
Fresh fruits	205	99	116	161	163	204	203	296
Fresh vegetables	207	112	133	134	163	177	215	305
Processed fruits	106	56	69	86	90	99	103	148
Processed vegetables	89	51	59	74	72	86	112	110
Other food at home	1,138	608	653	848	935	1,038	1,259	1,600
Sugar and other sweets	133	87	73	111	105	133	150	177
Fats and oils	96	60	71	88	94	94	93	118
Miscellaneous foods	540	266	288	390	412	483	594	790
Nonalcoholic beverages	306	179	200	230	275	270	358	401
Food prepared by consumer unit on trips	64	16	22	29	49	58	63	114
Food away from home	2,620	894	1,110	1,482	1,618	2,256	2,551	4,537
ALCOHOLIC BEVERAGES	455	152	192	234	243	256	410	878
HOUSING	15,113	7,421	8,884	9,777	11,404	12,145	14,900	24,037
Shelter	8,337	4,404	4,707	5,252	6,403	6,643	8,226	13,298
Owned dwellings	6,364	2,140	2,629	3,471	4,727	4,932	6,416	11,107
Mortgage interest and charges	2,988	867	1,051	1,523	2,018	2,430	3,032	5,385
Property taxes	1,823	761	819	1,085	1,350	1,485	1,825	3,064
Maintenance, repair, insurance, other expenses	1,553	511	760	864	1,359	1,018	1,560	2,658
Rented dwellings	1,223	2,046	1,879	1,508	1,357	1,315	1,234	543
Other lodging	751	217	199	273	319	396	576	1,647
Utilities, fuels, and public services	3,332	1,972	2,540	2,714	3,005	3,127	3,456	4,381
Natural gas	499	267	362	378	470	458	467	702
Electricity	1,218	759	1,018	1,037	1,105	1,169	1,253	1,533
Fuel oil and other fuels	169	97	127	148	197	158	186	200
Telephone services	1,062	658	774	835	880	968	1,129	1,434
Water and other public services	385	191	258	317	353	374	421	512
Household services	668	230	244	271	374	500	545	1,323
Personal services	57	28	17	12	10	91	35	113
Other household services	611	202	226	259	365	409	510	1,210
Housekeeping supplies	696	310	407	515	523	600	777	1,017
Laundry and cleaning supplies	154	82	81	157	138	140	157	205
Other household products	351	160	230	198	267	290	413	517
Postage and stationery	192	68	96	161	118	170	207	295

	total consumer units aged 55 to 64	under $10,000	$10,000–$19,999	$20,000–$29,999	$30,000–$39,999	$40,000–$49,999	$50,000–$69,999	$70,000 or more
Household furnishings and equipment	$2,079	$504	$985	$1,025	$1,098	$1,275	$1,896	$4,019
Household textiles	179	52	74	121	134	111	209	295
Furniture	511	123	348	221	215	282	379	1,037
Floor coverings	85	16	44	44	41	64	56	171
Major appliances	269	61	134	157	197	245	256	461
Small appliances, miscellaneous housewares	136	39	50	84	62	104	120	256
Miscellaneous household equipment	900	212	334	398	449	469	876	1,799
APPAREL AND RELATED SERVICES	1,823	754	743	697	1,151	1,469	1,600	3,373
Men and boys	367	198	173	143	208	365	323	644
Men, aged 16 or older	322	169	158	99	175	326	270	579
Boys, aged 2 to 15	45	29	15	43	33	40	53	65
Women and girls	751	266	281	256	471	521	723	1,418
Women, aged 16 or older	696	258	261	232	426	487	675	1,314
Girls, aged 2 to 15	54	8	20	24	45	33	49	104
Children under age 2	53	33	14	30	36	41	45	94
Footwear	325	130	128	135	254	363	325	522
Other apparel products and services	328	127	146	134	183	178	184	696
TRANSPORTATION	8,700	2,942	3,980	5,833	6,309	7,714	8,974	14,255
Vehicle purchases	3,717	1,128	1,431	2,601	2,303	3,490	3,694	6,329
Cars and trucks, new	2,355	1,058	766	1,556	1,099	1,635	1,841	4,562
Cars and trucks, used	1,292	71	665	1,042	1,193	1,739	1,736	1,644
Other vehicles	70	–	–	3	11	116	117	123
Gasoline and motor oil	1,888	763	1,144	1,432	1,715	1,776	2,107	2,659
Other vehicle expenses	2,522	903	1,262	1,602	2,005	2,141	2,691	4,037
Vehicle finance charges	313	71	119	204	291	311	376	474
Maintenance and repairs	738	268	454	472	496	598	849	1,155
Vehicle insurance	959	428	528	730	828	894	994	1,415
Vehicle rentals, leases, licenses, other charges	512	135	161	197	390	338	471	993
Public transportation	573	149	143	198	285	307	483	1,230
HEALTH CARE	3,352	1,758	2,081	2,645	3,065	3,665	3,645	4,406
Health insurance	1,580	845	1,039	1,312	1,340	1,665	1,727	2,081
Medical services	943	528	418	618	871	1,108	1,033	1,308
Drugs	682	308	552	617	746	767	699	800
Medical supplies	147	77	72	97	108	124	185	217
ENTERTAINMENT	2,627	859	1,140	2,406	1,673	1,678	2,864	4,310
Fees and admissions	631	197	162	205	337	333	574	1,322
Audio and visual equipment and services	838	433	510	622	793	774	887	1,173
Pets, toys, hobbies, playground equipment	479	164	254	229	413	401	426	814
Other entertainment products and services	680	65	215	1,349	129	169	977	1,001
PERSONAL CARE PRODUCTS AND SERVICES	590	212	287	380	356	534	563	996
READING	172	67	63	87	118	146	179	299
EDUCATION	727	96	82	244	142	233	416	1,855
TOBACCO PRODUCTS AND SMOKING SUPPLIES	318	279	329	308	418	351	340	273
MISCELLANEOUS	905	295	467	501	589	784	887	1,555
CASH CONTRIBUTIONS	1,864	521	594	815	1,054	1,282	1,893	3,588
PERSONAL INSURANCE AND PENSIONS	5,845	339	751	1,688	3,236	3,961	5,897	12,435
Life and other personal insurance	577	137	238	251	349	430	575	1,083
Pensions and Social Security	5,268	202	512	1,437	2,886	3,530	5,322	11,352
PERSONAL TAXES	3,047	205	29	439	849	1,393	2,406	7,616
Federal income taxes	2,187	71	–44	216	512	907	1,683	5,635
State and local income taxes	610	–6	11	83	171	257	477	1,546
Other taxes	251	140	63	140	166	229	246	435
GIFTS FOR PEOPLE IN OTHER HOUSEHOLDS	1,612	406	458	581	824	1,139	1,304	3,340

Note: "–" means sample is too small to make a reliable estimate.
Source: Bureau of Labor Statistics, 2004 and 2005 Consumer Expenditure Surveys, Internet site http://www.bls.gov/cex/; calculations by New Strategist

Table 17. Aged 55 to 64: Indexed spending by income, 2004–05

(indexed average annual spending of consumer units headed by people aged 55 to 64 by product and service category and before-tax income of consumer unit, 2004–05; index definition: an index of 100 is the average for all consumer units; an index of 132 means that spending by consumer units in that group is 32 percent above the average for all consumer units; an index of 68 indicates spending that is 32 percent below the average for all consumer units)

	total consumer units aged 55 to 64	under $10,000	$10,000– $19,999	$20,000– $29,999	$30,000– $39,999	$40,000– $49,999	$50,000– $69,999	$70,000 or more
Average spending of consumer units, total	$48,544	$18,463	$22,741	$29,838	$34,258	$39,634	$48,865	$81,501
Average spending of consumer units, index	100	38	47	61	71	82	101	168
FOOD	100	46	52	70	74	90	104	153
Food at home	100	55	59	80	84	92	109	137
Cereals and bakery products	100	61	59	80	88	94	113	131
Cereals and cereal products	100	64	60	79	91	88	109	133
Bakery products	100	59	59	81	86	96	115	131
Meats, poultry, fish, and eggs	100	53	59	91	87	92	108	133
Beef	100	48	62	84	89	82	109	137
Pork	100	57	58	104	95	103	118	116
Other meats	100	68	56	77	77	88	104	142
Poultry	100	55	61	101	84	105	111	123
Fish and seafood	100	38	49	82	76	83	95	157
Eggs	100	76	72	90	110	93	102	115
Dairy products	100	58	63	79	83	93	110	135
Fresh milk and cream	100	71	76	96	96	99	98	120
Other dairy products	100	49	55	69	76	89	116	144
Fruits and vegetables	100	53	62	75	81	93	104	142
Fresh fruits	100	48	57	79	80	100	99	144
Fresh vegetables	100	54	64	65	79	86	104	147
Processed fruits	100	53	65	81	85	93	97	140
Processed vegetables	100	57	66	83	81	97	126	124
Other food at home	100	53	57	75	82	91	111	141
Sugar and other sweets	100	65	55	83	79	100	113	133
Fats and oils	100	62	74	92	98	98	97	123
Miscellaneous foods	100	49	53	72	76	89	110	146
Nonalcoholic beverages	100	58	66	75	90	88	117	131
Food prepared by consumer unit on trips	100	26	34	45	77	91	98	178
Food away from home	100	34	42	57	62	86	97	173
ALCOHOLIC BEVERAGES	100	33	42	51	53	56	90	193
HOUSING	100	49	59	65	75	80	99	159
Shelter	100	53	56	63	77	80	99	160
Owned dwellings	100	34	41	55	74	77	101	175
Mortgage interest and charges	100	29	35	51	68	81	101	180
Property taxes	100	42	45	60	74	81	100	168
Maintenance, repair, insurance, other expenses	100	33	49	56	88	66	100	171
Rented dwellings	100	167	154	123	111	108	101	44
Other lodging	100	29	27	36	42	53	77	219
Utilities, fuels, and public services	100	59	76	81	90	94	104	131
Natural gas	100	54	73	76	94	92	94	141
Electricity	100	62	84	85	91	96	103	126
Fuel oil and other fuels	100	58	75	88	117	93	110	118
Telephone services	100	62	73	79	83	91	106	135
Water and other public services	100	49	67	82	92	97	109	133
Household services	100	34	36	41	56	75	82	198
Personal services	100	49	31	21	18	160	61	198
Other household services	100	33	37	42	60	67	83	198
Housekeeping supplies	100	45	59	74	75	86	112	146
Laundry and cleaning supplies	100	53	53	102	90	91	102	133
Other household products	100	46	65	56	76	83	118	147
Postage and stationery	100	36	50	84	61	89	108	154

	total consumer units aged 55 to 64	under $10,000	$10,000– $19,999	$20,000– $29,999	$30,000– $39,999	$40,000– $49,999	$50,000– $69,999	$70,000 or more
Household furnishings and equipment	100	24	47	49	53	61	91	193
Household textiles	100	29	42	68	75	62	117	165
Furniture	100	24	68	43	42	55	74	203
Floor coverings	100	19	52	52	48	75	66	201
Major appliances	100	23	50	58	73	91	95	171
Small appliances, miscellaneous housewares	100	28	37	62	46	76	88	188
Miscellaneous household equipment	100	24	37	44	50	52	97	200
APPAREL AND RELATED SERVICES	100	41	41	38	63	81	88	185
Men and boys	100	54	47	39	57	99	88	175
Men, aged 16 or older	100	52	49	31	54	101	84	180
Boys, aged 2 to 15	100	64	33	96	73	89	118	144
Women and girls	100	35	37	34	63	69	96	189
Women, aged 16 or older	100	37	38	33	61	70	97	189
Girls, aged 2 to 15	100	15	36	44	83	61	91	193
Children under age 2	100	63	27	57	68	77	85	177
Footwear	100	40	39	42	78	112	100	161
Other apparel products and services	100	39	45	41	56	54	56	212
TRANSPORTATION	100	34	46	67	73	89	103	164
Vehicle purchases	100	30	39	70	62	94	99	170
Cars and trucks, new	100	45	33	66	47	69	78	194
Cars and trucks, used	100	5	51	81	92	135	134	127
Other vehicles	100	–	–	4	16	166	167	176
Gasoline and motor oil	100	40	61	76	91	94	112	141
Other vehicle expenses	100	36	50	64	80	85	107	160
Vehicle finance charges	100	23	38	65	93	99	120	151
Maintenance and repairs	100	36	61	64	67	81	115	157
Vehicle insurance	100	45	55	76	86	93	104	148
Vehicle rentals, leases, licenses, other charges	100	26	31	38	76	66	92	194
Public transportation	100	26	25	35	50	54	84	215
HEALTH CARE	100	52	62	79	91	109	109	131
Health insurance	100	54	66	83	85	105	109	132
Medical services	100	56	44	66	92	117	110	139
Drugs	100	45	81	90	109	112	102	117
Medical supplies	100	52	49	66	73	84	126	148
ENTERTAINMENT	100	33	43	92	64	64	109	164
Fees and admissions	100	31	26	32	53	53	91	210
Audio and visual equipment and services	100	52	61	74	95	92	106	140
Pets, toys, hobbies, playground equipment	100	34	53	48	86	84	89	170
Other entertainment products and services	100	10	32	198	19	25	144	147
PERSONAL CARE PRODUCTS AND SERVICES	100	36	49	64	60	91	95	169
READING	100	39	37	51	69	85	104	174
EDUCATION	100	13	11	34	20	32	57	255
TOBACCO PRODUCTS AND SMOKING SUPPLIES	100	88	104	97	131	110	107	86
MISCELLANEOUS	100	33	52	55	65	87	98	172
CASH CONTRIBUTIONS	100	28	32	44	57	69	102	192
PERSONAL INSURANCE AND PENSIONS	100	6	13	29	55	68	101	213
Life and other personal insurance	100	24	41	44	60	75	100	188
Pensions and Social Security	100	4	10	27	55	67	101	215
PERSONAL TAXES	100	7	1	14	28	46	79	250
Federal income taxes	100	3	–2	10	23	41	77	258
State and local income taxes	100	–1	2	14	28	42	78	253
Other taxes	100	56	25	56	66	91	98	173
GIFTS FOR PEOPLE IN OTHER HOUSEHOLDS	100	25	28	36	51	71	81	207

Note: "–" means sample is too small to make a reliable estimate.
Source: Calculations by New Strategist based on the Bureau of Labor Statistics' 2004 and 2005 Consumer Expenditure Surveys

Table 18. Aged 65 or older: Average spending by income, 2004–05

(average annual spending of consumer units (CUs) headed by people aged 65 or older by product and service category and before-tax income of consumer unit, 2004–05)

	total consumer units 65 or older	under $10,000	$10,000–$19,999	$20,000–$29,999	$30,000–$39,999	$40,000–$49,999	$50,000–$69,999	$70,000 or more
Number of consumer units (in 000s)	22,786	2,947	6,687	4,124	2,765	1,774	1,958	2,530
Average number of persons per CU	1.7	1.2	1.3	1.7	1.9	2.0	2.2	2.5
Average before-tax income of CU	$36,034	$6,820	$14,699	$24,733	$34,669	$44,775	$58,974	$122,499
Average annual spending of CU	31,913	14,241	19,281	27,490	32,086	40,227	46,492	74,265
FOOD	4,183	2,262	2,648	3,726	4,160	5,105	6,039	8,378
Food at home	2,662	1,727	1,940	2,442	2,632	3,185	3,550	4,549
Cereals and bakery products	380	244	296	353	368	454	519	593
Cereals and cereal products	112	80	97	97	105	130	142	166
Bakery products	268	164	199	255	263	325	377	427
Meats, poultry, fish, and eggs	631	466	458	557	628	771	831	1,043
Beef	177	117	127	156	203	223	252	258
Pork	137	112	103	133	139	170	176	181
Other meats	85	53	61	71	72	98	105	185
Poultry	97	88	82	79	93	104	122	146
Fish and seafood	103	68	59	83	87	143	139	227
Eggs	33	26	27	35	34	32	38	46
Dairy products	310	197	232	301	318	384	402	482
Fresh milk and cream	118	99	94	111	120	137	146	166
Other dairy products	192	97	137	190	197	248	256	316
Fruits and vegetables	500	327	375	463	484	572	627	888
Fresh fruits	172	116	125	156	164	187	222	322
Fresh vegetables	157	112	118	147	146	169	190	291
Processed fruits	100	58	78	87	99	125	132	169
Processed vegetables	71	41	54	74	76	91	82	106
Other food at home	842	494	580	768	834	1,003	1,171	1,543
Sugar and other sweets	108	57	84	106	101	126	139	187
Fats and oils	74	61	57	71	69	91	99	103
Miscellaneous foods	422	229	282	370	424	534	596	792
Nonalcoholic beverages	202	135	150	201	197	219	274	328
Food prepared by consumer unit on trips	35	12	7	21	43	33	64	133
Food away from home	1,521	534	708	1,285	1,529	1,920	2,488	3,829
ALCOHOLIC BEVERAGES	254	109	110	203	232	298	353	755
HOUSING	10,673	5,994	7,710	9,780	10,660	12,592	13,760	21,471
Shelter	5,600	3,333	4,209	5,075	5,335	6,486	7,120	11,271
Owned dwellings	3,730	1,544	2,322	3,293	3,771	4,627	5,472	8,691
Mortgage interest and charges	978	355	423	707	902	1,265	1,707	2,928
Property taxes	1,468	678	991	1,336	1,520	1,855	2,029	3,101
Maintenance, repair, insurance, other expenses	1,285	511	907	1,250	1,349	1,507	1,737	2,662
Rented dwellings	1,444	1,736	1,789	1,490	1,202	1,297	881	919
Other lodging	426	53	98	292	361	561	767	1,661
Utilities, fuels, and public services	2,703	1,728	2,163	2,709	2,914	3,109	3,341	4,250
Natural gas	467	300	385	482	488	546	584	680
Electricity	995	646	795	989	1,057	1,136	1,191	1,624
Fuel oil and other fuels	181	106	163	217	196	160	182	251
Telephone services	716	482	549	690	792	828	924	1,147
Water and other public services	345	194	271	331	380	439	460	548
Household services	671	209	459	643	608	651	812	1,788
Personal services	153	64	144	202	57	88	166	344
Other household services	517	145	315	441	552	563	646	1,444
Housekeeping supplies	522	263	370	446	542	698	737	914
Laundry and cleaning supplies	109	64	84	98	116	160	146	148
Other household products	260	123	178	228	264	328	379	486
Postage and stationery	153	76	108	121	163	210	212	280

	total consumer units 65 or older	under $10,000	$10,000– $19,999	$20,000– $29,999	$30,000– $39,999	$40,000– $49,999	$50,000– $69,999	$70,000 or more
Household furnishings and equipment	$1,177	$461	$510	$907	$1,261	$1,648	$1,750	$3,247
Household textiles	122	34	49	128	124	173	184	292
Furniture	262	82	96	143	287	449	318	901
Floor coverings	35	23	13	19	22	58	115	74
Major appliances	192	69	116	158	178	226	257	521
Small appliances, miscellaneous housewares	92	30	58	77	115	117	108	208
Miscellaneous household equipment	474	223	178	381	535	625	767	1,250
APPAREL AND RELATED SERVICES	**930**	**463**	**446**	**675**	**771**	**1,214**	**1,630**	**2,360**
Men and boys	**197**	**90**	**70**	**157**	**166**	**285**	**306**	**554**
Men, aged 16 or older	174	75	57	146	140	253	257	511
Boys, aged 2 to 15	23	15	13	11	26	31	48	44
Women and girls	**439**	**195**	**216**	**322**	**351**	**549**	**815**	**1,104**
Women, aged 16 or older	413	186	204	304	312	520	781	1,030
Girls, aged 2 to 15	26	8	12	19	38	29	33	74
Children under age 2	**21**	**9**	**10**	**18**	**27**	**22**	**33**	**53**
Footwear	**141**	**112**	**88**	**93**	**98**	**167**	**294**	**264**
Other apparel products and services	**131**	**56**	**62**	**86**	**129**	**192**	**182**	**386**
TRANSPORTATION	**4,977**	**1,607**	**2,244**	**4,616**	**5,293**	**7,249**	**8,953**	**11,686**
Vehicle purchases	**1,946**	**447**	**574**	**1,909**	**1,978**	**3,274**	**4,062**	**4,771**
Cars and trucks, new	1,206	281	205	1,242	1,290	2,484	2,349	2,997
Cars and trucks, used	734	166	369	667	669	790	1,700	1,753
Other vehicles	6	–	–	–	19	–	13	21
Gasoline and motor oil	**1,086**	**497**	**640**	**998**	**1,310**	**1,442**	**1,709**	**2,118**
Other vehicle expenses	**1,566**	**574**	**900**	**1,425**	**1,719**	**1,978**	**2,467**	**3,542**
Vehicle finance charges	112	31	46	93	155	146	182	292
Maintenance and repairs	513	184	310	425	560	590	846	1,205
Vehicle insurance	683	291	441	684	739	908	1,062	1,261
Vehicle rentals, leases, licenses, other charges	257	68	104	224	265	334	377	784
Public transportation	**380**	**88**	**130**	**284**	**286**	**555**	**715**	**1,254**
HEALTH CARE	**4,052**	**2,121**	**3,124**	**3,994**	**4,694**	**4,745**	**5,383**	**6,589**
Health insurance	2,224	1,243	1,718	2,246	2,575	2,876	2,957	3,263
Medical services	726	283	501	680	752	691	941	1,742
Drugs	953	521	812	944	1,172	1,012	1,209	1,333
Medical supplies	148	73	93	124	195	166	276	251
ENTERTAINMENT	**1,472**	**471**	**748**	**1,037**	**1,396**	**2,490**	**2,310**	**3,933**
Fees and admissions	386	58	128	235	358	476	620	1,489
Audio and visual equipment and services	597	303	433	528	595	703	865	1,198
Pets, toys, hobbies, playground equipment	218	61	134	184	242	282	325	509
Other entertainment products and services	270	49	54	90	201	1,030	500	738
PERSONAL CARE PRODUCTS AND SERVICES	**465**	**184**	**298**	**430**	**500**	**605**	**727**	**888**
READING	**145**	**52**	**95**	**131**	**155**	**191**	**219**	**305**
EDUCATION	**243**	**78**	**52**	**98**	**110**	**204**	**299**	**1,298**
TOBACCO PRODUCTS AND SMOKING SUPPLIES	**155**	**110**	**127**	**161**	**176**	**193**	**181**	**202**
MISCELLANEOUS	**739**	**179**	**350**	**574**	**937**	**1,028**	**1,200**	**1,853**
CASH CONTRIBUTIONS	**1,941**	**464**	**995**	**1,435**	**1,760**	**2,499**	**2,444**	**6,407**
PERSONAL INSURANCE AND PENSIONS	**1,684**	**148**	**333**	**629**	**1,242**	**1,812**	**2,995**	**8,139**
Life and other personal insurance	388	124	192	258	415	464	529	1,233
Pensions and Social Security	1,296	24	141	371	828	1,348	2,467	6,906
PERSONAL TAXES	**933**	**43**	**199**	**935**	**312**	**615**	**1,159**	**4,632**
Federal income taxes	625	5	66	675	57	254	691	3,577
State and local income taxes	94	–5	8	24	25	50	139	620
Other taxes	214	43	125	236	230	310	328	435
GIFTS FOR PEOPLE IN OTHER HOUSEHOLDS	**944**	**355**	**569**	**663**	**666**	**939**	**1,203**	**3,109**

Note: Spending by category will not add to total spending because gift spending is also included in the preceding product and service categories and personal taxes are not included in the total. "–" means sample is too small to make a reliable estimate.
Source: Bureau of Labor Statistics, 2004 and 2005 Consumer Expenditure Surveys, Internet site http://www.bls.gov/cex/; calculations by New Strategist

Table 19. Aged 65 or older: Indexed spending by income, 2004–05

(indexed average annual spending of consumer units headed by people aged 65 or older by product and service category and before-tax income of consumer unit, 2004–05; index definition: an index of 100 is the average for all consumer units; an index of 132 means that spending by consumer units in that group is 32 percent above the average for all consumer units; an index of 68 indicates spending that is 32 percent below the average for all consumer units)

	total consumer units 65 or older	under $10,000	$10,000– $19,999	$20,000– $29,999	$30,000– $39,999	$40,000– $49,999	$50,000– $69,999	$70,000 or more
Average spending of consumer units, total	$31,913	$14,241	$19,281	$27,490	$32,086	$40,227	$46,492	$74,265
Average spending of consumer units, index	100	45	60	86	101	126	146	233
FOOD	100	54	63	89	99	122	144	200
Food at home	100	65	73	92	99	120	133	171
Cereals and bakery products	100	64	78	93	97	119	137	156
Cereals and cereal products	100	72	87	87	94	116	127	148
Bakery products	100	61	74	95	98	121	141	159
Meats, poultry, fish, and eggs	100	74	73	88	100	122	132	165
Beef	100	66	72	88	115	126	142	146
Pork	100	82	75	97	101	124	128	132
Other meats	100	63	72	84	85	115	124	218
Poultry	100	91	84	81	96	107	126	151
Fish and seafood	100	66	57	81	84	139	135	220
Eggs	100	78	82	106	103	97	115	139
Dairy products	100	63	75	97	103	124	130	155
Fresh milk and cream	100	84	80	94	102	116	124	141
Other dairy products	100	51	72	99	103	129	133	165
Fruits and vegetables	100	65	75	93	97	114	125	178
Fresh fruits	100	67	73	91	95	109	129	187
Fresh vegetables	100	71	75	94	93	108	121	185
Processed fruits	100	58	78	87	99	125	132	169
Processed vegetables	100	58	76	104	107	128	115	149
Other food at home	100	59	69	91	99	119	139	183
Sugar and other sweets	100	53	77	98	94	117	129	173
Fats and oils	100	83	77	96	93	123	134	139
Miscellaneous foods	100	54	67	88	100	127	141	188
Nonalcoholic beverages	100	67	74	100	98	108	136	162
Food prepared by consumer unit on trips	100	34	19	60	123	94	183	380
Food away from home	100	35	47	84	101	126	164	252
ALCOHOLIC BEVERAGES	100	43	43	80	91	117	139	297
HOUSING	100	56	72	92	100	118	129	201
Shelter	100	60	75	91	95	116	127	201
Owned dwellings	100	41	62	88	101	124	147	233
Mortgage interest and charges	100	36	43	72	92	129	175	299
Property taxes	100	46	68	91	104	126	138	211
Maintenance, repair, insurance, other expenses	100	40	71	97	105	117	135	207
Rented dwellings	100	120	124	103	83	90	61	64
Other lodging	100	12	23	69	85	132	180	390
Utilities, fuels, and public services	100	64	80	100	108	115	124	157
Natural gas	100	64	82	103	104	117	125	146
Electricity	100	65	80	99	106	114	120	163
Fuel oil and other fuels	100	59	90	120	108	88	101	139
Telephone services	100	67	77	96	111	116	129	160
Water and other public services	100	56	79	96	110	127	133	159
Household services	100	31	68	96	91	97	121	266
Personal services	100	42	94	132	37	58	108	225
Other household services	100	28	61	85	107	109	125	279
Housekeeping supplies	100	50	71	85	104	134	141	175
Laundry and cleaning supplies	100	58	77	90	106	147	134	136
Other household products	100	47	69	88	102	126	146	187
Postage and stationery	100	50	71	79	107	137	139	183

	total consumer units 65 or older	under $10,000	$10,000–$19,999	$20,000–$29,999	$30,000–$39,999	$40,000–$49,999	$50,000–$69,999	$70,000 or more
Household furnishings and equipment	100	39	43	77	107	140	149	276
Household textiles	100	28	40	105	102	142	151	239
Furniture	100	31	37	55	110	171	121	344
Floor coverings	100	65	37	54	63	166	329	211
Major appliances	100	36	60	82	93	118	134	271
Small appliances, miscellaneous housewares	100	33	63	84	125	127	117	226
Miscellaneous household equipment	100	47	38	80	113	132	162	264
APPAREL AND RELATED SERVICES	100	50	48	73	83	131	175	254
Men and boys	100	46	35	80	84	145	155	281
Men, aged 16 or older	100	43	33	84	80	145	148	294
Boys, aged 2 to 15	100	65	55	48	113	135	209	191
Women and girls	100	44	49	73	80	125	186	251
Women, aged 16 or older	100	45	50	74	76	126	189	249
Girls, aged 2 to 15	100	32	47	73	146	112	127	285
Children under age 2	100	45	49	86	129	105	157	252
Footwear	100	80	63	66	70	118	209	187
Other apparel products and services	100	43	47	66	98	147	139	295
TRANSPORTATION	100	32	45	93	106	146	180	235
Vehicle purchases	100	23	29	98	102	168	209	245
Cars and trucks, new	100	23	17	103	107	206	195	249
Cars and trucks, used	100	23	50	91	91	108	232	239
Other vehicles	100	–	–	–	317	–	217	350
Gasoline and motor oil	100	46	59	92	121	133	157	195
Other vehicle expenses	100	37	57	91	110	126	158	226
Vehicle finance charges	100	28	41	83	138	130	163	261
Maintenance and repairs	100	36	60	83	109	115	165	235
Vehicle insurance	100	43	65	100	108	133	155	185
Vehicle rentals, leases, licenses, other charges	100	27	40	87	103	130	147	305
Public transportation	100	23	34	75	75	146	188	330
HEALTH CARE	100	52	77	99	116	117	133	163
Health insurance	100	56	77	101	116	129	133	147
Medical services	100	39	69	94	104	95	130	240
Drugs	100	55	85	99	123	106	127	140
Medical supplies	100	49	63	84	132	112	186	170
ENTERTAINMENT	100	32	51	70	95	169	157	267
Fees and admissions	100	15	33	61	93	123	161	386
Audio and visual equipment and services	100	51	73	88	100	118	145	201
Pets, toys, hobbies, playground equipment	100	28	62	84	111	129	149	233
Other entertainment products and services	100	18	20	33	74	381	185	273
PERSONAL CARE PRODUCTS AND SERVICES	100	40	64	92	108	130	156	191
READING	100	36	65	90	107	132	151	210
EDUCATION	100	32	22	40	45	84	123	534
TOBACCO PRODUCTS AND SMOKING SUPPLIES	100	71	82	104	114	125	117	130
MISCELLANEOUS	100	24	47	78	127	139	162	251
CASH CONTRIBUTIONS	100	24	51	74	91	129	126	330
PERSONAL INSURANCE AND PENSIONS	100	9	20	37	74	108	178	483
Life and other personal insurance	100	32	50	66	107	120	136	318
Pensions and Social Security	100	2	11	29	64	104	190	533
PERSONAL TAXES	100	5	21	100	33	66	124	496
Federal income taxes	100	1	11	108	9	41	111	572
State and local income taxes	100	–6	9	26	27	53	148	660
Other taxes	100	20	59	110	107	145	153	203
GIFTS FOR PEOPLE IN OTHER HOUSEHOLDS	100	38	60	70	71	99	127	329

Note: "–" means sample is too small to make a reliable estimate.
Source: Calculations by New Strategist based on the Bureau of Labor Statistics' 2004 and 2005 Consumer Expenditure Surveys

Spending by Household Type, 2005

Married couples spent 30 percent more than the average household in 2005. Among married couples, those with school-aged or adult children at home spend the most, more than $68,000 in 2005. Behind the higher spending levels of married couples are their higher incomes, due primarily to the greater number of earners in the household. Married couples with children at home average 2.0 earners per household. Those with school-aged or adult children at home average 2.3 to 2.5 earners. The more earners, the greater the spending—particularly on products and services needed by workers such as food away from home, men's and women's clothes, and transportation.

Married couples with children under age 18 have distinct spending patterns. Couples with school-aged children spend 47 percent more than the average household overall. They spend 66 percent more than the average household on milk and 64 percent more on cereal. They spend more than twice the average household on fees and admissions to entertainment events and three times the average on children's clothes. The biggest spenders on household personal services (mostly day care) are married couples with preschoolers, while couples without children at home (mostly empty-nesters) spend the most on health care.

Single parents spend less than the average household on most items. Some of the exceptions are rent, children's clothes, and household personal services (mostly day care).

Table 20. Average spending by household type, 2005

(average annual spending of consumer units (CUs) by product and service category and type of consumer unit, 2005)

	total married couples	married couples, no children	married couples with children total	oldest child under 6	oldest child 6 to 17	oldest child 18 or older	single parent, at least one child <18	single person
Number of consumer units (in 000s)	59,337	25,293	29,528	5,659	15,477	8,393	6,902	34,339
Average number of persons per CU	3.2	2.0	3.9	3.5	4.1	3.9	2.8	1.0
Average before-tax income of CU	$79,679	$69,453	$87,527	$76,205	$89,981	$90,635	$33,286	$30,290
Average annual spending of CU	60,401	53,486	66,441	58,538	68,421	68,211	35,365	26,773
FOOD	7,698	6,351	8,764	6,943	9,156	9,308	5,283	3,073
Food at home	4,269	3,413	4,878	4,070	5,031	5,161	3,099	1,638
Cereals and bakery products	578	452	673	547	705	701	423	227
Cereals and cereal products	184	134	221	179	235	223	149	69
Bakery products	393	319	452	368	470	478	274	158
Meats, poultry, fish, and eggs	997	806	1,108	761	1,162	1,252	769	332
Beef	302	233	342	218	367	382	235	90
Pork	199	171	213	134	224	249	156	67
Other meats	135	110	150	107	159	162	105	45
Poultry	170	125	196	160	201	213	148	61
Fish and seafood	152	135	165	109	167	200	91	52
Eggs	40	33	43	33	44	47	33	18
Dairy products	493	376	582	509	613	573	347	193
Fresh milk and cream	187	131	229	212	243	215	146	74
Other dairy products	305	245	352	297	370	358	201	118
Fruits and vegetables	718	604	794	723	796	842	461	290
Fresh fruits	239	202	264	253	260	280	139	100
Fresh vegetables	229	197	248	214	246	276	132	91
Processed fruits	134	109	151	152	156	143	105	58
Processed vegetables	116	95	131	105	134	143	86	42
Other food at home	1,483	1,175	1,721	1,529	1,755	1,794	1,099	597
Sugar and other sweets	154	132	172	131	178	190	111	61
Fats and oils	108	91	120	89	123	137	81	44
Miscellaneous foods	781	600	929	917	936	926	607	312
Nonalcoholic beverages	381	291	442	343	460	480	283	161
Food prepared by consumer unit on trips	59	61	57	49	57	62	16	19
Food away from home	3,429	2,938	3,886	2,873	4,125	4,147	2,185	1,435
ALCOHOLIC BEVERAGES	488	505	476	496	446	521	221	327
HOUSING	18,902	16,359	21,057	21,734	21,887	19,084	12,905	9,835
Shelter	10,732	9,239	12,043	12,285	12,760	10,558	7,521	6,179
Owned dwellings	8,453	7,094	9,691	9,418	10,461	8,456	3,548	3,055
Mortgage interest and charges	4,816	3,391	6,026	6,297	6,557	4,863	2,265	1,429
Property taxes	2,151	2,114	2,238	2,002	2,359	2,174	729	907
Maintenance, repair, insurance, other expenses	1,485	1,589	1,427	1,119	1,544	1,419	554	720
Rented dwellings	1,523	1,264	1,643	2,528	1,567	1,185	3,802	2,889
Other lodging	756	881	709	338	732	917	170	235
Utilities, fuels, and public services	3,866	3,481	4,114	3,364	4,190	4,480	2,994	2,024
Natural gas	575	532	603	501	637	609	453	312
Electricity	1,397	1,265	1,482	1,243	1,517	1,577	1,145	719
Fuel oil and other fuels	188	190	189	103	187	249	54	99
Telephone services	1,247	1,073	1,359	1,104	1,354	1,538	1,042	664
Water and other public services	459	421	482	413	495	506	299	230
Household services	1,094	713	1,422	2,863	1,343	597	857	383
Personal services	474	40	830	2,313	710	50	598	42
Other household services	620	673	593	550	633	546	260	341
Housekeeping supplies	815	754	871	879	876	857	445	321
Laundry and cleaning supplies	173	140	195	182	194	207	137	66
Other household products	439	400	472	497	461	475	218	159
Postage and stationery	204	214	204	199	220	175	89	96
Household furnishings and equipment	2,394	2,172	2,607	2,343	2,719	2,593	1,089	928

	total married couples	married couples, no children	married couples with children				single parent, at least one child <18	single person
			total	oldest child under 6	oldest child 6 to 17	oldest child 18 or older		
Household textiles	$174	$160	$190	$154	$212	$176	$131	$65
Furniture	658	603	707	802	770	528	354	218
Floor coverings	83	76	98	86	119	67	25	25
Major appliances	317	306	333	187	399	307	72	104
Small appliances, miscellaneous housewares	139	145	136	146	123	155	71	62
Miscellaneous household equipment	1,023	882	1,142	969	1,096	1,360	436	454
APPAREL AND RELATED SERVICES	2,377	1,694	2,953	2,574	2,978	3,191	2,167	980
Men and boys	571	413	701	583	726	740	490	223
Men, aged 16 or older	448	388	497	475	422	662	239	212
Boys, aged 2 to 15	123	25	203	108	304	78	251	11
Women and girls	944	669	1,194	905	1,188	1,422	903	386
Women, aged 16 or older	769	630	901	755	764	1,277	628	370
Girls, aged 2 to 15	175	39	294	150	424	145	275	16
Children under age 2	124	47	176	531	103	64	81	16
Footwear	376	221	496	294	510	615	528	172
Other apparel products and services	361	343	386	261	451	351	164	183
TRANSPORTATION	11,333	10,192	12,319	10,647	12,267	13,543	5,910	4,030
Vehicle purchases	5,045	4,642	5,415	4,913	5,495	5,605	2,622	1,395
Cars and trucks, new	2,982	3,019	3,013	2,569	3,118	3,118	894	673
Cars and trucks, used	1,960	1,532	2,289	2,271	2,273	2,333	1,661	669
Other vehicles	104	91	112	74	104	155	67	54
Gasoline and motor oil	2,649	2,215	2,973	2,527	2,902	3,405	1,444	1,032
Other vehicle expenses	3,035	2,683	3,357	2,807	3,289	3,854	1,634	1,336
Vehicle finance charges	413	321	489	474	491	497	203	121
Maintenance and repairs	850	790	926	702	953	1,028	455	437
Vehicle insurance	1,163	995	1,292	1,014	1,179	1,689	687	521
Vehicle rentals, leases, licenses, other charges	609	577	649	616	666	640	288	258
Public transportation	604	652	574	400	582	679	211	267
HEALTH CARE	3,525	4,043	3,081	2,381	3,004	3,695	1,376	1,750
Health insurance	1,794	2,091	1,559	1,331	1,499	1,822	675	893
Medical services	924	935	905	647	917	1,056	433	424
Drugs	665	864	486	314	451	669	211	368
Medical supplies	141	154	131	89	137	149	56	65
ENTERTAINMENT	3,190	2,946	3,486	2,685	4,069	2,958	1,823	1,335
Fees and admissions	825	706	975	520	1,268	742	361	336
Audio and visual equipment and services	1,079	933	1,211	1,026	1,321	1,131	795	591
Pets, toys, hobbies, playground equipment	547	534	575	589	606	511	333	233
Other entertainment products and services	739	773	725	550	874	573	334	175
PERSONAL CARE PRODUCTS AND SERVICES	683	632	735	586	763	788	463	328
READING	158	174	152	106	170	149	57	103
EDUCATION	1,294	810	1,760	529	1,702	2,696	713	500
TOBACCO PRODUCTS AND SMOKING SUPPLIES	322	294	328	246	308	418	274	227
MISCELLANEOUS	999	1,069	922	797	902	1,044	541	563
CASH CONTRIBUTIONS	2,152	2,315	2,094	1,549	2,226	2,220	677	1,313
PERSONAL INSURANCE AND PENSIONS	7,280	6,102	8,313	7,267	8,543	8,595	2,955	2,409
Life and other personal insurance	557	516	575	390	611	632	158	162
Pensions and Social Security	6,723	5,586	7,738	6,877	7,932	7,962	2,796	2,247
PERSONAL TAXES	3,434	3,338	3,780	2,684	4,385	3,403	519	1,425
Federal income taxes	2,440	2,448	2,639	1,683	3,085	2,459	187	1,016
State and local income taxes	749	610	916	756	1,077	728	269	286
Other taxes	244	281	225	245	223	215	64	124
GIFTS FOR PEOPLE IN OTHER HOUSEHOLDS	1,426	1,874	1,102	667	1,111	1,379	697	769

Note: Spending by category will not add to total spending because gift spending is also included in the preceding product and service categories and personal taxes are not included in the total.

Source: Bureau of Labor Statistics, 2005 Consumer Expenditure Survey, Internet site http://www.bls.gov/cex/; calculations by New Strategist

Table 21. Indexed spending by household type, 2005

(indexed average annual spending of consumer units by product and service category and type of consumer unit, 2005; index definition: an index of 100 is the average for all consumer units; an index of 132 means that spending by consumer units in that group is 32 percent above the average for all consumer units; an index of 68 indicates spending that is 32 percent below the average for all consumer units)

	total married couples	married couples, no children	married couples with children				single parent, at least one child <18	single person
			total	oldest child under 6	oldest child 6 to 17	oldest child 18 or older		
Average spending of consumer units, total	$60,401	$53,486	$66,441	$58,538	$68,421	$68,211	$35,365	$26,773
Average spending of consumer units, index	130	115	143	126	147	147	76	58
FOOD	**130**	**107**	**148**	**117**	**154**	**157**	**89**	**52**
Food at home	**129**	**104**	**148**	**123**	**153**	**157**	**94**	**50**
Cereals and bakery products	130	102	151	123	158	158	95	51
Cereals and cereal products	129	94	155	125	164	156	104	48
Bakery products	130	106	150	122	156	158	91	52
Meats, poultry, fish, and eggs	130	105	145	100	152	164	101	43
Beef	132	102	150	96	161	168	103	39
Pork	130	112	139	88	146	163	102	44
Other meats	131	107	146	104	154	157	102	44
Poultry	127	93	146	119	150	159	110	46
Fish and seafood	135	119	146	96	148	177	81	46
Eggs	121	100	130	100	133	142	100	55
Dairy products	130	99	154	135	162	152	92	51
Fresh milk and cream	128	90	157	145	166	147	100	51
Other dairy products	131	106	152	128	159	154	87	51
Fruits and vegetables	130	109	144	131	144	153	84	53
Fresh fruits	131	111	145	139	143	154	76	55
Fresh vegetables	131	113	142	122	141	158	75	52
Processed fruits	126	103	142	143	147	135	99	55
Processed vegetables	130	107	147	118	151	161	97	47
Other food at home	128	101	149	132	152	155	95	52
Sugar and other sweets	129	111	145	110	150	160	93	51
Fats and oils	127	107	141	105	145	161	95	52
Miscellaneous foods	128	99	153	151	154	152	100	51
Nonalcoholic beverages	126	96	146	113	152	158	93	53
Food prepared by consumer unit on trips	144	149	139	120	139	151	39	46
Food away from home	**130**	**112**	**148**	**109**	**157**	**157**	**83**	**54**
ALCOHOLIC BEVERAGES	**115**	**119**	**112**	**116**	**105**	**122**	**52**	**77**
HOUSING	**125**	**108**	**139**	**143**	**144**	**126**	**85**	**65**
Shelter	**122**	**105**	**137**	**140**	**145**	**120**	**85**	**70**
Owned dwellings	142	119	163	158	176	142	60	51
Mortgage interest and charges	145	102	182	190	198	147	68	43
Property taxes	140	137	145	130	153	141	47	59
Maintenance, repair, insurance, other expenses	135	144	130	102	140	129	50	65
Rented dwellings	65	54	70	108	67	51	162	123
Other lodging	151	175	141	67	146	183	34	47
Utilities, fuels, and public services	**121**	**109**	**129**	**106**	**132**	**141**	**94**	**64**
Natural gas	122	112	127	106	135	129	96	66
Electricity	121	110	128	108	131	137	99	62
Fuel oil and other fuels	132	134	133	73	132	175	38	70
Telephone services	119	102	130	105	129	147	99	63
Water and other public services	125	115	132	113	135	138	82	63
Household services	**137**	**89**	**178**	**357**	**168**	**75**	**107**	**48**
Personal services	147	12	258	718	220	16	186	13
Other household services	129	141	124	115	132	114	54	71
Housekeeping supplies	**133**	**123**	**143**	**144**	**143**	**140**	**73**	**53**
Laundry and cleaning supplies	129	104	146	136	145	154	102	49
Other household products	137	125	148	155	144	148	68	50
Postage and stationery	130	136	130	127	140	111	57	61

	total married couples	married couples, no children	married couples with children				single parent, at least one child <18	single person
			total	oldest child under 6	oldest child 6 to 17	oldest child 18 or older		
Household furnishings and equipment	135	123	148	133	154	147	62	53
Household textiles	132	121	144	117	161	133	99	49
Furniture	141	129	151	172	165	113	76	47
Floor coverings	148	136	175	154	213	120	45	45
Major appliances	142	137	149	84	179	138	32	47
Small appliances, miscellaneous housewares	132	138	130	139	117	148	68	59
Miscellaneous household equipment	131	113	146	124	140	174	56	58
APPAREL AND RELATED SERVICES	126	90	157	136	158	169	115	52
Men and boys	130	94	159	133	165	168	111	51
Men, aged 16 or older	128	111	142	136	121	190	68	61
Boys, aged 2 to 15	135	27	223	119	334	86	276	12
Women and girls	125	89	158	120	158	189	120	51
Women, aged 16 or older	121	100	142	119	121	202	99	58
Girls, aged 2 to 15	145	32	243	124	350	120	227	13
Children under age 2	151	57	215	648	126	78	99	20
Footwear	118	69	155	92	159	192	165	54
Other apparel products and services	124	118	133	90	156	121	57	63
TRANSPORTATION	136	122	148	128	147	162	71	48
Vehicle purchases	142	131	153	139	155	158	74	39
Cars and trucks, new	154	156	156	133	161	161	46	35
Cars and trucks, used	128	100	150	148	148	152	108	44
Other vehicles	127	111	137	90	127	189	82	66
Gasoline and motor oil	132	110	148	126	144	169	72	51
Other vehicle expenses	130	115	144	120	141	165	70	57
Vehicle finance charges	139	108	165	160	165	167	68	41
Maintenance and repairs	127	118	138	105	142	153	68	65
Vehicle insurance	127	109	142	111	129	185	75	57
Vehicle rentals, leases, licenses, other charges	133	126	142	134	145	140	63	56
Public transportation	135	146	128	89	130	152	47	60
HEALTH CARE	132	152	116	89	113	139	52	66
Health insurance	132	154	115	98	110	134	50	66
Medical services	136	138	134	96	135	156	64	63
Drugs	128	166	93	60	87	128	40	71
Medical supplies	134	147	125	85	130	142	53	62
ENTERTAINMENT	134	123	146	112	170	124	76	56
Fees and admissions	140	120	166	88	216	126	61	57
Audio and visual equipment and services	122	105	136	116	149	127	90	67
Pets, toys, hobbies, playground equipment	130	127	137	140	144	122	79	55
Other entertainment products and services	150	157	147	112	178	116	68	36
PERSONAL CARE PRODUCTS AND SERVICES	126	117	136	108	141	146	86	61
READING	125	138	121	84	135	118	45	82
EDUCATION	138	86	187	56	181	287	76	53
TOBACCO PRODUCTS AND SMOKING SUPPLIES	101	92	103	77	97	131	86	71
MISCELLANEOUS	124	132	114	99	112	129	67	70
CASH CONTRIBUTIONS	129	139	126	93	134	133	41	79
PERSONAL INSURANCE AND PENSIONS	140	117	160	140	164	165	57	46
Life and other personal insurance	146	135	151	102	160	166	41	43
Pensions and Social Security	139	116	160	143	164	165	58	47
PERSONAL TAXES	143	139	157	111	182	141	22	59
Federal income taxes	144	144	156	99	182	145	11	60
State and local income taxes	140	114	172	142	202	136	50	54
Other taxes	138	159	127	138	126	121	36	70
GIFTS FOR PEOPLE IN OTHER HOUSEHOLDS	131	172	101	61	102	126	64	70

Note: Spending index for total consumer units is 100.
Source: Calculations by New Strategist based on the Bureau of Labor Statistics' 2005 Consumer Expenditure Survey

Spending by Household Type and Age, 2004–05

Women who live alone spent an annual average of $24,467 in 2004–05, only 54 percent of the $44,928 spent by the average household during that time period. Forty-one percent of women who live alone are aged 65 or older, many of them elderly widows with low incomes.

Among women who live alone, spending peaks in the 35-to-44 age group at $31,524 in 2004–05. Women under age 25 spend much more than the average household on education, with an index of 223. Women aged 45 to 54 who live alone spend 62 percent more than the average household on women's clothes. Among women who live alone, those aged 65 or older spend less than their middle-aged counterparts, an average of $20,699 in 2004–05. But they spend more than the average household on health care.

Men who live alone spent an annual average of $28,157 in 2004–05, only 63 percent of what the average household spent during the time period.

Among men who live alone, those under age 25 spend much more than the average household on education, with an index of 259. Men aged 25 to 34 who live alone spend twice the average on rent and 55 percent more than average on alcoholic beverages—more, in fact, than any other household type. Men aged 65 or older who live alone spend less than their middle-aged counterparts, an average of $24,277 in 2004–05. They spend only about half of what the average household spends on entertainment and food away from home.

Table 22. Average spending of single-person consumer units headed by women, by age, 2004–05

(average annual spending of single-person consumer units headed by women by product and service category and age, 2004–05)

	total single-person consumer units headed by women	under 25	25 to 34	35 to 44	45 to 54	55 to 64	65 or older
Number of consumer units (in 000s)	18,592	2,077	1,640	1,458	2,533	3,222	7,662
Average before-tax income of consumer units	$25,207	$10,741	$31,630	$39,407	$34,488	$32,796	$18,791
Average annual spending of consumer units	24,467	15,421	29,476	31,524	30,178	28,882	20,699
FOOD	**2,799**	**2,268**	**2,902**	**3,556**	**3,490**	**3,099**	**2,400**
Food at home	**1,704**	**980**	**1,397**	**1,847**	**2,106**	**2,001**	**1,685**
Cereals and bakery products	241	153	180	222	269	287	256
Cereals and cereal products	73	58	56	71	81	82	75
Bakery products	168	95	123	151	189	205	181
Meats, poultry, fish, and eggs	363	168	243	400	511	427	360
Beef	94	43	47	110	143	108	93
Pork	76	31	45	68	106	85	85
Other meats	44	19	40	45	60	48	44
Poultry	69	37	56	88	83	89	65
Fish and seafood	58	26	39	70	93	71	51
Eggs	22	11	16	19	27	26	23
Dairy products	200	119	169	214	228	220	208
Fresh milk and cream	73	41	57	71	80	83	81
Other dairy products	126	77	112	143	148	137	127
Fruits and vegetables	314	157	245	313	351	390	330
Fresh fruits	108	56	94	100	111	136	116
Fresh vegetables	102	40	82	106	120	139	103
Processed fruits	59	36	41	52	67	62	67
Processed vegetables	44	25	27	54	53	54	45
Other food at home	586	384	560	699	746	677	530
Sugar and other sweets	71	41	48	90	84	88	69
Fats and oils	48	20	34	54	60	59	50
Miscellaneous foods	300	219	290	358	370	340	271
Nonalcoholic beverages	150	87	165	175	213	164	131
Food prepared by consumer unit on trips	17	16	23	21	19	26	10
Food away from home	**1,095**	**1,288**	**1,505**	**1,708**	**1,384**	**1,099**	**715**
ALCOHOLIC BEVERAGES	**221**	**367**	**388**	**410**	**273**	**196**	**93**
HOUSING	**9,607**	**4,833**	**11,320**	**12,434**	**11,514**	**11,106**	**8,734**
Shelter	**5,831**	**3,366**	**7,889**	**8,395**	**7,083**	**6,505**	**4,874**
Owned dwellings	3,026	144	2,224	4,667	4,041	4,421	2,743
Mortgage interest and charges	1,241	56	1,504	3,113	2,297	1,850	544
Property taxes	908	71	428	951	1,014	1,239	1,056
Maintenance, repair, insurance, other expenses	876	17	292	602	730	1,332	1,143
Rented dwellings	2,577	2,949	5,470	3,500	2,695	1,756	1,988
Other lodging	229	274	194	228	347	329	143
Utilities, fuels, and public services	**2,002**	**723**	**1,828**	**2,122**	**2,235**	**2,420**	**2,111**
Natural gas	310	50	195	334	295	377	378
Electricity	702	253	615	710	813	853	741
Fuel oil and other fuels	104	6	13	57	83	105	165
Telephone services	657	383	871	816	794	789	554
Water and other public services	229	31	133	205	250	295	273
Household services	**498**	**76**	**298**	**361**	**363**	**491**	**730**
Personal services	121	3	10	13	4	9	284
Other household services	377	73	289	348	359	482	446
Housekeeping supplies	**372**	**151**	**265**	**358**	**557**	**453**	**365**
Laundry and cleaning supplies	77	36	56	87	125	91	70
Other household products	179	69	132	144	279	218	177
Postage and stationery	116	46	77	127	153	144	118

	total single-person consumer units headed by women	under 25	25 to 34	35 to 44	45 to 54	55 to 64	65 or older
Household furnishings and equipment	$903	$517	$1,040	$1,198	$1,276	$1,237	$654
Household textiles	98	36	64	113	171	150	74
Furniture	198	88	351	318	197	305	129
Floor coverings	26	5	10	38	19	66	18
Major appliances	107	31	133	73	133	155	102
Small appliances, miscellaneous housewares	75	48	69	50	88	90	80
Miscellaneous household equipment	398	308	414	605	668	470	252
APPAREL AND RELATED SERVICES	1,069	1,226	1,431	1,648	1,487	1,196	622
Men and boys	58	31	26	118	116	79	29
Men, aged 16 or older	44	30	23	106	98	49	18
Boys, aged 2 to 15	14	2	4	12	17	30	11
Women and girls	671	826	866	1,043	949	689	397
Women, aged 16 or older	654	824	857	1,025	924	670	379
Girls, aged 2 to 15	17	2	9	18	25	19	17
Children under age 2	18	12	14	16	21	35	13
Footwear	190	257	291	248	251	200	110
Other apparel products and services	133	99	233	223	151	194	73
TRANSPORTATION	3,272	2,151	5,231	4,461	4,555	4,255	2,094
Vehicle purchases	1,154	741	2,222	1,342	1,757	1,640	599
Cars and trucks, new	631	299	1,017	909	798	1,015	368
Cars and trucks, used	519	434	1,206	433	958	604	230
Other vehicles	5	8	–	–	1	21	–
Gasoline and motor oil	740	705	1,027	1,024	998	906	478
Other vehicle expenses	1,115	547	1,525	1,669	1,496	1,424	820
Vehicle finance charges	107	48	229	236	153	133	47
Maintenance and repairs	323	155	457	411	390	467	241
Vehicle insurance	480	199	597	626	636	547	423
Vehicle rentals, leases, licenses, other charges	205	146	243	397	317	277	109
Public transportation	263	158	456	427	303	284	196
HEALTH CARE	2,010	294	982	1,335	1,608	2,056	2,938
Health insurance	999	139	378	654	607	922	1,592
Medical services	448	52	320	359	600	557	503
Drugs	479	71	227	266	328	478	737
Medical supplies	84	31	56	56	73	99	107
ENTERTAINMENT	1,075	709	1,408	1,400	1,390	1,444	781
Fees and admissions	254	215	391	329	296	358	163
Audio and visual equipment and services	489	283	614	580	567	591	431
Pets, toys, hobbies, playground equipment	250	140	290	342	441	383	134
Other entertainment products and services	83	70	114	150	86	113	52
PERSONAL CARE PRODUCTS AND SERVICES	458	389	612	564	472	502	397
READING	106	40	100	98	108	139	112
EDUCATION	448	2,056	1,141	242	295	121	92
TOBACCO PRODUCTS AND SMOKING SUPPLIES	137	89	162	215	232	190	77
MISCELLANEOUS	417	154	398	596	514	551	371
CASH CONTRIBUTIONS	1,037	147	428	834	866	1,133	1,465
PERSONAL INSURANCE AND PENSIONS	1,811	698	2,976	3,732	3,375	2,894	525
Life and other personal insurance	154	9	92	135	228	191	169
Pensions and Social Security	1,657	689	2,884	3,597	3,147	2,703	356
PERSONAL TAXES	1,081	236	1,866	1,903	2,246	1,740	324
Federal income taxes	747	176	1,353	1,404	1,545	1,261	168
State and local income taxes	214	59	442	394	540	304	27
Other taxes	120	1	72	105	160	175	130
GIFTS FOR PEOPLE IN OTHER HOUSEHOLDS	770	300	451	981	1,209	865	732

Note: Spending by category will not add to total spending because gift spending is also included in the preceding product and service categories and personal taxes are not included in the total. "–" means value is less than 0.5.
Source: Bureau of Labor Statistics, 2004 and 2005 Consumer Expenditure Surveys, Internet site http://www.bls.gov/cex/

Table 23. Indexed spending of single-person consumer units headed by women, by age, 2004–05

(indexed average annual spending of single-person consumer units headed by women by product and service category and age, 2004–05; index definition: an index of 100 is the average for all consumer units; an index of 132 means that spending by consumer units in that group is 32 percent above the average for all consumer units; an index of 68 indicates spending that is 32 percent below the average for all consumer units)

	total single-person consumer units headed by women	under 25	25 to 34	35 to 44	45 to 54	55 to 64	65 or older
Average spending of consumer units, total	$24,467	$15,421	$29,476	$31,524	$30,178	$28,882	$20,699
Average spending of consumer units, index	54	34	66	70	67	64	46
FOOD	**48**	**39**	**50**	**61**	**60**	**53**	**41**
Food at home	**51**	**30**	**42**	**56**	**63**	**60**	**51**
Cereals and bakery products	53	34	40	49	59	63	57
Cereals and cereal products	49	39	38	48	55	55	51
Bakery products	55	31	40	50	62	67	59
Meats, poultry, fish, and eggs	44	20	30	49	62	52	44
Beef	38	17	19	45	58	44	38
Pork	46	19	27	41	63	51	51
Other meats	42	18	38	42	57	45	42
Poultry	48	26	39	61	57	61	45
Fish and seafood	48	21	32	58	77	59	42
Eggs	59	30	43	51	73	70	62
Dairy products	53	32	45	57	61	59	56
Fresh milk and cream	50	28	39	49	55	57	56
Other dairy products	55	34	49	62	65	60	55
Fruits and vegetables	56	28	44	56	63	70	59
Fresh fruits	59	30	51	54	60	74	63
Fresh vegetables	57	22	46	59	67	78	58
Processed fruits	55	33	38	48	62	57	62
Processed vegetables	52	29	32	64	62	64	53
Other food at home	53	34	50	63	67	61	47
Sugar and other sweets	58	33	39	73	68	72	56
Fats and oils	55	23	39	62	69	68	57
Miscellaneous foods	53	38	51	63	65	60	48
Nonalcoholic beverages	51	29	56	59	72	55	44
Food prepared by consumer unit on trips	41	39	56	51	46	63	24
Food away from home	**43**	**51**	**59**	**67**	**55**	**43**	**28**
ALCOHOLIC BEVERAGES	**50**	**83**	**88**	**93**	**62**	**44**	**21**
HOUSING	**66**	**33**	**78**	**85**	**79**	**76**	**60**
Shelter	**69**	**40**	**93**	**99**	**84**	**77**	**58**
Owned dwellings	53	3	39	82	71	78	48
Mortgage interest and charges	39	2	47	98	72	58	17
Property taxes	62	5	29	65	69	85	72
Maintenance, repair, insurance, other expenses	84	2	28	57	70	127	109
Rented dwellings	113	130	241	154	119	77	87
Other lodging	47	56	40	47	71	68	29
Utilities, fuels, and public services	**65**	**24**	**60**	**69**	**73**	**79**	**69**
Natural gas	69	11	44	75	66	84	84
Electricity	63	23	55	64	73	77	67
Fuel oil and other fuels	79	5	10	44	63	80	126
Telephone services	64	38	85	80	78	77	54
Water and other public services	66	9	38	59	72	85	79
Household services	**64**	**10**	**38**	**46**	**47**	**63**	**94**
Personal services	39	1	3	4	1	3	91
Other household services	81	16	62	75	77	103	96
Housekeeping supplies	**62**	**25**	**44**	**59**	**92**	**75**	**61**
Laundry and cleaning supplies	55	26	40	62	89	65	50
Other household products	59	23	43	47	91	71	58
Postage and stationery	74	29	49	81	98	92	76

	total single-person consumer units headed by women	under 25	25 to 34	35 to 44	45 to 54	55 to 64	65 or older
Household furnishings and equipment	53	30	61	70	75	73	38
Household textiles	68	25	44	78	118	103	51
Furniture	45	20	80	73	45	70	30
Floor coverings	48	9	19	70	35	122	33
Major appliances	50	14	62	34	62	72	48
Small appliances, miscellaneous housewares	71	46	66	48	84	86	76
Miscellaneous household equipment	53	41	55	81	90	63	34
APPAREL AND RELATED SERVICES	58	66	77	89	80	65	34
Men and boys	14	7	6	28	27	19	7
Men, aged 16 or older	13	9	7	32	29	15	5
Boys, aged 2 to 15	16	2	4	13	19	33	12
Women and girls	90	111	116	140	127	92	53
Women, aged 16 or older	103	130	136	162	146	106	60
Girls, aged 2 to 15	15	2	8	16	22	17	15
Children under age 2	23	15	18	20	26	44	16
Footwear	59	79	90	77	77	62	34
Other apparel products and services	48	36	84	81	55	70	26
TRANSPORTATION	40	27	65	55	56	53	26
Vehicle purchases	33	21	64	39	51	47	17
Cars and trucks, new	35	16	56	50	44	56	20
Cars and trucks, used	33	28	77	27	61	38	15
Other vehicles	–	–	–	–	–	–	–
Gasoline and motor oil	41	39	57	57	55	50	26
Other vehicle expenses	47	23	65	71	64	60	35
Vehicle finance charges	35	15	74	76	49	43	15
Maintenance and repairs	49	23	69	62	59	71	36
Vehicle insurance	51	21	63	66	68	58	45
Vehicle rentals, leases, licenses, other charges	46	33	55	90	72	63	25
Public transportation	59	36	103	96	68	64	44
HEALTH CARE	77	11	37	51	61	78	112
Health insurance	74	10	28	49	45	68	118
Medical services	67	8	48	54	90	84	76
Drugs	95	14	45	53	65	95	147
Medical supplies	77	28	51	51	67	91	98
ENTERTAINMENT	47	31	62	61	61	63	34
Fees and admissions	46	39	70	59	53	64	29
Audio and visual equipment and services	58	34	73	69	68	71	51
Pets, toys, hobbies, playground equipment	62	35	72	85	110	96	33
Other entertainment products and services	17	15	24	31	18	23	11
PERSONAL CARE PRODUCTS AND SERVICES	82	69	109	101	84	89	71
READING	83	31	78	77	84	109	88
EDUCATION	48	223	123	26	32	13	10
TOBACCO PRODUCTS AND SMOKING SUPPLIES	45	29	53	71	77	63	25
MISCELLANEOUS	56	21	53	79	68	73	49
CASH CONTRIBUTIONS	68	10	28	54	56	74	95
PERSONAL INSURANCE AND PENSIONS	36	14	59	75	67	58	10
Life and other personal insurance	40	2	24	35	59	49	44
Pensions and Social Security	36	15	62	78	68	59	8
PERSONAL TAXES	48	10	82	84	99	76	14
Federal income taxes	47	11	85	88	97	79	11
State and local income taxes	43	12	88	79	108	61	5
Other taxes	68	1	41	60	91	99	74
GIFTS FOR PEOPLE IN OTHER HOUSEHOLDS	67	26	39	85	105	75	63

Note: Spending index for total consumer units is 100. "–" means sample is too small to make a reliable estimate.
Source: Calculations by New Strategist based on the Bureau of Labor Statistics' 2004–05 Consumer Expenditure Surveys

Table 24. Average spending of single-person consumer units headed by men, by age, 2004–05

(average annual spending of single-person consumer units headed by men by product and service category and age, 2004–05)

	total single-person consumer units headed by men	under 25	25 to 34	35 to 44	45 to 54	55 to 64	65 or older
Number of consumer units (in 000s)	15,405	2,343	2,732	2,563	2,628	2,130	3,010
Average before-tax income of consumer units	$33,995	$13,680	$35,950	$43,434	$45,833	$39,335	$25,883
Average annual spending of consumer units	28,157	18,189	30,218	33,021	32,706	30,222	24,277
FOOD	3,449	2,360	3,649	3,952	3,858	3,558	3,149
Food at home	1,602	886	1,414	1,781	1,968	1,685	1,748
Cereals and bakery products	210	124	181	224	249	215	249
Cereals and cereal products	68	44	67	69	87	59	76
Bakery products	142	81	114	155	161	156	173
Meats, poultry, fish, and eggs	383	226	299	470	502	406	374
Beef	115	69	96	133	160	138	93
Pork	74	46	45	86	89	88	86
Other meats	51	29	42	58	60	55	55
Poultry	66	40	63	94	80	58	58
Fish and seafood	57	33	36	75	88	49	56
Eggs	20	9	17	23	24	17	25
Dairy products	173	93	156	182	194	184	211
Fresh milk and cream	69	36	59	69	81	74	88
Other dairy products	104	58	97	113	113	109	122
Fruits and vegetables	267	124	226	286	327	279	331
Fresh fruits	90	33	70	101	113	106	110
Fresh vegetables	78	39	74	86	95	76	90
Processed fruits	61	33	53	60	73	57	80
Processed vegetables	38	20	29	38	47	40	51
Other food at home	569	318	552	619	697	601	583
Sugar and other sweets	50	22	47	52	61	49	61
Fats and oils	42	21	35	35	61	53	44
Miscellaneous foods	284	177	281	310	324	286	305
Nonalcoholic beverages	169	88	168	194	229	176	148
Food prepared by consumer unit on trips	24	11	21	28	22	37	25
Food away from home	1,847	1,474	2,235	2,171	1,890	1,873	1,401
ALCOHOLIC BEVERAGES	501	590	684	593	469	465	236
HOUSING	9,445	5,236	10,364	11,671	10,993	9,946	8,254
Shelter	6,249	3,784	7,259	7,790	7,364	6,209	4,994
Owned dwellings	2,959	472	2,489	4,165	4,290	3,799	2,539
Mortgage interest and charges	1,618	283	1,779	2,703	2,586	1,845	584
Property taxes	811	150	470	926	1,079	1,136	1,072
Maintenance, repair, insurance, other expenses	530	38	240	536	625	818	884
Rented dwellings	3,014	3,026	4,601	3,439	2,716	2,088	2,116
Other lodging	276	287	168	185	358	322	338
Utilities, fuels, and public services	1,834	819	1,796	2,042	2,137	2,186	1,967
Natural gas	271	66	201	289	366	329	355
Electricity	661	302	651	744	749	801	703
Fuel oil and other fuels	77	8	21	71	73	155	136
Telephone services	641	399	759	750	710	684	539
Water and other public services	184	44	164	189	240	216	234
Household services	306	96	241	331	344	390	412
Personal services	32	5	20	36	15	24	84
Other household services	273	91	222	295	329	366	328
Housekeeping supplies	246	85	235	237	311	296	288
Laundry and cleaning supplies	59	25	53	57	64	75	73
Other household products	120	38	137	94	156	147	132
Postage and stationery	68	21	45	86	91	73	84

	total single-person consumer units headed by men	under 25	25 to 34	35 to 44	45 to 54	55 to 64	65 or older
Household furnishings and equipment	$811	$453	$833	$1,271	$838	$866	$594
Household textiles	47	5	94	45	26	23	67
Furniture	178	130	248	269	156	200	79
Floor coverings	23	13	9	9	22	64	26
Major appliances	80	22	51	84	122	141	70
Small appliances, miscellaneous housewares	41	20	54	38	36	39	50
Miscellaneous household equipment	442	264	377	826	476	398	302
APPAREL AND RELATED SERVICES	823	667	992	968	996	893	448
Men and boys	375	341	412	465	474	330	228
Men, aged 16 or older	362	337	396	452	445	318	224
Boys, aged 2 to 15	13	4	16	13	29	12	4
Women and girls	49	15	55	46	72	38	59
Women, aged 16 or older	35	13	37	12	59	29	52
Girls, aged 2 to 15	14	2	17	34	13	9	7
Children under age 2	9	2	19	8	5	11	6
Footwear	165	160	260	193	172	134	68
Other apparel products and services	225	149	246	255	273	380	88
TRANSPORTATION	4,930	3,773	6,137	4,997	5,086	5,138	4,399
Vehicle purchases	2,000	1,735	2,575	1,841	1,923	1,908	1,950
Cars and trucks, new	874	524	1,223	603	603	997	1,211
Cars and trucks, used	1,042	1,106	1,261	1,155	1,300	691	721
Other vehicles	83	105	91	84	20	220	17
Gasoline and motor oil	1,135	886	1,299	1,267	1,186	1,306	901
Other vehicle expenses	1,540	988	1,924	1,592	1,707	1,670	1,339
Vehicle finance charges	143	81	224	182	155	165	61
Maintenance and repairs	539	409	635	518	558	579	528
Vehicle insurance	584	342	711	602	690	590	545
Vehicle rentals, leases, licenses, other charges	273	156	353	290	305	336	206
Public transportation	257	164	340	296	269	254	210
HEALTH CARE	1,377	288	665	952	1,223	1,866	3,018
Health insurance	713	185	413	558	626	911	1,464
Medical services	360	56	153	179	326	551	835
Drugs	252	36	89	172	229	337	591
Medical supplies	52	12	10	42	42	67	128
ENTERTAINMENT	1,459	1,136	1,665	1,649	1,580	1,535	1,192
Fees and admissions	377	290	413	490	411	273	357
Audio and visual equipment and services	632	473	788	673	712	629	512
Pets, toys, hobbies, playground equipment	171	51	231	210	163	235	133
Other entertainment products and services	279	322	233	275	294	398	190
PERSONAL CARE PRODUCTS AND SERVICES	196	117	241	203	229	202	173
READING	93	47	77	83	112	124	110
EDUCATION	714	2,395	846	282	521	348	79
TOBACCO PRODUCTS AND SMOKING SUPPLIES	266	191	210	358	383	281	185
MISCELLANEOUS	707	168	557	807	885	939	854
CASH CONTRIBUTIONS	1,322	216	888	2,022	1,925	1,584	1,269
PERSONAL INSURANCE AND PENSIONS	2,872	1,003	3,242	4,486	4,445	3,341	911
Life and other personal insurance	155	17	100	139	206	316	167
Pensions and Social Security	2,717	985	3,143	4,347	4,239	3,026	744
PERSONAL TAXES	1,791	367	1,975	2,243	3,264	2,414	621
Federal income taxes	1,309	272	1,490	1,624	2,469	1,812	317
State and local income taxes	365	91	446	504	675	432	71
Other taxes	116	4	39	115	120	170	233
GIFTS FOR PEOPLE IN OTHER HOUSEHOLDS	880	290	568	1,113	1,067	1,168	1,040

Note: Spending by category will not add to total spending because gift spending is also included in the preceding product and service categories and personal taxes are not included in the total.
Source: Bureau of Labor Statistics, 2004 and 2005 Consumer Expenditure Surveys, Internet site http://www.bls.gov/cex/

Table 25. Indexed spending of single-person consumer units headed by men, by age, 2004–05

(indexed average annual spending of single-person consumer units headed by men by product and service category and age, 2004–05; index definition: an index of 100 is the average for all consumer units; an index of 132 means that spending by consumer units in that group is 32 percent above the average for all consumer units; an index of 68 indicates spending that is 32 percent below the average for all consumer units)

	total single-person consumer units headed by men	under 25	25 to 34	35 to 44	45 to 54	55 to 64	65 or older
Average spending of consumer units, total	$28,157	$18,189	$30,218	$33,021	$32,706	$30,222	$24,277
Average spending of consumer units, index	63	40	67	73	73	67	54
FOOD	**59**	**40**	**62**	**67**	**66**	**61**	**54**
Food at home	**48**	**27**	**43**	**54**	**59**	**51**	**53**
Cereals and bakery products	46	27	40	49	55	47	55
Cereals and cereal products	46	30	45	47	59	40	51
Bakery products	47	27	37	51	53	51	57
Meats, poultry, fish, and eggs	47	27	36	57	61	49	45
Beef	47	28	39	54	65	56	38
Pork	44	28	27	51	53	53	51
Other meats	48	27	40	55	57	52	52
Poultry	46	28	43	65	55	40	40
Fish and seafood	47	27	30	62	73	40	46
Eggs	54	24	46	62	65	46	68
Dairy products	46	25	42	49	52	49	56
Fresh milk and cream	48	25	41	48	56	51	61
Other dairy products	45	25	42	49	49	48	53
Fruits and vegetables	48	22	41	51	59	50	60
Fresh fruits	49	18	38	55	61	58	60
Fresh vegetables	44	22	41	48	53	42	50
Processed fruits	56	31	49	56	68	53	74
Processed vegetables	45	24	34	45	55	47	60
Other food at home	51	28	49	55	62	54	52
Sugar and other sweets	41	18	38	42	50	40	50
Fats and oils	48	24	40	40	70	61	51
Miscellaneous foods	50	31	49	54	57	50	54
Nonalcoholic beverages	57	30	57	66	77	59	50
Food prepared by consumer unit on trips	59	27	51	68	54	90	61
Food away from home	**73**	**58**	**88**	**86**	**75**	**74**	**55**
ALCOHOLIC BEVERAGES	**113**	**133**	**155**	**134**	**106**	**105**	**53**
HOUSING	**65**	**36**	**71**	**80**	**75**	**68**	**57**
Shelter	**74**	**45**	**86**	**92**	**87**	**73**	**59**
Owned dwellings	52	8	44	73	75	67	45
Mortgage interest and charges	51	9	56	85	81	58	18
Property taxes	55	10	32	63	74	78	73
Maintenance, repair, insurance, other expenses	51	4	23	51	60	78	84
Rented dwellings	133	133	202	151	119	92	93
Other lodging	57	59	34	38	74	66	69
Utilities, fuels, and public services	**60**	**27**	**59**	**67**	**70**	**72**	**64**
Natural gas	60	15	45	65	82	73	79
Electricity	59	27	59	67	67	72	63
Fuel oil and other fuels	59	6	16	54	56	118	104
Telephone services	63	39	74	74	70	67	53
Water and other public services	53	13	47	54	69	62	67
Household services	**39**	**12**	**31**	**43**	**44**	**50**	**53**
Personal services	10	2	6	12	5	8	27
Other household services	59	20	48	63	71	79	70
Housekeeping supplies	**41**	**14**	**39**	**39**	**52**	**49**	**48**
Laundry and cleaning supplies	42	18	38	40	45	53	52
Other household products	39	12	45	31	51	48	43
Postage and stationery	44	13	29	55	58	47	54

	total single-person consumer units headed by men	under 25	25 to 34	35 to 44	45 to 54	55 to 64	65 or older
Household furnishings and equipment	48	27	49	75	49	51	35
Household textiles	32	3	65	31	18	16	46
Furniture	41	30	57	62	36	46	18
Floor coverings	43	24	17	17	41	119	48
Major appliances	37	10	24	39	57	66	33
Small appliances, miscellaneous housewares	39	19	51	36	34	37	48
Miscellaneous household equipment	59	35	51	111	64	53	40
APPAREL AND RELATED SERVICES	44	36	54	52	54	48	24
Men and boys	89	81	97	110	112	78	54
Men, aged 16 or older	109	101	119	136	134	95	67
Boys, aged 2 to 15	14	4	18	14	32	13	4
Women and girls	7	2	7	6	10	5	8
Women, aged 16 or older	6	2	6	2	9	5	8
Girls, aged 2 to 15	12	2	15	30	11	8	6
Children under age 2	11	3	24	10	6	14	8
Footwear	51	49	80	60	53	41	21
Other apparel products and services	81	54	89	92	99	137	32
TRANSPORTATION	61	47	76	62	63	64	54
Vehicle purchases	58	50	74	53	55	55	56
Cars and trucks, new	48	29	67	33	33	55	66
Cars and trucks, used	66	70	80	73	82	44	46
Other vehicles	112	142	123	114	27	297	23
Gasoline and motor oil	63	49	72	70	66	72	50
Other vehicle expenses	65	42	82	68	73	71	57
Vehicle finance charges	46	26	72	59	50	53	20
Maintenance and repairs	82	62	96	78	84	88	80
Vehicle insurance	62	36	75	64	73	63	58
Vehicle rentals, leases, licenses, other charges	62	35	80	66	69	76	47
Public transportation	58	37	77	67	61	57	47
HEALTH CARE	52	11	25	36	47	71	115
Health insurance	53	14	31	41	46	68	109
Medical services	54	8	23	27	49	83	126
Drugs	50	7	18	34	46	67	117
Medical supplies	48	11	9	39	39	61	117
ENTERTAINMENT	64	50	73	72	69	67	52
Fees and admissions	68	52	74	88	74	49	64
Audio and visual equipment and services	75	56	94	80	85	75	61
Pets, toys, hobbies, playground equipment	43	13	58	52	41	59	33
Other entertainment products and services	58	67	48	57	61	83	39
PERSONAL CARE PRODUCTS AND SERVICES	35	21	43	36	41	36	31
READING	73	37	60	65	88	97	86
EDUCATION	77	259	92	31	56	38	9
TOBACCO PRODUCTS AND SMOKING SUPPLIES	88	63	69	118	126	93	61
MISCELLANEOUS	94	22	74	107	118	125	114
CASH CONTRIBUTIONS	86	14	58	132	125	103	83
PERSONAL INSURANCE AND PENSIONS	57	20	65	90	89	67	18
Life and other personal insurance	40	4	26	36	53	82	43
Pensions and Social Security	59	21	68	94	92	66	16
PERSONAL TAXES	79	16	87	99	143	106	27
Federal income taxes	82	17	93	102	155	113	20
State and local income taxes	73	18	89	101	135	86	14
Other taxes	66	2	22	65	68	97	132
GIFTS FOR PEOPLE IN OTHER HOUSEHOLDS	76	25	49	96	92	101	90

Note: Spending index for total consumer units is 100.
Source: Calculations by New Strategist based on the Bureau of Labor Statistics' 2004 and 2005 Consumer Expenditure Surveys

Spending by Region, 2005

Households in the West spent $52,891 in 2005, 14 percent more than the average household and greater than households in any other region. Spending by households in the Northeast is 3 percent above average, at $47,921. Households in the Midwest spent $45,027, or just slightly below the average amount. In the South, average household spending was 8 percent below average at $42,504 in 2005.

Households in the Northeast and West spend more than the average household on most products and services. Those in the Midwest spend close to the average, while households in the South spend less than average on most items. Households in the Northeast spend the most on property taxes. Those in the West spend the most on mortgage interest and rent. Households in the Midwest spend the most on tobacco. Households in the South spend 18 percent less than average on alcoholic beverages.

The biggest consumers of natural gas are households in the Midwest, spending 53 percent more than the average household on this item. Households in the South spend the most on electricity, while those in the Northeast spend the most on fuel oil. Western households spend 25 percent more than the average household on water and other public services.

Households in the West spend the most on entertainment. Public transportation spending is highest in the Northeast. Spending on women's apparel is 14 percent above average in the Northeast. Households in the Midwest and South spend 7 percent more than average on drugs.

Table 26. Average spending by region, 2005

(average annual spending of consumer units by product and service category and region of residence, 2005)

	total	Northeast	Midwest	South	West
Number of consumer units (in 000s)	117,356	22,356	27,005	42,120	25,875
Average number of persons per consumer unit	2.5	2.4	2.4	2.5	2.6
Average before-tax income of consumer units	$58,712	$63,068	$56,606	$53,311	$65,938
Average annual spending of consumer units	46,409	47,921	45,027	42,504	52,891
FOOD	**5,931**	**6,495**	**5,754**	**5,491**	**6,339**
Food at home	**3,297**	**3,645**	**3,232**	**3,011**	**3,527**
Cereals and bakery products	445	508	454	400	456
Cereals and cereal products	143	162	143	129	148
Bakery products	302	346	311	270	307
Meats, poultry, fish, and eggs	764	885	712	732	767
Beef	228	243	220	227	222
Pork	153	163	150	157	143
Other meats	103	125	109	89	101
Poultry	134	159	121	129	135
Fish and seafood	113	158	85	100	125
Eggs	33	37	26	30	40
Dairy products	378	424	391	332	401
Fresh milk and cream	146	151	150	137	152
Other dairy products	232	273	240	195	249
Fruits and vegetables	552	652	517	475	624
Fresh fruits	182	214	175	148	214
Fresh vegetables	175	217	150	149	206
Processed fruits	106	127	106	89	117
Processed vegetables	89	95	87	89	87
Other food at home	1,158	1,176	1,158	1,072	1,279
Sugar and other sweets	119	126	119	109	128
Fats and oils	85	93	83	79	90
Miscellaneous foods	609	614	615	563	673
Nonalcoholic beverages	303	306	300	291	324
Food prepared by consumer unit on trips	41	37	40	30	64
Food away from home	**2,634**	**2,850**	**2,522**	**2,480**	**2,813**
ALCOHOLIC BEVERAGES	**426**	**441**	**460**	**350**	**503**
HOUSING	**15,167**	**16,421**	**14,151**	**13,402**	**18,016**
Shelter	**8,805**	**10,071**	**7,886**	**7,167**	**11,337**
Owned dwellings	5,958	6,681	5,688	4,900	7,337
Mortgage interest and charges	3,317	3,049	3,001	2,815	4,693
Property taxes	1,541	2,344	1,671	1,085	1,452
Maintenance, repair, insurance, other expenses	1,101	1,288	1,016	1,000	1,192
Rented dwellings	2,345	2,765	1,664	1,911	3,398
Other lodging	502	624	534	355	601
Utilities, fuels, and public services	**3,183**	**3,409**	**3,158**	**3,240**	**2,923**
Natural gas	473	621	725	294	375
Electricity	1,155	1,102	994	1,401	969
Fuel oil and other fuels	142	391	106	75	73
Telephone services	1,048	1,035	1,000	1,085	1,047
Water and other public services	366	261	333	385	459
Household services	**801**	**765**	**759**	**777**	**913**
Personal services	322	307	346	313	323
Other household services	479	458	413	464	590
Housekeeping supplies	**611**	**654**	**618**	**573**	**629**
Laundry and cleaning supplies	134	118	140	141	130
Other household products	320	342	317	298	338
Postage and stationery	157	194	162	133	161

	total consumer units	Northeast	Midwest	South	West
Household furnishings and equipment	$1,767	$1,522	$1,730	$1,646	$2,214
Household textiles	132	132	144	128	128
Furniture	467	385	395	463	621
Floor coverings	56	58	56	56	55
Major appliances	223	210	210	214	264
Small appliances, miscellaneous housewares	105	99	108	88	136
Miscellaneous household equipment	782	638	817	697	1,009
APPAREL AND RELATED SERVICES	1,886	2,036	1,750	1,836	1,975
Men and boys	440	467	388	421	499
Men, aged 16 or older	349	379	310	315	416
Boys, aged 2 to 15	91	88	78	106	83
Women and girls	754	848	728	738	724
Women, aged 16 or older	633	722	621	617	594
Girls, aged 2 to 15	121	126	107	121	130
Children under age 2	82	87	77	76	93
Footwear	320	354	280	322	330
Other apparel products and services	290	281	278	279	329
TRANSPORTATION	8,344	7,732	7,753	7,990	10,068
Vehicle purchases	3,544	2,911	3,085	3,543	4,572
Cars and trucks, new	1,931	1,760	1,700	1,777	2,571
Cars and trucks, used	1,531	1,114	1,298	1,689	1,874
Other vehicles	82	36	86	77	127
Gasoline and motor oil	2,013	1,761	1,975	2,069	2,180
Other vehicle expenses	2,339	2,424	2,313	2,085	2,708
Vehicle finance charges	297	241	274	336	304
Maintenance and repairs	671	641	648	587	860
Vehicle insurance	913	967	845	879	993
Vehicle rentals, leases, licenses, other charges	458	574	546	282	550
Public transportation	448	637	380	293	608
HEALTH CARE	2,664	2,581	2,841	2,606	2,647
Health insurance	1,361	1,429	1,409	1,353	1,264
Medical services	677	563	755	600	820
Drugs	521	482	558	557	459
Medical supplies	105	107	119	96	105
ENTERTAINMENT	2,388	2,263	2,384	2,112	2,950
Fees and admissions	588	615	614	451	760
Audio and visual equipment and services	888	903	839	868	959
Pets, toys, hobbies, playground equipment	420	394	411	396	491
Other entertainment products and services	492	352	520	397	741
PERSONAL CARE PRODUCTS AND SERVICES	541	540	514	508	623
READING	126	148	132	94	155
EDUCATION	940	1,387	998	674	926
TOBACCO PRODUCTS AND SMOKING SUPPLIES	319	330	374	318	254
MISCELLANEOUS	808	822	837	654	1,016
CASH CONTRIBUTIONS	1,663	1,370	1,868	1,710	1,627
PERSONAL INSURANCE AND PENSIONS	5,204	5,353	5,212	4,760	5,789
Life and other personal insurance	381	374	380	419	326
Pensions and Social Security	4,823	4,980	4,832	4,341	5,462
PERSONAL TAXES	2,408	2,160	2,326	2,265	2,938
Federal income taxes	1,696	1,412	1,533	1,694	2,117
State and local income taxes	534	509	572	435	677
Other taxes	177	239	221	136	144
GIFTS FOR PEOPLE IN OTHER HOUSEHOLDS	1,091	1,353	1,055	916	1,188

Note: Spending by category will not add to total spending because gift spending is also included in the preceding product and service categories and personal taxes are not included in the total.
Source: Bureau of Labor Statistics, 2005 Consumer Expenditure Survey, Internet site http://www.bls.gov/cex/

Table 27. Indexed spending by region, 2005

(indexed average annual spending of consumer units by product and service category and region of residence, 2005; index definition: an index of 100 is the average for all consumer units; an index of 132 means that spending by consumer units in that group is 32 percent above the average for all consumer units; an index of 68 indicates spending that is 32 percent below the average for all consumer units)

	total	Northeast	Midwest	South	West
Average spending of consumer units, total	$46,409	$47,921	$45,027	$42,504	$52,891
Average spending of consumer units, index	100	103	97	92	114
FOOD	100	110	97	93	107
Food at home	100	111	98	91	107
Cereals and bakery products	100	114	102	90	102
Cereals and cereal products	100	113	100	90	103
Bakery products	100	115	103	89	102
Meats, poultry, fish, and eggs	100	116	93	96	100
Beef	100	107	96	100	97
Pork	100	107	98	103	93
Other meats	100	121	106	86	98
Poultry	100	119	90	96	101
Fish and seafood	100	140	75	88	111
Eggs	100	112	79	91	121
Dairy products	100	112	103	88	106
Fresh milk and cream	100	103	103	94	104
Other dairy products	100	118	103	84	107
Fruits and vegetables	100	118	94	86	113
Fresh fruits	100	118	96	81	118
Fresh vegetables	100	124	86	85	118
Processed fruits	100	120	100	84	110
Processed vegetables	100	107	98	100	98
Other food at home	100	102	100	93	110
Sugar and other sweets	100	106	100	92	108
Fats and oils	100	109	98	93	106
Miscellaneous foods	100	101	101	92	111
Nonalcoholic beverages	100	101	99	96	107
Food prepared by consumer unit on trips	100	90	98	73	156
Food away from home	100	108	96	94	107
ALCOHOLIC BEVERAGES	100	104	108	82	118
HOUSING	100	108	93	88	119
Shelter	100	114	90	81	129
Owned dwellings	100	112	95	82	123
Mortgage interest and charges	100	92	90	85	141
Property taxes	100	152	108	70	94
Maintenance, repair, insurance, other expenses	100	117	92	91	108
Rented dwellings	100	118	71	81	145
Other lodging	100	124	106	71	120
Utilities, fuels, and public services	100	107	99	102	92
Natural gas	100	131	153	62	79
Electricity	100	95	86	121	84
Fuel oil and other fuels	100	275	75	53	51
Telephone services	100	99	95	104	100
Water and other public services	100	71	91	105	125
Household services	100	96	95	97	114
Personal services	100	95	107	97	100
Other household services	100	96	86	97	123
Housekeeping supplies	100	107	101	94	103
Laundry and cleaning supplies	100	88	104	105	97
Other household products	100	107	99	93	106
Postage and stationery	100	124	103	85	103

	total consumer units	Northeast	Midwest	South	West
Household furnishings and equipment	100	86	98	93	125
Household textiles	100	100	109	97	97
Furniture	100	82	85	99	133
Floor coverings	100	104	100	100	98
Major appliances	100	94	94	96	118
Small appliances, miscellaneous housewares	100	94	103	84	130
Miscellaneous household equipment	100	82	104	89	129
APPAREL AND RELATED SERVICES	100	108	93	97	105
Men and boys	100	106	88	96	113
Men, aged 16 or older	100	109	89	90	119
Boys, aged 2 to 15	100	97	86	116	91
Women and girls	100	112	97	98	96
Women, aged 16 or older	100	114	98	97	94
Girls, aged 2 to 15	100	104	88	100	107
Children under age 2	100	106	94	93	113
Footwear	100	111	88	101	103
Other apparel products and services	100	97	96	96	113
TRANSPORTATION	100	93	93	96	121
Vehicle purchases	100	82	87	100	129
Cars and trucks, new	100	91	88	92	133
Cars and trucks, used	100	73	85	110	122
Other vehicles	100	44	105	94	155
Gasoline and motor oil	100	87	98	103	108
Other vehicle expenses	100	104	99	89	116
Vehicle finance charges	100	81	92	113	102
Maintenance and repairs	100	96	97	87	128
Vehicle insurance	100	106	93	96	109
Vehicle rentals, leases, licenses, other charges	100	125	119	62	120
Public transportation	100	142	85	65	136
HEALTH CARE	100	97	107	98	99
Health insurance	100	105	104	99	93
Medical services	100	83	112	89	121
Drugs	100	93	107	107	88
Medical supplies	100	102	113	91	100
ENTERTAINMENT	100	95	100	88	124
Fees and admissions	100	105	104	77	129
Audio and visual equipment and services	100	102	94	98	108
Pets, toys, hobbies, playground equipment	100	94	98	94	117
Other entertainment products and services	100	72	106	81	151
PERSONAL CARE PRODUCTS AND SERVICES	100	100	95	94	115
READING	100	117	105	75	123
EDUCATION	100	148	106	72	99
TOBACCO PRODUCTS AND SMOKING SUPPLIES	100	103	117	100	80
MISCELLANEOUS	100	102	104	81	126
CASH CONTRIBUTIONS	100	82	112	103	98
PERSONAL INSURANCE AND PENSIONS	100	103	100	91	111
Life and other personal insurance	100	98	100	110	86
Pensions and Social Security	100	103	100	90	113
PERSONAL TAXES	100	90	97	94	122
Federal income taxes	100	83	90	100	125
State and local income taxes	100	95	107	81	127
Other taxes	100	135	125	77	81
GIFTS FOR PEOPLE IN OTHER HOUSEHOLDS	100	124	97	84	109

Source: Calculations by New Strategist based on the Bureau of Labor Statistics' 2005 Consumer Expenditure Survey

Spending by Region and Income, 2004–05

Households with incomes of $70,000 or more are most commonly found in the Northeast and West, accounting for 31 and 30 percent of households in those regions, respectively. In the Midwest, 27 percent of households have incomes of $70,000-plus, while in the South the proportion is a smaller 24 percent.

In every region, spending rises with income. The most affluent households in the Northeast spend 70 percent more than the average northeastern household, $80,061 versus $47,005 in 2004–05. The spending gap is greatest for items such as mortgage interest, other lodging (a category that includes vacation homes and hotels and motels on out of town trips), fees and admissions to entertainment events, and education.

In the Midwest, the most affluent households spent $77,691 in 2004–05, or 75 percent more than the $44,322 spent by the average Midwestern household. Households with incomes of $70,000 or more in the Midwest spend more than twice as much as the average household on such things as public transportation and fees and admissions to entertainment events.

The most affluent households in the South spend 82 percent more than the average Southern household, $74,618 versus $40,903 in 2004–05. The richest households in the South spend more than two times as much as the average household on other lodging. They spend 7 percent less than the average household in the South on tobacco, and 42 percent less on rent.

The most affluent households in the West spend 70 percent more than the average Western household, $85,401 versus $50,305 in 2004–05. The gap is greatest for items such as mortgage interest, other lodging, furniture, and fees and admissions to entertainment events.

Table 28. Average spending in the Northeast by income, 2004–05

(average annual spending of consumer units (CUs) in the Northeast by product and service category and before-tax income of consumer unit, 2004–05)

	total consumer units in Northeast	under $10,000	$10,000 to $19,999	$20,000 to $29,999	$30,000 to $39,999	$40,000 to $49,999	$50,000 to $69,999	$70,000 or more
Number of consumer units (in 000s)	22,184	2,109	3,042	2,495	2,297	2,047	3,257	6,936
Average number of persons per CU	2.4	1.5	1.7	2.0	2.3	2.4	2.7	3.1
Average before-tax income of CU	$62,002	$4,913	$14,847	$24,792	$34,676	$44,809	$59,394	$128,771
Average annual spending of CU	47,005	17,523	21,119	27,742	32,699	39,065	47,974	80,061
FOOD	**6,430**	**3,553**	**3,149**	**4,021**	**4,628**	**5,538**	**6,696**	**9,920**
Food at home	3,640	2,401	2,111	2,444	2,789	3,118	3,978	5,172
Cereals and bakery products	515	362	311	350	412	442	569	711
Cereals and cereal products	169	138	116	116	148	139	173	228
Bakery products	346	224	194	235	264	302	396	483
Meats, poultry, fish, and eggs	946	664	548	601	754	840	1,034	1,326
Beef	261	181	155	149	211	220	275	378
Pork	176	124	115	115	139	166	212	228
Other meats	130	86	65	84	104	124	141	185
Poultry	177	115	106	102	148	148	213	243
Fish and seafood	161	124	74	121	111	144	149	240
Eggs	42	34	32	29	40	38	42	53
Dairy products	421	265	249	296	317	378	456	592
Fresh milk and cream	154	121	102	115	121	149	165	200
Other dairy products	267	144	147	181	196	229	291	392
Fruits and vegetables	645	389	392	459	481	593	678	914
Fresh fruits	214	123	119	156	152	195	220	312
Fresh vegetables	213	120	130	149	151	185	227	308
Processed fruits	127	83	88	93	97	119	133	172
Processed vegetables	92	63	55	61	82	94	98	123
Other food at home	1,114	722	612	738	825	865	1,240	1,630
Sugar and other sweets	131	78	80	95	91	97	138	196
Fats and oils	93	73	60	66	84	92	97	119
Miscellaneous foods	560	377	303	363	389	407	622	837
Nonalcoholic beverages	293	182	154	199	233	246	340	413
Food prepared by consumer unit on trips	37	12	15	15	28	24	44	65
Food away from home	**2,790**	**1,152**	**1,039**	**1,577**	**1,839**	**2,420**	**2,718**	**4,748**
ALCOHOLIC BEVERAGES	**532**	**148**	**176**	**288**	**372**	**594**	**463**	**908**
HOUSING	**16,121**	**6,746**	**8,864**	**10,749**	**12,242**	**13,378**	**16,178**	**26,039**
Shelter	**9,887**	**4,283**	**5,555**	**6,497**	**7,611**	**8,169**	**9,969**	**15,932**
Owned dwellings	6,571	1,235	2,275	2,593	3,949	4,743	6,781	12,818
Mortgage interest and charges	3,096	376	582	704	1,517	2,155	3,589	6,456
Property taxes	2,235	640	973	1,199	1,545	1,711	2,224	4,036
Maintenance, repair, insurance, other expenses	1,239	219	719	691	888	877	968	2,326
Rented dwellings	2,726	2,946	3,217	3,707	3,425	3,097	2,767	1,732
Other lodging	590	102	64	197	237	329	421	1,382
Utilities, fuels, and public services	**3,257**	**1,433**	**2,125**	**2,596**	**2,805**	**3,146**	**3,548**	**4,590**
Natural gas	596	276	431	535	568	602	620	783
Electricity	1,043	476	660	821	862	1,023	1,165	1,473
Fuel oil and other fuels	356	117	273	299	300	329	362	510
Telephone services	1,010	492	606	758	864	942	1,097	1,464
Water and other public services	251	73	155	184	211	250	305	360
Household services	**779**	**211**	**458**	**526**	**445**	**432**	**610**	**1,477**
Personal services	329	112	268	292	120	145	241	600
Other household services	450	100	190	235	326	287	368	877
Housekeeping supplies	**620**	**295**	**255**	**396**	**415**	**545**	**594**	**1,010**
Laundry and cleaning supplies	132	71	64	86	106	158	136	184
Other household products	318	139	127	183	192	257	317	537
Postage and stationery	170	84	64	127	117	131	141	288

	total consumer units in Northeast	under $10,000	$10,000 to $19,999	$20,000 to $29,999	$30,000 to $39,999	$40,000 to $49,999	$50,000 to $69,999	$70,000 or more
Household furnishings and equipment	$1,577	$524	$471	$733	$966	$1,086	$1,458	$3,031
Household textiles	170	48	44	96	71	173	175	302
Furniture	383	125	94	171	277	246	344	757
Floor coverings	51	12	31	17	14	68	29	102
Major appliances	214	35	57	137	130	151	243	394
Small appliances, miscellaneous housewares	97	28	44	49	75	74	81	173
Miscellaneous household equipment	662	276	200	262	400	374	585	1,302
APPAREL AND RELATED SERVICES	2,106	1,030	917	1,040	1,556	1,448	1,920	3,677
Men and boys	463	168	239	196	257	343	439	832
Men, aged 16 or older	373	97	193	132	193	277	331	698
Boys, aged 2 to 15	91	71	45	63	64	65	108	134
Women and girls	890	427	327	396	591	583	810	1,612
Women, aged 16 or older	765	372	282	330	512	509	708	1,376
Girls, aged 2 to 15	125	55	45	67	79	74	102	236
Children under age 2	78	53	43	65	55	43	76	124
Footwear	390	254	202	225	451	313	369	565
Other apparel products and services	284	126	106	158	202	166	226	544
TRANSPORTATION	7,646	2,210	2,740	4,841	4,905	6,832	8,862	13,023
Vehicle purchases	3,031	666	1,001	2,082	1,666	2,690	3,805	5,172
Cars and trucks, new	1,666	371	330	1,012	888	1,582	2,074	2,971
Cars and trucks, used	1,301	277	664	1,070	750	1,060	1,645	2,067
Other vehicles	64	41	12	–	28	48	85	134
Gasoline and motor oil	1,572	555	651	996	1,262	1,605	1,890	2,436
Other vehicle expenses	2,405	777	877	1,404	1,603	2,073	2,699	4,148
Vehicle finance charges	248	39	59	109	200	246	326	425
Maintenance and repairs	612	318	253	425	373	513	692	995
Vehicle insurance	977	292	436	675	744	943	1,111	1,555
Vehicle rentals, leases, licenses, other charges	568	128	130	194	286	370	570	1,173
Public transportation	637	211	212	359	374	464	468	1,266
HEALTH CARE	2,476	953	2,033	2,214	2,193	2,454	2,491	3,312
Health insurance	1,366	577	1,126	1,325	1,259	1,395	1,370	1,751
Medical services	582	155	429	336	461	490	603	925
Drugs	429	183	406	498	405	476	417	481
Medical supplies	99	38	72	56	68	92	101	155
ENTERTAINMENT	2,137	852	822	1,135	1,506	1,821	2,188	3,718
Fees and admissions	577	179	122	230	319	389	576	1,162
Audio and visual equipment and services	871	428	474	602	805	753	947	1,298
Pets, toys, hobbies, playground equipment	376	147	168	225	247	377	430	595
Other entertainment products and services	313	98	58	78	134	302	234	663
PERSONAL CARE PRODUCTS AND SERVICES	586	217	255	382	400	532	611	952
READING	146	47	82	101	122	132	134	240
EDUCATION	1,256	674	160	289	388	467	731	3,021
TOBACCO PRODUCTS AND SMOKING SUPPLIES	314	220	290	351	338	332	421	275
MISCELLANEOUS	793	329	338	417	674	902	897	1,209
CASH CONTRIBUTIONS	1,241	294	681	553	815	1,032	1,006	2,334
PERSONAL INSURANCE AND PENSIONS	5,223	251	612	1,361	2,558	3,605	5,376	11,433
Life and other personal insurance	371	64	124	159	205	255	353	747
Pensions and Social Security	4,851	187	488	1,202	2,353	3,350	5,023	10,686
PERSONAL TAXES	2,260	0	25	284	764	813	1,901	5,731
Federal income taxes	1,494	–68	–92	45	388	358	1,103	4,070
State and local income taxes	532	–3	9	45	218	254	503	1,299
Other taxes	234	69	108	194	158	201	295	362
GIFTS FOR PEOPLE IN OTHER HOUSEHOLDS	1,428	387	525	466	803	672	952	3,098

Note: Spending by category will not add to total spending because gift spending is also included in the preceding product and service categories and personal taxes are not included in the total. "–" means sample is too small to make a reliable estimate.
Source: Bureau of Labor Statistics, 2004 and 2005 Consumer Expenditure Surveys, Internet site http://www.bls.gov/cex/; calculations by New Strategist

Table 29. Indexed spending in the Northeast by income, 2004–05

(indexed average annual spending of consumer units in the Northeast by product and service category and before-tax income of consumer unit, 2004–05; index definition: an index of 100 is the average for all consumer units; an index of 132 means that spending by consumer units in that group is 32 percent above the average for all consumer units; an index of 68 indicates spending that is 32 percent below the average for all consumer units)

	total consumer units in Northeast	under $10,000	$10,000 to $19,999	$20,000 to $29,999	$30,000 to $39,999	$40,000 to $49,999	$50,000 to $69,999	$70,000 or more
Average spending of consumer units, total	$47,005	$17,523	$21,119	$27,742	$32,699	$39,065	$47,974	$80,061
Average spending of consumer units, index	100	37	45	59	70	83	102	170
FOOD	100	55	49	63	72	86	104	154
Food at home	100	66	58	67	77	86	109	142
Cereals and bakery products	100	70	60	68	80	86	110	138
Cereals and cereal products	100	82	69	69	88	82	102	135
Bakery products	100	65	56	68	76	87	114	140
Meats, poultry, fish, and eggs	100	70	58	64	80	89	109	140
Beef	100	69	59	57	81	84	105	145
Pork	100	70	66	65	79	94	120	130
Other meats	100	66	50	65	80	95	108	142
Poultry	100	65	60	58	84	84	120	137
Fish and seafood	100	77	46	75	69	89	93	149
Eggs	100	80	76	69	95	90	100	126
Dairy products	100	63	59	70	75	90	108	141
Fresh milk and cream	100	78	66	75	79	97	107	130
Other dairy products	100	54	55	68	73	86	109	147
Fruits and vegetables	100	60	61	71	75	92	105	142
Fresh fruits	100	57	55	73	71	91	103	146
Fresh vegetables	100	56	61	70	71	87	107	145
Processed fruits	100	65	70	73	76	94	105	135
Processed vegetables	100	69	60	66	89	102	107	134
Other food at home	100	65	55	66	74	78	111	146
Sugar and other sweets	100	60	61	73	69	74	105	150
Fats and oils	100	78	65	71	90	99	104	128
Miscellaneous foods	100	67	54	65	69	73	111	149
Nonalcoholic beverages	100	62	52	68	80	84	116	141
Food prepared by consumer unit on trips	100	32	39	41	76	65	119	176
Food away from home	100	41	37	57	66	87	97	170
ALCOHOLIC BEVERAGES	100	28	33	54	70	112	87	171
HOUSING	100	42	55	67	76	83	100	162
Shelter	100	43	56	66	77	83	101	161
Owned dwellings	100	19	35	39	60	72	103	195
Mortgage interest and charges	100	12	19	23	49	70	116	209
Property taxes	100	29	44	54	69	77	100	181
Maintenance, repair, insurance, other expenses	100	18	58	56	72	71	78	188
Rented dwellings	100	108	118	136	126	114	102	64
Other lodging	100	17	11	33	40	56	71	234
Utilities, fuels, and public services	100	44	65	80	86	97	109	141
Natural gas	100	46	72	90	95	101	104	131
Electricity	100	46	63	79	83	98	112	141
Fuel oil and other fuels	100	33	77	84	84	92	102	143
Telephone services	100	49	60	75	86	93	109	145
Water and other public services	100	29	62	73	84	100	122	143
Household services	100	27	59	68	57	55	78	190
Personal services	100	34	82	89	36	44	73	182
Other household services	100	22	42	52	72	64	82	195
Housekeeping supplies	100	48	41	64	67	88	96	163
Laundry and cleaning supplies	100	54	49	65	80	120	103	139
Other household products	100	44	40	58	60	81	100	169
Postage and stationery	100	50	38	75	69	77	83	169

	total consumer units in Northeast	under $10,000	$10,000 to $19,999	$20,000 to $29,999	$30,000 to $39,999	$40,000 to $49,999	$50,000 to $69,999	$70,000 or more
Household furnishings and equipment	100	33	30	46	61	69	92	192
Household textiles	100	28	26	56	42	102	103	178
Furniture	100	33	25	45	72	64	90	198
Floor coverings	100	24	61	33	27	133	57	200
Major appliances	100	16	27	64	61	71	114	184
Small appliances, miscellaneous housewares	100	29	46	51	77	76	84	178
Miscellaneous household equipment	100	42	30	40	60	56	88	197
APPAREL AND RELATED SERVICES	100	49	44	49	74	69	91	175
Men and boys	100	36	52	42	56	74	95	180
Men, aged 16 or older	100	26	52	35	52	74	89	187
Boys, aged 2 to 15	100	78	50	69	70	71	119	147
Women and girls	100	48	37	44	66	66	91	181
Women, aged 16 or older	100	49	37	43	67	67	93	180
Girls, aged 2 to 15	100	44	36	54	63	59	82	189
Children under age 2	100	68	56	83	71	55	97	159
Footwear	100	65	52	58	116	80	95	145
Other apparel products and services	100	44	37	56	71	58	80	192
TRANSPORTATION	100	29	36	63	64	89	116	170
Vehicle purchases	100	22	33	69	55	89	126	171
Cars and trucks, new	100	22	20	61	53	95	124	178
Cars and trucks, used	100	21	51	82	58	81	126	159
Other vehicles	100	64	19	–	44	75	133	209
Gasoline and motor oil	100	35	41	63	80	102	120	155
Other vehicle expenses	100	32	36	58	67	86	112	172
Vehicle finance charges	100	16	24	44	81	99	131	171
Maintenance and repairs	100	52	41	69	61	84	113	163
Vehicle insurance	100	30	45	69	76	97	114	159
Vehicle rentals, leases, licenses, other charges	100	23	23	34	50	65	100	207
Public transportation	100	33	33	56	59	73	73	199
HEALTH CARE	100	38	82	89	89	99	101	134
Health insurance	100	42	82	97	92	102	100	128
Medical services	100	27	74	58	79	84	104	159
Drugs	100	43	95	116	94	111	97	112
Medical supplies	100	39	72	57	69	93	102	157
ENTERTAINMENT	100	40	38	53	70	85	102	174
Fees and admissions	100	31	21	40	55	67	100	201
Audio and visual equipment and services	100	49	54	69	92	86	109	149
Pets, toys, hobbies, playground equipment	100	39	45	60	66	100	114	158
Other entertainment products and services	100	31	19	25	43	96	75	212
PERSONAL CARE PRODUCTS AND SERVICES	100	37	44	65	68	91	104	162
READING	100	32	56	69	84	90	92	164
EDUCATION	100	54	13	23	31	37	58	241
TOBACCO PRODUCTS AND SMOKING SUPPLIES	100	70	92	112	108	106	134	88
MISCELLANEOUS	100	42	43	53	85	114	113	152
CASH CONTRIBUTIONS	100	24	55	45	66	83	81	188
PERSONAL INSURANCE AND PENSIONS	100	5	12	26	49	69	103	219
Life and other personal insurance	100	17	33	43	55	69	95	201
Pensions and Social Security	100	4	10	25	49	69	104	220
PERSONAL TAXES	100	0	1	13	34	36	84	254
Federal income taxes	100	–5	–6	3	26	24	74	272
State and local income taxes	100	0	2	8	41	48	95	244
Other taxes	100	30	46	83	68	86	126	155
GIFTS FOR PEOPLE IN OTHER HOUSEHOLDS	100	27	37	33	56	47	67	217

Note: "–" means sample is too small to make a reliable estimate.
Source: Calculations by New Strategist based on the Bureau of Labor Statistics' 2004 and 2005 Consumer Expenditure Surveys

Table 30. Average spending in the Midwest by income, 2004–05

(average annual spending of consumer units (CUs) in the Midwest by product and service category and before-tax income of consumer unit, 2004–05)

	total consumer units in Midwest	under $10,000	$10,000 to $19,999	$20,000 to $29,999	$30,000 to $39,999	$40,000 to $49,999	$50,000 to $69,999	$70,000 or more
Number of consumer units (in 000s)	26,767	2,464	3,682	3,332	3,095	2,684	4,242	7,267
Average number of persons per CU	2.4	1.5	1.7	2.0	2.3	2.4	2.8	3.2
Average before-tax income of CU	$55,215	$4,646	$14,788	$24,891	$34,886	$44,802	$59,222	$116,916
Average annual spending of CU	44,322	16,344	20,134	27,049	33,472	38,549	48,361	77,691
FOOD	5,672	2,272	2,866	3,875	4,605	5,094	6,422	8,940
Food at home	3,210	1,397	1,944	2,416	2,754	2,986	3,577	4,694
Cereals and bakery products	450	214	279	346	386	407	516	641
Cereals and cereal products	142	67	87	116	119	131	158	204
Bakery products	308	146	192	230	267	276	358	438
Meats, poultry, fish, and eggs	747	346	455	578	688	727	807	1,057
Beef	231	96	131	186	236	211	250	326
Pork	160	81	107	129	154	171	175	209
Other meats	114	43	66	82	99	125	125	165
Poultry	124	65	76	86	100	123	131	184
Fish and seafood	88	42	50	67	70	73	93	137
Eggs	29	18	24	27	29	24	33	35
Dairy products	374	152	220	282	331	355	435	537
Fresh milk and cream	144	66	96	112	140	146	156	193
Other dairy products	231	85	125	170	191	209	278	343
Fruits and vegetables	514	213	324	413	447	463	547	753
Fresh fruits	173	68	111	142	146	154	184	257
Fresh vegetables	149	65	88	111	125	138	161	222
Processed fruits	109	42	72	93	100	98	113	156
Processed vegetables	83	38	53	67	76	73	89	118
Other food at home	1,126	474	666	796	902	1,035	1,272	1,706
Sugar and other sweets	124	66	73	83	97	116	151	182
Fats and oils	83	36	52	71	69	83	89	117
Miscellaneous foods	587	223	345	395	468	544	655	909
Nonalcoholic beverages	289	133	187	225	239	264	341	407
Food prepared by consumer unit on trips	42	16	10	23	29	28	36	91
Food away from home	2,462	875	921	1,459	1,851	2,108	2,846	4,246
ALCOHOLIC BEVERAGES	443	177	215	221	355	328	448	795
HOUSING	13,852	6,229	7,529	9,132	10,933	12,609	14,540	22,980
Shelter	7,665	3,842	4,259	5,009	5,951	6,958	7,939	12,735
Owned dwellings	5,527	1,405	1,832	2,642	3,612	4,910	6,005	10,883
Mortgage interest and charges	2,931	615	532	977	1,786	2,543	3,336	6,224
Property taxes	1,600	515	742	948	1,129	1,518	1,659	2,900
Maintenance, repair, insurance, other expenses	995	275	558	717	697	849	1,011	1,760
Rented dwellings	1,608	2,270	2,312	2,186	2,094	1,759	1,449	593
Other lodging	530	167	115	181	245	289	484	1,260
Utilities, fuels, and public services	3,064	1,503	2,122	2,562	2,829	3,020	3,396	4,226
Natural gas	676	326	483	596	614	663	710	943
Electricity	980	515	727	854	923	965	1,059	1,306
Fuel oil and other fuels	105	37	80	89	128	126	129	117
Telephone services	976	504	633	762	865	942	1,134	1,375
Water and other public services	327	122	197	260	299	324	365	485
Household services	734	178	311	408	429	554	676	1,515
Personal services	323	48	108	152	153	222	314	717
Other household services	411	130	203	257	276	332	363	797
Housekeeping supplies	640	226	352	361	504	554	750	1,032
Laundry and cleaning supplies	147	70	81	112	127	133	191	201
Other household products	328	106	176	155	272	255	372	558
Postage and stationery	165	50	95	94	105	166	187	272

	total consumer units in Midwest	under $10,000	$10,000 to $19,999	$20,000 to $29,999	$30,000 to $39,999	$40,000 to $49,999	$50,000 to $69,999	$70,000 or more
Household furnishings and equipment	$1,749	$481	$487	$792	$1,220	$1,523	$1,779	$3,473
Household textiles	135	36	48	76	133	106	119	249
Furniture	412	99	114	173	173	342	477	870
Floor coverings	56	9	15	21	21	41	87	110
Major appliances	223	46	86	75	154	363	176	419
Small appliances, miscellaneous housewares	103	40	57	64	79	72	96	184
Miscellaneous household equipment	821	250	166	384	659	600	824	1,642
APPAREL AND RELATED SERVICES	**1,711**	**752**	**772**	**877**	**1,371**	**1,367**	**1,748**	**3,056**
Men and boys	**398**	**149**	**160**	**202**	**273**	**396**	**428**	**709**
Men, aged 16 or older	314	136	122	156	189	330	339	559
Boys, aged 2 to 15	84	13	38	45	84	66	88	150
Women and girls	**693**	**335**	**321**	**345**	**600**	**483**	**730**	**1,216**
Women, aged 16 or older	583	313	283	281	521	399	615	1,005
Girls, aged 2 to 15	110	22	38	64	79	84	115	211
Children under age 2	**78**	**33**	**29**	**39**	**80**	**75**	**87**	**126**
Footwear	**275**	**133**	**164**	**172**	**285**	**193**	**315**	**414**
Other apparel products and services	266	101	98	119	133	220	188	592
TRANSPORTATION	**7,795**	**2,541**	**2,934**	**5,080**	**6,047**	**6,925**	**9,839**	**13,150**
Vehicle purchases	**3,259**	**1,087**	**818**	**2,182**	**2,242**	**2,756**	**4,535**	**5,599**
Cars and trucks, new	1,651	384	263	927	984	1,368	2,081	3,253
Cars and trucks, used	1,524	701	555	1,206	1,242	1,312	2,231	2,226
Other vehicles	84	6	–	49	15	77	224	121
Gasoline and motor oil	**1,801**	**666**	**964**	**1,265**	**1,572**	**1,746**	**2,158**	**2,764**
Other vehicle expenses	**2,365**	**613**	**1,049**	**1,480**	**2,044**	**2,201**	**2,775**	**3,982**
Vehicle finance charges	303	37	76	146	267	294	403	540
Maintenance and repairs	651	195	353	427	659	572	754	1,018
Vehicle insurance	886	264	440	660	742	903	1,055	1,384
Vehicle rentals, leases, licenses, other charges	525	117	181	247	375	432	563	1,041
Public transportation	**371**	**175**	**103**	**154**	**189**	**221**	**371**	**804**
HEALTH CARE	**2,859**	**1,054**	**2,120**	**2,520**	**2,805**	**2,843**	**3,176**	**3,835**
Health insurance	1,456	510	1,170	1,332	1,461	1,522	1,683	1,819
Medical services	737	250	364	557	599	649	802	1,225
Drugs	544	241	536	570	623	526	555	598
Medical supplies	122	54	49	61	122	145	136	192
ENTERTAINMENT	**2,293**	**794**	**870**	**1,117**	**1,477**	**1,753**	**2,441**	**4,489**
Fees and admissions	602	183	125	205	291	369	549	1,417
Audio and visual equipment and services	805	394	464	566	641	749	948	1,232
Pets, toys, hobbies, playground equipment	392	83	173	190	343	405	410	690
Other entertainment products and services	494	133	107	155	202	231	534	1,150
PERSONAL CARE PRODUCTS AND SERVICES	**539**	**212**	**289**	**377**	**394**	**469**	**549**	**915**
READING	**141**	**54**	**77**	**83**	**114**	**120**	**153**	**243**
EDUCATION	**951**	**1,091**	**444**	**354**	**435**	**531**	**733**	**1,934**
TOBACCO PRODUCTS AND SMOKING SUPPLIES	**356**	**217**	**253**	**358**	**384**	**459**	**428**	**363**
MISCELLANEOUS	**821**	**254**	**464**	**523**	**724**	**794**	**875**	**1,343**
CASH CONTRIBUTIONS	**1,828**	**292**	**666**	**965**	**1,150**	**1,560**	**1,616**	**3,846**
PERSONAL INSURANCE AND PENSIONS	**5,058**	**405**	**635**	**1,567**	**2,678**	**3,696**	**5,395**	**11,800**
Life and other personal insurance	411	97	125	179	245	314	384	890
Pensions and Social Security	4,648	307	509	1,388	2,433	3,382	5,011	10,909
PERSONAL TAXES	**2,381**	**–34**	**–7**	**187**	**586**	**1,224**	**2,414**	**6,587**
Federal income taxes	1,568	–63	–107	–68	222	695	1,623	4,582
State and local income taxes	580	3	14	102	210	326	541	1,555
Other taxes	234	27	87	153	154	203	250	451
GIFTS FOR PEOPLE IN OTHER HOUSEHOLDS	**1,154**	**303**	**538**	**662**	**637**	**747**	**1,182**	**2,300**

Note: Spending by category will not add to total spending because gift spending is also included in the preceding product and service categories and personal taxes are not included in the total. "–" means sample is too small to make a reliable estimate.
Source: Bureau of Labor Statistics, 2004 and 2005 Consumer Expenditure Surveys, Internet site http://www.bls.gov/cex/; calculations by New Strategist

Table 31. Indexed spending in the Midwest by income, 2004–05

(indexed average annual spending of consumer units in the Midwest by product and service category and before-tax income of consumer unit, 2004–05; index definition: an index of 100 is the average for all consumer units; an index of 132 means that spending by consumer units in that group is 32 percent above the average for all consumer units; an index of 68 indicates spending that is 32 percent below the average for all consumer units)

	total consumer units in Midwest	under $10,000	$10,000 to $19,999	$20,000 to $29,999	$30,000 to $39,999	$40,000 to $49,999	$50,000 to $69,999	$70,000 or more
Average spending of consumer units, total	$44,322	$16,344	$20,134	$27,049	$33,472	$38,549	$48,361	$77,691
Average spending of consumer units, index	100	37	45	61	76	87	109	175
FOOD	100	40	51	68	81	90	113	158
Food at home	100	44	61	75	86	93	111	146
Cereals and bakery products	100	47	62	77	86	90	115	142
Cereals and cereal products	100	47	62	82	84	92	111	144
Bakery products	100	47	62	75	87	90	116	142
Meats, poultry, fish, and eggs	100	46	61	77	92	97	108	141
Beef	100	42	57	81	102	91	108	141
Pork	100	51	67	81	96	107	109	131
Other meats	100	38	58	72	87	110	110	145
Poultry	100	53	61	69	81	99	106	148
Fish and seafood	100	47	57	76	80	83	106	156
Eggs	100	61	82	93	100	83	114	121
Dairy products	100	41	59	75	89	95	116	144
Fresh milk and cream	100	46	67	78	97	101	108	134
Other dairy products	100	37	54	74	83	90	120	148
Fruits and vegetables	100	41	63	80	87	90	106	146
Fresh fruits	100	39	64	82	84	89	106	149
Fresh vegetables	100	43	59	74	84	93	108	149
Processed fruits	100	39	66	85	92	90	104	143
Processed vegetables	100	46	63	81	92	88	107	142
Other food at home	100	42	59	71	80	92	113	152
Sugar and other sweets	100	53	58	67	78	94	122	147
Fats and oils	100	43	62	86	83	100	107	141
Miscellaneous foods	100	38	59	67	80	93	112	155
Nonalcoholic beverages	100	46	65	78	83	91	118	141
Food prepared by consumer unit on trips	100	38	24	55	69	67	86	217
Food away from home	100	36	37	59	75	86	116	172
ALCOHOLIC BEVERAGES	100	40	49	50	80	74	101	179
HOUSING	100	45	54	66	79	91	105	166
Shelter	100	50	56	65	78	91	104	166
Owned dwellings	100	25	33	48	65	89	109	197
Mortgage interest and charges	100	21	18	33	61	87	114	212
Property taxes	100	32	46	59	71	95	104	181
Maintenance, repair, insurance, other expenses	100	28	56	72	70	85	102	177
Rented dwellings	100	141	144	136	130	109	90	37
Other lodging	100	31	22	34	46	55	91	238
Utilities, fuels, and public services	100	49	69	84	92	99	111	138
Natural gas	100	48	71	88	91	98	105	139
Electricity	100	53	74	87	94	98	108	133
Fuel oil and other fuels	100	36	76	85	122	120	123	111
Telephone services	100	52	65	78	89	97	116	141
Water and other public services	100	37	60	80	91	99	112	148
Household services	100	24	42	56	58	75	92	206
Personal services	100	15	33	47	47	69	97	222
Other household services	100	32	49	63	67	81	88	194
Housekeeping supplies	100	35	55	56	79	87	117	161
Laundry and cleaning supplies	100	47	55	76	86	90	130	137
Other household products	100	32	54	47	83	78	113	170
Postage and stationery	100	31	57	57	64	101	113	165

	total consumer units in Midwest	under $10,000	$10,000 to $19,999	$20,000 to $29,999	$30,000 to $39,999	$40,000 to $49,999	$50,000 to $69,999	$70,000 or more
Household furnishings and equipment	100	27	28	45	70	87	102	199
Household textiles	100	27	35	56	99	79	88	184
Furniture	100	24	28	42	42	83	116	211
Floor coverings	100	16	27	38	38	73	155	196
Major appliances	100	20	38	34	69	163	79	188
Small appliances, miscellaneous housewares	100	39	56	62	77	70	93	179
Miscellaneous household equipment	100	30	20	47	80	73	100	200
APPAREL AND RELATED SERVICES	100	44	45	51	80	80	102	179
Men and boys	100	37	40	51	69	99	108	178
Men, aged 16 or older	100	43	39	50	60	105	108	178
Boys, aged 2 to 15	100	15	45	54	100	79	105	179
Women and girls	100	48	46	50	87	70	105	175
Women, aged 16 or older	100	54	49	48	89	68	105	172
Girls, aged 2 to 15	100	20	34	58	72	76	105	192
Children under age 2	100	43	37	50	103	96	112	162
Footwear	100	48	60	63	104	70	115	151
Other apparel products and services	100	38	37	45	50	83	71	223
TRANSPORTATION	100	33	38	65	78	89	126	169
Vehicle purchases	100	33	25	67	69	85	139	172
Cars and trucks, new	100	23	16	56	60	83	126	197
Cars and trucks, used	100	46	36	79	81	86	146	146
Other vehicles	100	7	–	58	18	92	267	144
Gasoline and motor oil	100	37	54	70	87	97	120	153
Other vehicle expenses	100	26	44	63	86	93	117	168
Vehicle finance charges	100	12	25	48	88	97	133	178
Maintenance and repairs	100	30	54	66	101	88	116	156
Vehicle insurance	100	30	50	74	84	102	119	156
Vehicle rentals, leases, licenses, other charges	100	22	34	47	71	82	107	198
Public transportation	100	47	28	42	51	60	100	217
HEALTH CARE	100	37	74	88	98	99	111	134
Health insurance	100	35	80	91	100	105	116	125
Medical services	100	34	49	76	81	88	109	166
Drugs	100	44	99	105	115	97	102	110
Medical supplies	100	44	40	50	100	119	111	157
ENTERTAINMENT	100	35	38	49	64	76	106	196
Fees and admissions	100	30	21	34	48	61	91	235
Audio and visual equipment and services	100	49	58	70	80	93	118	153
Pets, toys, hobbies, playground equipment	100	21	44	48	88	103	105	176
Other entertainment products and services	100	27	22	31	41	47	108	233
PERSONAL CARE PRODUCTS AND SERVICES	100	39	54	70	73	87	102	170
READING	100	39	55	59	81	85	109	172
EDUCATION	100	115	47	37	46	56	77	203
TOBACCO PRODUCTS AND SMOKING SUPPLIES	100	61	71	101	108	129	120	102
MISCELLANEOUS	100	31	56	64	88	97	107	164
CASH CONTRIBUTIONS	100	16	36	53	63	85	88	210
PERSONAL INSURANCE AND PENSIONS	100	8	13	31	53	73	107	233
Life and other personal insurance	100	24	31	44	60	76	93	217
Pensions and Social Security	100	7	11	30	52	73	108	235
PERSONAL TAXES	100	–1	0	8	25	51	101	277
Federal income taxes	100	–4	–7	–4	14	44	104	292
State and local income taxes	100	0	2	18	36	56	93	268
Other taxes	100	12	37	65	66	87	107	193
GIFTS FOR PEOPLE IN OTHER HOUSEHOLDS	100	26	47	57	55	65	102	199

Note: "–" means sample is too small to make a reliable estimate.
Source: Calculations by New Strategist based on the Bureau of Labor Statistics' 2004 and 2005 Consumer Expenditure Surveys

Table 32. Average spending in the South by income, 2004–05

(average annual spending of consumer units (CUs) in the South by product and service category and before-tax income of consumer unit, 2004–05)

	total consumer units in South	under $10,000	$10,000 to $19,999	$20,000 to $29,999	$30,000 to $39,999	$40,000 to $49,999	$50,000 to $69,999	$70,000 or more
Number of consumer units (in 000s)	41,986	4,494	6,391	5,696	5,108	4,185	5,930	10,183
Average number of persons per CU	2.5	1.6	2.0	2.3	2.5	2.7	2.8	3.0
Average before-tax income of CU	$52,066	$5,582	$14,814	$24,867	$34,608	$44,493	$59,095	$118,948
Average annual spending of CU	40,903	15,074	19,894	27,489	33,320	37,938	45,943	74,618
FOOD	5,404	2,633	3,290	3,896	4,649	5,116	6,100	8,648
Food at home	3,065	1,773	2,256	2,572	2,742	2,930	3,390	4,329
Cereals and bakery products	413	253	321	340	370	392	451	577
Cereals and cereal products	136	86	111	110	120	129	154	185
Bakery products	277	167	210	230	250	264	296	392
Meats, poultry, fish, and eggs	790	473	595	695	701	761	899	1,068
Beef	245	123	178	190	220	232	309	341
Pork	173	117	136	179	154	172	188	212
Other meats	90	64	78	80	77	85	94	120
Poultry	139	92	108	125	122	137	148	185
Fish and seafood	108	52	65	84	92	98	125	171
Eggs	35	26	30	36	36	35	34	40
Dairy products	331	193	246	280	312	309	366	459
Fresh milk and cream	135	93	111	119	134	127	141	174
Other dairy products	196	99	135	161	179	182	225	286
Fruits and vegetables	488	277	372	401	429	479	510	704
Fresh fruits	154	89	112	127	132	162	153	228
Fresh vegetables	158	90	119	126	133	142	167	237
Processed fruits	91	50	71	70	89	88	97	128
Processed vegetables	85	49	71	77	75	87	93	111
Other food at home	1,043	577	723	857	930	989	1,165	1,520
Sugar and other sweets	114	66	85	100	92	103	128	162
Fats and oils	82	56	68	75	75	83	86	103
Miscellaneous foods	527	264	347	430	470	485	590	797
Nonalcoholic beverages	289	181	214	240	262	286	324	393
Food prepared by consumer unit on trips	32	8	7	12	30	32	38	65
Food away from home	2,340	859	1,034	1,324	1,907	2,186	2,710	4,319
ALCOHOLIC BEVERAGES	349	144	168	233	266	332	379	627
HOUSING	12,862	6,055	7,316	8,950	10,805	11,972	13,591	22,436
Shelter	6,936	3,339	3,653	4,669	5,776	6,359	7,335	12,438
Owned dwellings	4,719	1,249	1,528	2,161	3,228	4,049	5,210	10,421
Mortgage interest and charges	2,712	510	578	1,037	1,752	2,419	3,129	6,318
Property taxes	1,064	408	504	572	689	876	1,108	2,219
Maintenance, repair, insurance, other expenses	943	330	445	552	787	754	973	1,884
Rented dwellings	1,867	1,960	2,051	2,364	2,368	2,098	1,858	1,092
Other lodging	350	129	75	144	181	212	266	924
Utilities, fuels, and public services	3,108	1,796	2,347	2,652	2,913	3,186	3,408	4,312
Natural gas	273	154	207	211	235	272	267	426
Electricity	1,344	817	1,077	1,183	1,262	1,381	1,449	1,801
Fuel oil and other fuels	73	55	72	71	73	67	61	93
Telephone services	1,060	577	725	893	1,007	1,102	1,232	1,485
Water and other public services	358	193	267	294	336	365	400	507
Household services	725	177	299	423	490	576	745	1,569
Personal services	285	49	95	178	186	233	295	632
Other household services	440	129	205	245	304	343	450	937
Housekeeping supplies	561	267	354	394	466	539	613	910
Laundry and cleaning supplies	144	86	94	123	126	156	158	202
Other household products	283	121	190	182	245	255	309	472
Postage and stationery	133	60	70	89	95	128	147	236

	total consumer units in South	under $10,000	$10,000 to $19,999	$20,000 to $29,999	$30,000 to $39,999	$40,000 to $49,999	$50,000 to $69,999	$70,000 or more
Household furnishings and equipment	$1,532	$476	$662	$812	$1,160	$1,312	$1,489	$3,207
Household textiles	139	34	59	119	108	117	139	263
Furniture	404	110	210	179	267	370	328	910
Floor coverings	45	12	7	27	17	31	42	115
Major appliances	187	50	112	105	140	142	223	360
Small appliances, miscellaneous housewares	93	28	45	62	93	62	77	189
Miscellaneous household equipment	663	241	230	321	534	591	681	1,370
APPAREL AND RELATED SERVICES	1,740	758	877	1,097	1,327	1,574	1,864	3,202
Men and boys	399	169	156	217	309	410	469	736
Men, aged 16 or older	302	129	113	131	215	327	353	576
Boys, aged 2 to 15	98	40	43	86	94	83	116	160
Women and girls	700	291	359	482	494	610	780	1,272
Women, aged 16 or older	591	253	306	391	403	522	651	1,083
Girls, aged 2 to 15	109	39	53	91	91	87	129	189
Children under age 2	74	35	47	64	77	58	71	120
Footwear	317	174	217	226	299	330	336	472
Other apparel products and services	249	88	97	108	148	166	209	602
TRANSPORTATION	7,620	2,079	3,250	5,720	6,734	7,643	9,666	13,111
Vehicle purchases	3,366	586	1,032	2,569	2,941	3,338	4,642	5,985
Cars and trucks, new	1,690	188	293	1,083	1,312	1,168	2,329	3,603
Cars and trucks, used	1,612	397	738	1,450	1,623	2,062	2,195	2,258
Other vehicles	63	1	–	35	6	108	117	124
Gasoline and motor oil	1,835	788	1,044	1,456	1,791	1,956	2,233	2,744
Other vehicle expenses	2,132	627	1,094	1,565	1,845	2,133	2,538	3,668
Vehicle finance charges	347	61	108	205	268	422	467	642
Maintenance and repairs	583	205	374	439	452	523	629	1,024
Vehicle insurance	920	278	522	729	885	978	1,138	1,425
Vehicle rentals, leases, licenses, other charges	282	84	91	192	240	210	305	577
Public transportation	288	78	80	130	156	216	253	715
HEALTH CARE	2,569	1,172	1,734	2,142	2,434	2,706	2,802	3,818
Health insurance	1,323	578	933	1,120	1,213	1,472	1,484	1,909
Medical services	598	236	262	426	536	627	638	1,060
Drugs	548	307	486	515	589	526	557	691
Medical supplies	101	51	54	82	95	81	123	159
ENTERTAINMENT	2,124	639	799	1,561	1,659	1,771	2,346	4,155
Fees and admissions	426	92	97	150	279	340	400	1,057
Audio and visual equipment and services	811	353	492	583	724	829	921	1,311
Pets, toys, hobbies, playground equipment	381	126	156	261	371	338	422	688
Other entertainment products and services	507	68	55	566	285	265	603	1,099
PERSONAL CARE PRODUCTS AND SERVICES	525	227	294	357	446	508	557	908
READING	96	33	48	67	66	88	109	180
EDUCATION	662	275	274	223	246	374	540	1,715
TOBACCO PRODUCTS AND SMOKING SUPPLIES	304	227	281	324	373	342	318	283
MISCELLANEOUS	587	240	259	399	512	516	665	1,072
CASH CONTRIBUTIONS	1,479	327	563	895	1,003	1,259	1,500	3,204
PERSONAL INSURANCE AND PENSIONS	4,583	267	739	1,624	2,799	3,736	5,507	11,260
Life and other personal insurance	406	102	172	202	298	326	432	873
Pensions and Social Security	4,177	164	568	1,422	2,501	3,410	5,075	10,387
PERSONAL TAXES	1,959	–9	–112	426	479	1,009	2,137	6,015
Federal income taxes	1,437	–51	–194	228	183	571	1,538	4,719
State and local income taxes	379	–3	28	105	191	268	419	1,037
Other taxes	143	45	54	93	104	170	179	259
GIFTS FOR PEOPLE IN OTHER HOUSEHOLDS	958	355	388	488	614	657	900	2,147

Note: Spending by category will not add to total spending because gift spending is also included in the preceding product and service categories and personal taxes are not included in the total. "–" means value is less than 0.5.
Source: Bureau of Labor Statistics, 2004 and 2005 Consumer Expenditure Surveys, Internet site http://www.bls.gov/cex/; calculations by New Strategist

Table 33. Indexed spending in the South by income, 2004–05

(indexed average annual spending of consumer units in the South by product and service category and before-tax income of consumer unit, 2004–05; index definition: an index of 100 is the average for all consumer units; an index of 132 means that spending by consumer units in that group is 32 percent above the average for all consumer units; an index of 68 indicates spending that is 32 percent below the average for all consumer units)

	total consumer units in South	under $10,000	$10,000 to $19,999	$20,000 to $29,999	$30,000 to $39,999	$40,000 to $49,999	$50,000 to $69,999	$70,000 or more
Average spending of consumer units, total	$40,903	$15,074	$19,894	$27,489	$33,320	$37,938	$45,943	$74,618
Average spending of consumer units, index	100	37	49	67	81	93	112	182
FOOD	**100**	**49**	**61**	**72**	**86**	**95**	**113**	**160**
Food at home	**100**	**58**	**74**	**84**	**89**	**96**	**111**	**141**
Cereals and bakery products	100	61	78	82	90	95	109	140
Cereals and cereal products	100	63	82	81	88	95	113	136
Bakery products	100	60	76	83	90	95	107	142
Meats, poultry, fish, and eggs	100	60	75	88	89	96	114	135
Beef	100	50	72	78	90	95	126	139
Pork	100	68	79	103	89	99	109	123
Other meats	100	71	86	89	86	94	104	133
Poultry	100	66	78	90	88	99	106	133
Fish and seafood	100	48	60	78	85	91	116	158
Eggs	100	74	86	103	103	100	97	114
Dairy products	100	58	74	85	94	93	111	139
Fresh milk and cream	100	69	82	88	99	94	104	129
Other dairy products	100	51	69	82	91	93	115	146
Fruits and vegetables	100	57	76	82	88	98	105	144
Fresh fruits	100	58	72	82	86	105	99	148
Fresh vegetables	100	57	75	80	84	90	106	150
Processed fruits	100	55	78	77	98	97	107	141
Processed vegetables	100	58	83	91	88	102	109	131
Other food at home	100	55	69	82	89	95	112	146
Sugar and other sweets	100	58	75	88	81	90	112	142
Fats and oils	100	68	83	91	91	101	105	126
Miscellaneous foods	100	50	66	82	89	92	112	151
Nonalcoholic beverages	100	63	74	83	91	99	112	136
Food prepared by consumer unit on trips	100	26	23	38	94	100	119	203
Food away from home	**100**	**37**	**44**	**57**	**81**	**93**	**116**	**185**
ALCOHOLIC BEVERAGES	**100**	**41**	**48**	**67**	**76**	**95**	**109**	**180**
HOUSING	**100**	**47**	**57**	**70**	**84**	**93**	**106**	**174**
Shelter	**100**	**48**	**53**	**67**	**83**	**92**	**106**	**179**
Owned dwellings	100	26	32	46	68	86	110	221
Mortgage interest and charges	100	19	21	38	65	89	115	233
Property taxes	100	38	47	54	65	82	104	209
Maintenance, repair, insurance, other expenses	100	35	47	59	83	80	103	200
Rented dwellings	100	105	110	127	127	112	100	58
Other lodging	100	37	21	41	52	61	76	264
Utilities, fuels, and public services	**100**	**58**	**76**	**85**	**94**	**103**	**110**	**139**
Natural gas	100	56	76	77	86	100	98	156
Electricity	100	61	80	88	94	103	108	134
Fuel oil and other fuels	100	75	98	97	100	92	84	127
Telephone services	100	54	68	84	95	104	116	140
Water and other public services	100	54	75	82	94	102	112	142
Household services	**100**	**24**	**41**	**58**	**68**	**79**	**103**	**216**
Personal services	100	17	33	62	65	82	104	222
Other household services	100	29	47	56	69	78	102	213
Housekeeping supplies	**100**	**48**	**63**	**70**	**83**	**96**	**109**	**162**
Laundry and cleaning supplies	100	59	66	85	88	108	110	140
Other household products	100	43	67	64	87	90	109	167
Postage and stationery	100	45	52	67	71	96	111	177

	total consumer units in South	under $10,000	$10,000 to $19,999	$20,000 to $29,999	$30,000 to $39,999	$40,000 to $49,999	$50,000 to $69,999	$70,000 or more
Household furnishings and equipment	100	31	43	53	76	86	97	209
Household textiles	100	24	43	86	78	84	100	189
Furniture	100	27	52	44	66	92	81	225
Floor coverings	100	27	15	60	38	69	93	256
Major appliances	100	27	60	56	75	76	119	193
Small appliances, miscellaneous housewares	100	30	48	67	100	67	83	203
Miscellaneous household equipment	100	36	35	48	81	89	103	207
APPAREL AND RELATED SERVICES	100	44	50	63	76	90	107	184
Men and boys	100	42	39	54	77	103	118	184
Men, aged 16 or older	100	43	37	43	71	108	117	191
Boys, aged 2 to 15	100	41	44	88	96	85	118	163
Women and girls	100	42	51	69	71	87	111	182
Women, aged 16 or older	100	43	52	66	68	88	110	183
Girls, aged 2 to 15	100	36	49	83	83	80	118	173
Children under age 2	100	48	64	86	104	78	96	162
Footwear	100	55	69	71	94	104	106	149
Other apparel products and services	100	35	39	43	59	67	84	242
TRANSPORTATION	100	27	43	75	88	100	127	172
Vehicle purchases	100	17	31	76	87	99	138	178
Cars and trucks, new	100	11	17	64	78	69	138	213
Cars and trucks, used	100	25	46	90	101	128	136	140
Other vehicles	100	2	–	56	10	171	186	197
Gasoline and motor oil	100	43	57	79	98	107	122	150
Other vehicle expenses	100	29	51	73	87	100	119	172
Vehicle finance charges	100	18	31	59	77	122	135	185
Maintenance and repairs	100	35	64	75	78	90	108	176
Vehicle insurance	100	30	57	79	96	106	124	155
Vehicle rentals, leases, licenses, other charges	100	30	32	68	85	74	108	205
Public transportation	100	27	28	45	54	75	88	248
HEALTH CARE	100	46	67	83	95	105	109	149
Health insurance	100	44	70	85	92	111	112	144
Medical services	100	39	44	71	90	105	107	177
Drugs	100	56	89	94	107	96	102	126
Medical supplies	100	51	53	81	94	80	122	157
ENTERTAINMENT	100	30	38	73	78	83	110	196
Fees and admissions	100	22	23	35	65	80	94	248
Audio and visual equipment and services	100	44	61	72	89	102	114	162
Pets, toys, hobbies, playground equipment	100	33	41	69	97	89	111	181
Other entertainment products and services	100	13	11	112	56	52	119	217
PERSONAL CARE PRODUCTS AND SERVICES	100	43	56	68	85	97	106	173
READING	100	34	50	70	69	92	114	188
EDUCATION	100	42	41	34	37	56	82	259
TOBACCO PRODUCTS AND SMOKING SUPPLIES	100	75	92	107	123	113	105	93
MISCELLANEOUS	100	41	44	68	87	88	113	183
CASH CONTRIBUTIONS	100	22	38	61	68	85	101	217
PERSONAL INSURANCE AND PENSIONS	100	6	16	35	61	82	120	246
Life and other personal insurance	100	25	42	50	73	80	106	215
Pensions and Social Security	100	4	14	34	60	82	121	249
PERSONAL TAXES	100	0	–6	22	24	52	109	307
Federal income taxes	100	–4	–14	16	13	40	107	328
State and local income taxes	100	–1	7	28	50	71	111	274
Other taxes	100	31	38	65	73	119	125	181
GIFTS FOR PEOPLE IN OTHER HOUSEHOLDS	100	37	40	51	64	69	94	224

Note: "–" means sample is too small to make a reliable estimate.
Source: Calculations by New Strategist based on the Bureau of Labor Statistics' 2004 and 2005 Consumer Expenditure Surveys

Table 34. Average spending in the West by income, 2004–05

(average annual spending of consumer units (CUs) in the West by product and service category and before-tax income of consumer unit, 2004–05)

	total consumer units in West	under $10,000	$10,000 to $19,999	$20,000 to $29,999	$30,000 to $39,999	$40,000 to $49,999	$50,000 to $69,999	$70,000 or more
Number of consumer units (in 000s)	25,872	2,317	3,422	2,901	3,033	2,503	4,023	7,673
Average number of persons per CU	2.6	1.6	1.9	2.2	2.5	2.8	2.8	3.2
Average before-tax income of CU	$60,730	$4,782	$14,944	$24,905	$34,506	$44,603	$59,109	$128,063
Average annual spending of CU	50,305	18,471	24,152	30,723	36,532	43,071	52,310	85,401
FOOD	**6,280**	**2,981**	**3,582**	**4,394**	**5,267**	**5,884**	**6,729**	**9,308**
Food at home	**3,580**	**1,893**	**2,404**	**2,789**	**3,208**	**3,578**	**3,814**	**4,841**
Cereals and bakery products	467	251	326	354	445	501	486	615
Cereals and cereal products	157	102	117	111	160	163	162	199
Bakery products	311	149	209	243	285	338	324	416
Meats, poultry, fish, and eggs	843	492	549	700	768	844	922	1,103
Beef	252	160	164	214	228	249	277	326
Pork	157	99	102	144	150	151	178	196
Other meats	100	50	59	79	75	97	117	142
Poultry	149	88	103	120	151	123	161	197
Fish and seafood	139	65	84	100	113	175	142	193
Eggs	45	31	38	41	51	48	47	50
Dairy products	406	209	283	312	361	415	422	550
Fresh milk and cream	156	91	121	140	149	164	161	192
Other dairy products	249	118	163	172	212	251	261	358
Fruits and vegetables	635	349	462	482	563	598	646	873
Fresh fruits	218	116	159	160	192	201	209	311
Fresh vegetables	215	126	161	168	187	186	231	291
Processed fruits	118	62	82	89	109	121	115	164
Processed vegetables	83	45	59	64	75	90	91	107
Other food at home	1,228	592	783	942	1,071	1,220	1,338	1,701
Sugar and other sweets	131	64	88	91	117	117	143	186
Fats and oils	95	49	86	76	82	100	100	119
Miscellaneous foods	623	291	379	487	531	628	670	875
Nonalcoholic beverages	320	174	209	259	295	326	363	413
Food prepared by consumer unit on trips	59	14	21	28	47	49	63	108
Food away from home	**2,701**	**1,088**	**1,178**	**1,605**	**2,059**	**2,306**	**2,916**	**4,467**
ALCOHOLIC BEVERAGES	**517**	**279**	**198**	**261**	**364**	**477**	**623**	**828**
HOUSING	**16,828**	**6,968**	**9,249**	**11,379**	**13,111**	**14,731**	**17,103**	**27,208**
Shelter	**10,480**	**4,787**	**5,934**	**7,364**	**7,990**	**9,158**	**10,700**	**16,706**
Owned dwellings	6,670	1,255	1,970	2,830	3,686	4,947	7,193	13,321
Mortgage interest and charges	4,255	637	804	1,419	2,312	3,281	4,685	8,820
Property taxes	1,309	319	552	641	694	952	1,334	2,546
Maintenance, repair, insurance, other expenses	1,105	299	614	769	680	714	1,174	1,955
Rented dwellings	3,231	3,259	3,734	4,338	4,088	3,935	3,046	2,108
Other lodging	579	273	230	196	216	277	461	1,277
Utilities, fuels, and public services	**2,795**	**1,284**	**1,728**	**2,209**	**2,438**	**2,770**	**3,041**	**3,969**
Natural gas	370	152	234	294	302	350	404	540
Electricity	925	462	624	767	833	888	954	1,291
Fuel oil and other fuels	58	37	46	61	44	68	66	67
Telephone services	1,009	479	587	793	904	1,044	1,138	1,402
Water and other public services	432	153	235	293	356	418	479	668
Household services	**904**	**198**	**340**	**429**	**503**	**623**	**792**	**1,859**
Personal services	325	38	65	89	149	250	273	740
Other household services	579	159	275	341	355	373	520	1,119
Housekeeping supplies	**618**	**257**	**424**	**393**	**561**	**543**	**677**	**895**
Laundry and cleaning supplies	140	72	108	111	144	152	155	168
Other household products	305	131	197	183	251	231	324	477
Postage and stationery	173	53	119	100	166	160	198	250

	total consumer units in West	under $10,000	$10,000 to $19,999	$20,000 to $29,999	$30,000 to $39,999	$40,000 to $49,999	$50,000 to $69,999	$70,000 or more
Household furnishings and equipment	$2,030	$443	$824	$984	$1,618	$1,637	$1,893	$3,779
Household textiles	143	36	91	77	171	101	164	212
Furniture	560	115	187	198	365	410	445	1,183
Floor coverings	68	11	12	19	14	67	80	144
Major appliances	249	48	114	139	164	197	263	454
Small appliances, miscellaneous housewares	133	34	71	95	105	118	116	226
Miscellaneous household equipment	878	201	349	455	799	744	825	1,560
APPAREL AND RELATED SERVICES	1,954	883	911	1,305	1,549	1,392	1,993	3,260
Men and boys	453	178	186	282	371	298	452	788
Men, aged 16 or older	370	141	147	224	309	223	353	661
Boys, aged 2 to 15	83	37	38	58	62	76	99	127
Women and girls	750	361	310	459	567	496	850	1,252
Women, aged 16 or older	633	338	261	407	488	377	728	1,044
Girls, aged 2 to 15	117	24	49	51	79	120	122	207
Children under age 2	94	35	64	112	66	83	83	138
Footwear	331	209	185	250	312	276	342	475
Other apparel products and services	326	100	166	202	232	238	266	608
TRANSPORTATION	9,498	2,617	3,739	5,684	7,097	8,406	10,706	16,256
Vehicle purchases	4,268	970	1,403	2,387	2,904	3,533	4,858	7,722
Cars and trucks, new	2,369	348	497	1,221	1,268	1,427	2,572	4,883
Cars and trucks, used	1,808	600	900	1,140	1,635	2,058	2,156	2,635
Other vehicles	91	22	12	26	1	48	130	204
Gasoline and motor oil	1,966	721	988	1,402	1,687	1,964	2,284	2,936
Other vehicle expenses	2,658	762	1,114	1,595	2,181	2,539	2,965	4,386
Vehicle finance charges	310	45	71	146	242	296	401	543
Maintenance and repairs	838	287	402	523	706	727	935	1,354
Vehicle insurance	1,004	304	462	704	916	1,087	1,182	1,484
Vehicle rentals, leases, licenses, other charges	506	127	178	222	317	428	446	1,005
Public transportation	606	165	234	299	326	371	599	1,212
HEALTH CARE	2,602	1,027	1,819	1,963	2,009	2,689	2,715	3,811
Health insurance	1,262	546	845	979	1,001	1,341	1,431	1,760
Medical services	773	217	455	555	529	720	730	1,302
Drugs	450	226	440	353	388	535	418	567
Medical supplies	117	39	78	76	91	93	136	182
ENTERTAINMENT	2,636	831	1,260	1,406	1,689	2,219	2,778	4,684
Fees and admissions	711	186	244	306	364	421	643	1,500
Audio and visual equipment and services	887	329	456	603	727	783	956	1,417
Pets, toys, hobbies, playground equipment	464	169	218	204	321	375	453	845
Other entertainment products and services	573	147	342	292	277	640	726	923
PERSONAL CARE PRODUCTS AND SERVICES	621	263	327	422	459	605	624	991
READING	153	63	74	89	105	139	148	264
EDUCATION	1,039	1,476	696	495	320	585	701	1,871
TOBACCO PRODUCTS AND SMOKING SUPPLIES	239	179	218	205	315	244	282	224
MISCELLANEOUS	910	267	474	525	702	760	1,160	1,441
CASH CONTRIBUTIONS	1,576	363	770	968	920	1,178	1,421	3,003
PERSONAL INSURANCE AND PENSIONS	5,451	273	835	1,627	2,624	3,760	5,326	12,252
Life and other personal insurance	343	47	130	118	166	282	318	715
Pensions and Social Security	5,108	226	706	1,509	2,459	3,478	5,008	11,537
PERSONAL TAXES	2,689	–82	65	599	739	1,061	1,862	7,224
Federal income taxes	1,979	–110	–18	399	452	710	1,336	5,453
State and local income taxes	592	–1	35	153	238	280	418	1,519
Other taxes	118	29	48	48	49	70	107	252
GIFTS FOR PEOPLE IN OTHER HOUSEHOLDS	1,245	264	636	615	999	769	1,035	2,398

Note: Spending by category will not add to total spending because gift spending is also included in the preceding product and service categories and personal taxes are not included in the total.
Source: Bureau of Labor Statistics, 2004 and 2005 Consumer Expenditure Surveys, Internet site http://www.bls.gov/cex/; calculations by New Strategist

Table 35. Indexed spending in the West by income, 2004–05

(indexed average annual spending of consumer units in the West by product and service category and before-tax income of consumer unit, 2004–05; index definition: an index of 100 is the average for all consumer units; an index of 132 means that spending by consumer units in that group is 32 percent above the average for all consumer units; an index of 68 indicates spending that is 32 percent below the average for all consumer units)

	total consumer units in West	under $10,000	$10,000 to $19,999	$20,000 to $29,999	$30,000 to $39,999	$40,000 to $49,999	$50,000 to $69,999	$70,000 or more
Average spending of consumer units, total	$50,305	$18,471	$24,152	$30,723	$36,532	$43,071	$52,310	$85,401
Average spending of consumer units, index	100	37	48	61	73	86	104	170
FOOD	**100**	**47**	**57**	**70**	**84**	**94**	**107**	**148**
Food at home	**100**	**53**	**67**	**78**	**90**	**100**	**107**	**135**
Cereals and bakery products	100	54	70	76	95	107	104	132
Cereals and cereal products	100	65	75	71	102	104	103	127
Bakery products	100	48	67	78	92	109	104	134
Meats, poultry, fish, and eggs	100	58	65	83	91	100	109	131
Beef	100	63	65	85	90	99	110	129
Pork	100	63	65	92	96	96	113	125
Other meats	100	50	59	79	75	97	117	142
Poultry	100	59	69	81	101	83	108	132
Fish and seafood	100	47	60	72	81	126	102	139
Eggs	100	69	84	91	113	107	104	111
Dairy products	100	51	70	77	89	102	104	135
Fresh milk and cream	100	58	78	90	96	105	103	123
Other dairy products	100	47	65	69	85	101	105	144
Fruits and vegetables	100	55	73	76	89	94	102	137
Fresh fruits	100	53	73	73	88	92	96	143
Fresh vegetables	100	58	75	78	87	87	107	135
Processed fruits	100	52	70	75	92	103	97	139
Processed vegetables	100	55	72	77	90	108	110	129
Other food at home	100	48	64	77	87	99	109	139
Sugar and other sweets	100	49	67	69	89	89	109	142
Fats and oils	100	52	91	80	86	105	105	125
Miscellaneous foods	100	47	61	78	85	101	108	140
Nonalcoholic beverages	100	54	65	81	92	102	113	129
Food prepared by consumer unit on trips	100	23	36	47	80	83	107	183
Food away from home	**100**	**40**	**44**	**59**	**76**	**85**	**108**	**165**
ALCOHOLIC BEVERAGES	**100**	**54**	**38**	**50**	**70**	**92**	**121**	**160**
HOUSING	**100**	**41**	**55**	**68**	**78**	**88**	**102**	**162**
Shelter	**100**	**46**	**57**	**70**	**76**	**87**	**102**	**159**
Owned dwellings	100	19	30	42	55	74	108	200
Mortgage interest and charges	100	15	19	33	54	77	110	207
Property taxes	100	24	42	49	53	73	102	194
Maintenance, repair, insurance, other expenses	100	27	56	70	62	65	106	177
Rented dwellings	100	101	116	134	127	122	94	65
Other lodging	100	47	40	34	37	48	80	221
Utilities, fuels, and public services	**100**	**46**	**62**	**79**	**87**	**99**	**109**	**142**
Natural gas	100	41	63	79	82	95	109	146
Electricity	100	50	68	83	90	96	103	140
Fuel oil and other fuels	100	64	80	105	76	117	114	116
Telephone services	100	47	58	79	90	103	113	139
Water and other public services	100	36	54	68	82	97	111	155
Household services	**100**	**22**	**38**	**47**	**56**	**69**	**88**	**206**
Personal services	100	12	20	27	46	77	84	228
Other household services	100	28	47	59	61	64	90	193
Housekeeping supplies	**100**	**42**	**69**	**64**	**91**	**88**	**110**	**145**
Laundry and cleaning supplies	100	52	77	79	103	109	111	120
Other household products	100	43	65	60	82	76	106	156
Postage and stationery	100	30	69	58	96	92	114	145

	total consumer units in West	under $10,000	$10,000 to $19,999	$20,000 to $29,999	$30,000 to $39,999	$40,000 to $49,999	$50,000 to $69,999	$70,000 or more
Household furnishings and equipment	100	22	41	48	80	81	93	186
Household textiles	100	25	64	54	120	71	115	148
Furniture	100	20	33	35	65	73	79	211
Floor coverings	100	16	17	28	21	99	118	212
Major appliances	100	19	46	56	66	79	106	182
Small appliances, miscellaneous housewares	100	26	53	71	79	89	87	170
Miscellaneous household equipment	100	23	40	52	91	85	94	178
APPAREL AND RELATED SERVICES	100	45	47	67	79	71	102	167
Men and boys	100	39	41	62	82	66	100	174
Men, aged 16 or older	100	38	40	61	84	60	95	179
Boys, aged 2 to 15	100	44	46	70	75	92	119	153
Women and girls	100	48	41	61	76	66	113	167
Women, aged 16 or older	100	53	41	64	77	60	115	165
Girls, aged 2 to 15	100	20	42	44	68	103	104	177
Children under age 2	100	37	69	119	70	88	88	147
Footwear	100	63	56	76	94	83	103	144
Other apparel products and services	100	31	51	62	71	73	82	187
TRANSPORTATION	100	28	39	60	75	89	113	171
Vehicle purchases	100	23	33	56	68	83	114	181
Cars and trucks, new	100	15	21	52	54	60	109	206
Cars and trucks, used	100	33	50	63	90	114	119	146
Other vehicles	100	24	13	29	1	53	143	224
Gasoline and motor oil	100	37	50	71	86	100	116	149
Other vehicle expenses	100	29	42	60	82	96	112	165
Vehicle finance charges	100	14	23	47	78	95	129	175
Maintenance and repairs	100	34	48	62	84	87	112	162
Vehicle insurance	100	30	46	70	91	108	118	148
Vehicle rentals, leases, licenses, other charges	100	25	35	44	63	85	88	199
Public transportation	100	27	39	49	54	61	99	200
HEALTH CARE	100	39	70	75	77	103	104	146
Health insurance	100	43	67	78	79	106	113	139
Medical services	100	28	59	72	68	93	94	168
Drugs	100	50	98	78	86	119	93	126
Medical supplies	100	33	67	65	78	79	116	156
ENTERTAINMENT	100	32	48	53	64	84	105	178
Fees and admissions	100	26	34	43	51	59	90	211
Audio and visual equipment and services	100	37	51	68	82	88	108	160
Pets, toys, hobbies, playground equipment	100	36	47	44	69	81	98	182
Other entertainment products and services	100	26	60	51	48	112	127	161
PERSONAL CARE PRODUCTS AND SERVICES	100	42	53	68	74	97	100	160
READING	100	41	49	58	69	91	97	173
EDUCATION	100	142	67	48	31	56	67	180
TOBACCO PRODUCTS AND SMOKING SUPPLIES	100	75	91	86	132	102	118	94
MISCELLANEOUS	100	29	52	58	77	84	127	158
CASH CONTRIBUTIONS	100	23	49	61	58	75	90	191
PERSONAL INSURANCE AND PENSIONS	100	5	15	30	48	69	98	225
Life and other personal insurance	100	14	38	34	48	82	93	208
Pensions and Social Security	100	4	14	30	48	68	98	226
PERSONAL TAXES	100	–3	2	22	27	39	69	269
Federal income taxes	100	–6	–1	20	23	36	68	276
State and local income taxes	100	0	6	26	40	47	71	257
Other taxes	100	24	40	41	42	59	91	214
GIFTS FOR PEOPLE IN OTHER HOUSEHOLDS	100	21	51	49	80	62	83	193

Source: Calculations by New Strategist based on the Bureau of Labor Statistics' 2004 and 2005 Consumer Expenditure Surveys

Spending by Metropolitan Area, 2004–05

Within regions, spending levels vary considerably by metropolitan area. Among the four northeastern metropolitan areas examined by the Consumer Expenditure Survey, average household spending ranged from $39,891 in Pittsburgh to $54,121 in New York in 2004–05. In the Midwest, spending ranged from $38,476 in Cleveland to $58,900 in Minneapolis-St. Paul. Among selected metropolitan areas in the South, spending was greatest in Washington, D.C. ($55,977) and lowest in Miami ($37,673). In the West, San Francisco had the highest household spending ($60,992)—not only for the region, but among all the metropolitan areas included in the survey. Among western metropolitan areas, household spending was lowest in Phoenix ($49,009).

Spending levels by metropolitan area vary significantly by product and service category. Households in Boston spend more on alcoholic beverages (with an index of 157) than the households in Pittsburgh (with an index of 73). Households in Pittsburgh spend more on tobacco than those in the other three metropolitan areas (with an index of 148).

Households in Minneapolis–St. Paul spend nearly twice as much as households in Detroit on alcoholic beverages. But households in Detroit spend more than those in Minneapolis-St. Paul on tobacco.

In the South, households in Miami spend much less than those in other southern metropolitan areas on reading materials. Households in Washington, D.C., spend more than households in other southern metropolitan areas on alcoholic beverages.

In the West, spending on tobacco is 25 percent lower than the western average in Los Angeles and 40 percent lower in San Francisco. But spending on tobacco is 84 percent above the western average in Anchorage. Spending on food away from home is 43 percent above the western average in Honolulu and 9 percent below average in Denver.

Table 36. Average spending in selected Northeastern metros, 2004–05

(average annual spending of consumer units in selected Northeastern metropolitan areas by product and service category, 2004–05)

	total consumer units in the Northeast	Boston	New York	Philadelphia	Pittsburgh
Number of consumer units (in 000s)	22,184	2,876	7,687	2,620	1,154
Average number of persons per consumer unit	2.4	2.4	2.6	2.5	2.3
Average income before taxes	$62,002	$67,927	$74,851	$61,496	$52,637
Average annual spending	47,005	51,679	54,121	47,289	39,891
FOOD	6,430	7,223	7,283	6,481	5,205
Food at home	3,640	3,977	4,014	3,620	2,785
Cereals and bakery products	515	579	568	522	399
Meats, poultry, fish, and eggs	946	998	1,109	963	681
Dairy products	421	410	462	408	331
Fruits and vegetables	645	686	766	611	460
Other food at home	1,114	1,304	1,111	1,116	915
Food away from home	2,790	3,247	3,269	2,861	2,420
ALCOHOLIC BEVERAGES	532	834	553	567	387
HOUSING	16,121	17,805	20,065	15,915	12,031
Shelter	9,887	11,364	13,271	9,289	6,429
Owned dwellings	6,571	7,882	8,277	6,344	4,454
Rented dwellings	2,726	2,899	4,245	2,470	1,524
Other lodging	590	583	749	475	451
Utilities, fuels, and public services	3,257	3,169	3,528	3,600	3,103
Household services	779	917	957	687	563
Housekeeping supplies	620	684	579	628	549
Household furnishings and equipment	1,577	1,670	1,730	1,709	1,386
APPAREL AND RELATED SERVICES	2,106	1,929	2,858	2,279	1,747
TRANSPORTATION	7,646	8,586	7,581	8,084	7,456
Vehicle purchases	3,031	3,759	2,316	3,802	3,307
Gasoline and motor oil	1,572	1,747	1,495	1,477	1,538
Other vehicle expenses	2,405	2,502	2,716	2,310	2,218
Public transportation	637	579	1,054	495	393
HEALTH CARE	2,476	2,624	2,412	2,254	2,528
ENTERTAINMENT	2,137	2,347	2,330	1,895	2,102
PERSONAL CARE PRODUCTS AND SERVICES	586	591	687	643	479
READING	146	195	144	132	144
EDUCATION	1,256	1,744	1,643	1,235	879
TOBACCO PRODUCTS AND SMOKING SUPPLIES	314	287	265	275	465
MISCELLANEOUS	793	599	1,064	729	662
CASH CONTRIBUTIONS	1,241	1,063	1,168	1,227	1,817
PERSONAL INSURANCE AND PENSIONS	5,223	5,851	6,068	5,573	3,989
Life and other personal insurance	371	393	422	350	378
Pensions and Social Security	4,851	5,458	5,646	5,222	3,611

Source: Bureau of Labor Statistics, 2004 and 2005 Consumer Expenditure Surveys, Internet site http://www.bls.gov/cex/

Table 37. Indexed spending in selected Northeastern metros, 2004–05

(indexed average annual spending of consumer units in selected Northeastern metropolitan areas by product and service category, 2004–05; index definition: an index of 100 is the average for all consumer units; an index of 132 means that spending by consumer units in that group is 32 percent above the average for all consumer units; an index of 68 indicates spending that is 32 percent below the average for all consumer units)

	total consumer units in the Northeast	Boston	New York	Philadelphia	Pittsburgh
Average spending of consumer unit, total	$47,005	$51,679	$54,121	$47,289	$39,891
Average spending of consumer unit, index	100	110	115	101	85
FOOD	100	112	113	101	81
Food at home	100	109	110	99	77
Cereals and bakery products	100	112	110	101	77
Meats, poultry, fish, and eggs	100	105	117	102	72
Dairy products	100	97	110	97	79
Fruits and vegetables	100	106	119	95	71
Other food at home	100	117	100	100	82
Food away from home	100	116	117	103	87
ALCOHOLIC BEVERAGES	100	157	104	107	73
HOUSING	100	110	124	99	75
Shelter	100	115	134	94	65
Owned dwellings	100	120	126	97	68
Rented dwellings	100	106	156	91	56
Other lodging	100	99	127	81	76
Utilities, fuels, and public services	100	97	108	111	95
Household services	100	118	123	88	72
Housekeeping supplies	100	110	93	101	89
Household furnishings and equipment	100	106	110	108	88
APPAREL AND RELATED SERVICES	100	92	136	108	83
TRANSPORTATION	100	112	99	106	98
Vehicle purchases	100	124	76	125	109
Gasoline and motor oil	100	111	95	94	98
Other vehicle expenses	100	104	113	96	92
Public transportation	100	91	165	78	62
HEALTH CARE	100	106	97	91	102
ENTERTAINMENT	100	110	109	89	98
PERSONAL CARE PRODUCTS AND SERVICES	100	101	117	110	82
READING	100	134	99	90	99
EDUCATION	100	139	131	98	70
TOBACCO PRODUCTS AND SMOKING SUPPLIES	100	91	84	88	148
MISCELLANEOUS	100	76	134	92	83
CASH CONTRIBUTIONS	100	86	94	99	146
PERSONAL INSURANCE AND PENSIONS	100	112	116	107	76
Life and other personal insurance	100	106	114	94	102
Pensions and Social Security	100	113	116	108	74

Source: Calculations by New Strategist based on the Bureau of Labor Statistics' 2004 and 2005 Consumer Expenditure Surveys

Table 38. Average spending in selected Midwestern metros, 2004–05

(average annual spending of consumer units (CUs) in selected Midwestern metropolitan areas by product and service category, 2004–05)

	total consumer units in the Midwest	Chicago	Cleveland	Detroit	Minneapolis–St. Paul	St. Louis
Number of consumer units (in 000s)	26,767	3,189	1,161	2,123	1,293	1,075
Average number of persons per CU	2.4	2.6	2.4	2.7	2.3	2.4
Average income before taxes	$55,215	$67,726	$51,602	$66,189	$78,388	$61,535
Average annual spending	44,322	54,935	38,476	51,219	58,900	48,365
FOOD	5,672	6,456	4,526	6,780	6,850	6,266
Food at home	3,210	3,453	2,788	3,965	3,567	3,452
Cereals and bakery products	450	473	391	545	493	494
Meats, poultry, fish, and eggs	747	815	726	1,047	713	854
Dairy products	374	365	320	405	458	395
Fruits and vegetables	514	609	455	635	600	536
Other food at home	1,126	1,192	896	1,333	1,303	1,173
Food away from home	2,462	3,002	1,738	2,815	3,282	2,814
ALCOHOLIC BEVERAGES	443	581	435	380	750	738
HOUSING	13,852	18,962	13,349	16,490	19,341	14,409
Shelter	7,665	11,440	7,560	9,656	11,245	7,620
Owned dwellings	5,527	8,510	5,333	7,389	8,463	5,568
Rented dwellings	1,608	2,138	1,613	1,462	1,896	1,494
Other lodging	530	792	614	805	886	558
Utilities, fuels, and public services	3,064	3,541	3,412	3,511	3,070	3,251
Household services	734	1,063	434	864	1,126	921
Housekeeping supplies	640	792	570	568	810	581
Household furnishings and equipment	1,749	2,124	1,373	1,890	3,090	2,035
APPAREL AND RELATED SERVICES	1,711	2,318	1,156	2,251	2,472	2,015
TRANSPORTATION	7,795	8,875	6,095	9,246	8,550	8,649
Vehicle purchases	3,259	4,013	2,056	2,914	3,140	4,095
Gasoline and motor oil	1,801	1,754	1,449	2,129	1,853	1,853
Other vehicle expenses	2,365	2,464	2,328	3,759	2,826	2,287
Public transportation	371	644	263	444	731	415
HEALTH CARE	2,859	2,933	2,600	2,261	3,100	2,980
ENTERTAINMENT	2,293	2,629	2,213	2,619	3,656	2,477
PERSONAL CARE PRODUCTS AND SERVICES	539	664	439	568	700	563
READING	141	162	147	149	179	127
EDUCATION	951	1,456	719	1,140	1,296	1,370
TOBACCO PRODUCTS AND SMOKING SUPPLIES	356	346	364	480	346	348
MISCELLANEOUS	821	920	926	895	1,177	699
CASH CONTRIBUTIONS	1,828	2,969	1,027	1,528	2,275	2,177
PERSONAL INSURANCE AND PENSIONS	5,058	5,665	4,478	6,430	8,210	5,546
Life and other personal insurance	411	384	294	451	414	555
Pensions and Social Security	4,648	5,282	4,184	5,979	7,796	4,991

Source: Bureau of Labor Statistics, 2004 and 2005 Consumer Expenditure Surveys, Internet site http://www.bls.gov/cex/

Table 39. Indexed spending in selected Midwestern metros, 2004–05

(indexed average annual spending of consumer units in selected Midwestern metropolitan areas by product and service category, 2004–05; index definition: an index of 100 is the average for all consumer units; an index of 132 means that spending by consumer units in that group is 32 percent above the average for all consumer units; an index of 68 indicates spending that is 32 percent below the average for all consumer units)

	total consumer units in the Midwest	Chicago	Cleveland	Detroit	Minneapolis–St. Paul	St. Louis
Average spending of consumer units, total	$44,322	$54,935	$38,476	$51,219	$58,900	$48,365
Average spending of consumer units, index	100	124	87	116	133	109
FOOD	**100**	**114**	**80**	**120**	**121**	**110**
Food at home	**100**	**108**	**87**	**124**	**111**	**108**
Cereals and bakery products	100	105	87	121	110	110
Meats, poultry, fish, and eggs	100	109	97	140	95	114
Dairy products	100	98	86	108	122	106
Fruits and vegetables	100	118	89	124	117	104
Other food at home	100	106	80	118	116	104
Food away from home	**100**	**122**	**71**	**114**	**133**	**114**
ALCOHOLIC BEVERAGES	**100**	**131**	**98**	**86**	**169**	**167**
HOUSING	**100**	**137**	**96**	**119**	**140**	**104**
Shelter	**100**	**149**	**99**	**126**	**147**	**99**
Owned dwellings	100	154	96	134	153	101
Rented dwellings	100	133	100	91	118	93
Other lodging	100	149	116	152	167	105
Utilities, fuels, and public services	**100**	**116**	**111**	**115**	**100**	**106**
Household services	**100**	**145**	**59**	**118**	**153**	**125**
Housekeeping supplies	**100**	**124**	**89**	**89**	**127**	**91**
Household furnishings and equipment	**100**	**121**	**79**	**108**	**177**	**116**
APPAREL AND RELATED SERVICES	**100**	**135**	**68**	**132**	**144**	**118**
TRANSPORTATION	**100**	**114**	**78**	**119**	**110**	**111**
Vehicle purchases	100	123	63	89	96	126
Gasoline and motor oil	100	97	80	118	103	103
Other vehicle expenses	100	104	98	159	119	97
Public transportation	100	174	71	120	197	112
HEALTH CARE	**100**	**103**	**91**	**79**	**108**	**104**
ENTERTAINMENT	**100**	**115**	**97**	**114**	**159**	**108**
PERSONAL CARE PRODUCTS AND SERVICES	**100**	**123**	**81**	**105**	**130**	**104**
READING	**100**	**115**	**104**	**106**	**127**	**90**
EDUCATION	**100**	**153**	**76**	**120**	**136**	**144**
TOBACCO PRODUCTS AND SMOKING SUPPLIES	**100**	**97**	**102**	**135**	**97**	**98**
MISCELLANEOUS	**100**	**112**	**113**	**109**	**143**	**85**
CASH CONTRIBUTIONS	**100**	**162**	**56**	**84**	**124**	**119**
PERSONAL INSURANCE AND PENSIONS	**100**	**112**	**89**	**127**	**162**	**110**
Life and other personal insurance	100	93	72	110	101	135
Pensions and Social Security	100	114	90	129	168	107

Source: Calculations by New Strategist based on the Bureau of Labor Statistics' 2004 and 2005 Consumer Expenditure Surveys

Table 40. Average spending in selected Southern metros, 2004–05

(average annual spending of consumer units in selected Southern metropolitan areas by product and service category, 2004–05)

	total consumer units in the South	Atlanta	Baltimore	Dallas–Fort Worth	Houston	Miami	Washington, D.C.
Number of consumer units (in 000s)	41,986	1,989	1,169	2,054	1,751	1,779	2,344
Average number of persons per consumer unit	2.5	2.5	2.3	2.8	2.9	2.6	2.5
Average income before taxes	$52,066	$59,942	$63,372	$61,753	$69,557	$51,799	$86,526
Average annual spending	40,903	39,992	39,217	50,637	52,998	37,673	55,977
FOOD	5,404	5,496	4,324	6,426	5,862	5,522	5,831
Food at home	3,065	2,676	2,655	3,560	3,118	3,793	3,055
Cereals and bakery products	413	364	374	489	422	507	407
Meats, poultry, fish, and eggs	790	750	737	805	776	1,029	766
Dairy products	331	255	275	414	338	470	337
Fruits and vegetables	488	502	448	579	556	736	597
Other food at home	1,043	804	820	1,273	1,025	1,052	949
Food away from home	2,340	2,820	1,670	2,867	2,744	1,729	2,776
ALCOHOLIC BEVERAGES	349	337	354	540	430	272	551
HOUSING	12,862	14,346	14,714	16,706	16,609	14,807	21,523
Shelter	6,936	8,497	9,487	9,453	9,245	9,465	13,997
Owned dwellings	4,719	6,019	6,644	6,818	6,373	6,150	10,250
Rented dwellings	1,867	2,202	2,366	2,147	2,255	3,027	3,178
Other lodging	350	276	476	488	617	289	570
Utilities, fuels, and public services	3,108	3,430	2,944	3,833	3,877	3,140	3,618
Household services	725	717	614	929	1,067	741	1,326
Housekeeping supplies	561	518	417	645	653	525	567
Household furnishings and equipment	1,532	1,184	1,253	1,845	1,767	936	2,015
APPAREL AND RELATED SERVICES	1,740	1,744	1,641	2,228	2,265	954	2,224
TRANSPORTATION	7,620	6,044	5,799	8,838	10,326	6,282	7,876
Vehicle purchases	3,366	2,359	2,052	3,587	4,584	2,013	2,758
Gasoline and motor oil	1,835	1,695	1,541	1,982	2,249	1,633	1,726
Other vehicle expenses	2,132	1,748	1,844	2,799	3,107	2,284	2,601
Public transportation	288	242	363	469	386	353	790
HEALTH CARE	2,569	1,837	2,215	3,027	2,942	2,003	2,510
ENTERTAINMENT	2,124	2,079	1,696	2,111	2,338	1,412	2,632
PERSONAL CARE PRODUCTS AND SERVICES	525	397	507	767	746	516	637
READING	96	65	80	118	129	33	166
EDUCATION	662	773	998	921	1,061	576	1,610
TOBACCO PRODUCTS AND SMOKING SUPPLIES	304	142	219	228	246	141	188
MISCELLANEOUS	587	421	395	783	879	455	847
CASH CONTRIBUTIONS	1,479	1,047	1,228	1,855	2,677	852	1,667
PERSONAL INSURANCE AND PENSIONS	4,583	5,265	5,046	6,090	6,488	3,846	7,713
Life and other personal insurance	406	364	235	437	425	218	609
Pensions and Social Security	4,177	4,901	4,811	5,652	6,063	3,628	7,104

Source: Bureau of Labor Statistics, 2004 and 2005 Consumer Expenditure Surveys, Internet site http://www.bls.gov/cex/

Table 41. Indexed spending in selected Southern metros, 2004–05

(indexed average annual spending of consumer units in selected Southern metropolitan areas by product and service category, 2004–05; index definition: an index of 100 is the average for all consumer units; an index of 132 means that spending by consumer units in that group is 32 percent above the average for all consumer units; an index of 68 indicates spending that is 32 percent below the average for all consumer units)

	total consumer units in the South	Atlanta	Baltimore	Dallas–Fort Worth	Houston	Miami	Washington, D.C.
Average spending of consumer units, total	$40,903	$39,992	$39,217	$50,637	$52,998	$37,673	$55,977
Average spending of consumer units, index	100	98	96	124	130	92	137
FOOD	100	102	80	119	108	102	108
Food at home	100	87	87	116	102	124	100
Cereals and bakery products	100	88	91	118	102	123	99
Meats, poultry, fish, and eggs	100	95	93	102	98	130	97
Dairy products	100	77	83	125	102	142	102
Fruits and vegetables	100	103	92	119	114	151	122
Other food at home	100	77	79	122	98	101	91
Food away from home	100	121	71	123	117	74	119
ALCOHOLIC BEVERAGES	100	97	101	155	123	78	158
HOUSING	100	112	114	130	129	115	167
Shelter	100	123	137	136	133	136	202
Owned dwellings	100	128	141	144	135	130	217
Rented dwellings	100	118	127	115	121	162	170
Other lodging	100	79	136	139	176	83	163
Utilities, fuels, and public services	100	110	95	123	125	101	116
Household services	100	99	85	128	147	102	183
Housekeeping supplies	100	92	74	115	116	94	101
Household furnishings and equipment	100	77	82	120	115	61	132
APPAREL AND RELATED SERVICES	100	100	94	128	130	55	128
TRANSPORTATION	100	79	76	116	136	82	103
Vehicle purchases	100	70	61	107	136	60	82
Gasoline and motor oil	100	92	84	108	123	89	94
Other vehicle expenses	100	82	86	131	146	107	122
Public transportation	100	84	126	163	134	123	274
HEALTH CARE	100	72	86	118	115	78	98
ENTERTAINMENT	100	98	80	99	110	66	124
PERSONAL CARE PRODUCTS AND SERVICES	100	76	97	146	142	98	121
READING	100	68	83	123	134	34	173
EDUCATION	100	117	151	139	160	87	243
TOBACCO PRODUCTS AND SMOKING SUPPLIES	100	47	72	75	81	46	62
MISCELLANEOUS	100	72	67	133	150	78	144
CASH CONTRIBUTIONS	100	71	83	125	181	58	113
PERSONAL INSURANCE AND PENSIONS	100	115	110	133	142	84	168
Life and other personal insurance	100	90	58	108	105	54	150
Pensions and Social Security	100	117	115	135	145	87	170

Source: Calculations by New Strategist based on the Bureau of Labor Statistics' 2004 and 2005 Consumer Expenditure Surveys

Table 42. Average spending in selected Western metros, 2004–05

(average annual spending of consumer units in selected Western metropolitan areas by product and service category, 2004–05)

	total consumer units in the West	Anchorage	Denver	Honolulu	Los Angeles	Phoenix	Portland	San Diego	San Francisco	Seattle
Number of consumer units (in 000s)	25,872	119	1,270	278	5,112	1,423	1,052	892	2,724	1,801
Average number of persons per consumer unit	2.6	2.5	2.4	2.8	2.9	2.6	2.5	2.6	2.6	2.3
Average income before taxes	$60,730	$71,031	$65,224	$70,104	$65,810	$60,726	$56,702	$69,067	$86,935	$63,888
Average annual spending	50,305	59,427	49,996	54,937	55,760	49,009	50,313	59,805	60,992	54,027
FOOD	**6,280**	**6,412**	**6,251**	**8,089**	**7,062**	**6,434**	**6,377**	**6,437**	**7,581**	**6,904**
Food at home	**3,580**	**3,713**	**3,789**	**4,231**	**3,876**	**3,599**	**3,557**	**3,462**	**3,909**	**3,908**
Cereals and bakery products	467	457	511	556	492	470	453	458	519	475
Meats, poultry, fish, and eggs	843	846	886	1,090	976	859	783	761	888	840
Dairy products	406	437	428	335	411	415	432	404	445	457
Fruits and vegetables	635	605	619	831	749	632	650	606	772	666
Other food at home	1,228	1,369	1,344	1,419	1,248	1,222	1,239	1,233	1,285	1,469
Food away from home	**2,701**	**2,698**	**2,462**	**3,858**	**3,185**	**2,835**	**2,820**	**2,976**	**3,672**	**2,996**
ALCOHOLIC BEVERAGES	**517**	**636**	**635**	**463**	**485**	**585**	**526**	**613**	**628**	**781**
HOUSING	**16,828**	**18,764**	**15,772**	**17,400**	**19,911**	**14,719**	**16,039**	**21,484**	**22,885**	**17,483**
Shelter	**10,480**	**11,391**	**10,078**	**10,887**	**13,030**	**8,414**	**9,862**	**14,511**	**15,947**	**10,741**
Owned dwellings	6,670	7,814	6,613	6,516	8,122	5,911	6,650	9,118	10,068	7,144
Rented dwellings	3,231	2,850	2,936	3,960	4,383	2,100	2,535	4,627	4,928	2,737
Other lodging	579	727	530	411	524	402	677	767	951	860
Utilities, fuels, and public services	**2,795**	**3,228**	**3,013**	**2,813**	**2,908**	**3,057**	**2,878**	**2,767**	**2,711**	**2,769**
Household services	**904**	**985**	**722**	**692**	**1,224**	**984**	**933**	**1,561**	**1,384**	**725**
Housekeeping supplies	**618**	**771**	**548**	**817**	**632**	**605**	**553**	**646**	**634**	**706**
Household furnishings and equipment	**2,030**	**2,388**	**1,411**	**2,191**	**2,119**	**1,659**	**1,813**	**1,999**	**2,210**	**2,541**
APPAREL AND RELATED SERVICES	**1,954**	**1,820**	**1,755**	**2,157**	**2,386**	**1,876**	**1,822**	**1,935**	**2,382**	**1,833**
TRANSPORTATION	**9,498**	**12,596**	**8,646**	**9,921**	**10,972**	**10,549**	**8,845**	**11,301**	**9,518**	**9,491**
Vehicle purchases	4,268	6,082	3,529	4,768	4,996	5,490	3,964	5,681	3,347	3,897
Gasoline and motor oil	1,966	2,157	1,755	1,658	2,312	1,769	1,742	2,094	1,922	1,914
Other vehicle expenses	2,658	3,239	2,573	2,427	3,029	2,911	2,542	2,587	3,296	2,813
Public transportation	606	1,119	789	1,069	635	380	596	939	953	867
HEALTH CARE	**2,602**	**3,397**	**2,724**	**2,600**	**2,275**	**2,890**	**2,693**	**3,038**	**2,773**	**2,910**
ENTERTAINMENT	**2,636**	**3,420**	**3,227**	**3,126**	**2,719**	**2,355**	**3,057**	**2,653**	**2,938**	**3,002**
PERSONAL CARE PRODUCTS, SERVICES	**621**	**615**	**636**	**772**	**798**	**666**	**578**	**805**	**664**	**625**
READING	**153**	**218**	**144**	**128**	**158**	**132**	**188**	**192**	**212**	**214**
EDUCATION	**1,039**	**842**	**1,573**	**1,320**	**960**	**739**	**1,200**	**1,245**	**1,107**	**1,217**
TOBACCO PRODUCTS, SMOKING SUPPLIES	**239**	**440**	**308**	**241**	**179**	**373**	**344**	**136**	**143**	**236**
MISCELLANEOUS	**910**	**1,227**	**1,010**	**861**	**848**	**786**	**1,303**	**940**	**1,014**	**1,004**
CASH CONTRIBUTIONS	**1,576**	**1,853**	**1,624**	**1,112**	**1,272**	**1,662**	**1,775**	**2,520**	**1,607**	**2,070**
PERSONAL INSURANCE AND PENSIONS	**5,451**	**7,187**	**5,689**	**6,746**	**5,736**	**5,243**	**5,565**	**6,507**	**7,538**	**6,256**
Life and other personal insurance	343	581	240	520	298	400	367	423	336	346
Pensions and Social Security	5,108	6,606	5,449	6,226	5,438	4,843	5,198	6,084	7,202	5,910

Source: Bureau of Labor Statistics, 2004 and 2005 Consumer Expenditure Surveys, Internet site http://www.bls.gov/cex/

Table 43. Indexed spending in selected Western metros, 2004–05

(indexed average annual spending of consumer units in selected Western metropolitan areas by product and service category, 2004–05; index definition: an index of 100 is the average for all consumer units; an index of 132 means that spending by consumer units in that group is 32 percent above the average for all consumer units; an index of 68 indicates spending that is 32 percent below the average for all consumer units)

	total consumer units in the West	Anchorage	Denver	Honolulu	Los Angeles	Phoenix	Portland	San Diego	San Francisco	Seattle
Average spending of consumer units, total	$50,305	$59,427	$49,996	$54,937	$55,760	$49,009	$50,313	$59,805	$60,992	$54,027
Average spending of consumer units, index	100	118	99	109	111	97	100	119	121	107
FOOD	100	102	100	129	112	102	102	103	121	110
Food at home	100	104	106	118	108	101	99	97	109	109
Cereals and bakery products	100	98	109	119	105	101	97	98	111	102
Meats, poultry, fish, and eggs	100	100	105	129	116	102	93	90	105	100
Dairy products	100	108	105	83	101	102	106	100	110	113
Fruits and vegetables	100	95	97	131	118	100	102	95	122	105
Other food at home	100	111	109	116	102	100	101	100	105	120
Food away from home	100	100	91	143	118	105	104	110	136	111
ALCOHOLIC BEVERAGES	100	123	123	90	94	113	102	119	121	151
HOUSING	100	112	94	103	118	87	95	128	136	104
Shelter	100	109	96	104	124	80	94	138	152	102
Owned dwellings	100	117	99	98	122	89	100	137	151	107
Rented dwellings	100	88	91	123	136	65	78	143	153	85
Other lodging	100	126	92	71	91	69	117	132	164	149
Utilities, fuels, and public services	100	115	108	101	104	109	103	99	97	99
Household services	100	109	80	77	135	109	103	173	153	80
Housekeeping supplies	100	125	89	132	102	98	89	105	103	114
Household furnishings and equipment	100	118	70	108	104	82	89	98	109	125
APPAREL AND RELATED SERVICES	100	93	90	110	122	96	93	99	122	94
TRANSPORTATION	100	133	91	104	116	111	93	119	100	100
Vehicle purchases	100	143	83	112	117	129	93	133	78	91
Gasoline and motor oil	100	110	89	84	118	90	89	107	98	97
Other vehicle expenses	100	122	97	91	114	110	96	97	124	106
Public transportation	100	185	130	176	105	63	98	155	157	143
HEALTH CARE	100	131	105	100	87	111	103	117	107	112
ENTERTAINMENT	100	130	122	119	103	89	116	101	111	114
PERSONAL CARE PRODUCTS, SERVICES	100	99	102	124	129	107	93	130	107	101
READING	100	142	94	84	103	86	123	125	139	140
EDUCATION	100	81	151	127	92	71	115	120	107	117
TOBACCO PRODUCTS, SMOKING SUPPLIES	100	184	129	101	75	156	144	57	60	99
MISCELLANEOUS	100	135	111	95	93	86	143	103	111	110
CASH CONTRIBUTIONS	100	118	103	71	81	105	113	160	102	131
PERSONAL INSURANCE AND PENSIONS	100	132	104	124	105	96	102	119	138	115
Life and other personal insurance	100	169	70	152	87	117	107	123	98	101
Pensions and Social Security	100	129	107	122	106	95	102	119	141	116

Source: Calculations by New Strategist based on the Bureau of Labor Statistics' 2004 and 2005 Consumer Expenditure Surveys

Spending by Race and Hispanic Origin, 2005

Asians spend more than the average household while Hispanics and blacks spend less. The $52,054 spent by Asians in 2005 was 12 percent above average and surpassed the spending of every other racial or ethnic group. Black households spent $32,849 in 2005, or 29 percent less than average. Hispanic spending, at $40,123, was 14 percent below average.

Asian spending reflects their above-average incomes, a consequence of their high educational attainment. Asian households spend nearly twice the average on education and more than twice the average on public transportation (mostly airline fares).

Hispanic and black spending exceeds that of the average household in many categories. Because of their larger families, Hispanic households spend 15 percent more than the average household on meats, poultry, fish, and eggs. They spend 65 percent more than the average household on rented dwellings and 82 percent more on clothes for infants.

Blacks spend 34 percent more the average household on rented dwellings, 11 percent more on pork and 32 percent more on poultry. They spend 7 to 35 percent more on clothes for boys and girls, and 54 percent more on shoes.

Table 44. Average spending by race and Hispanic origin of householder, 2005

(average annual spending of consumer units by product and service category and by race and Hispanic origin of consumer unit reference person, 2005)

	total consumer units	Asian	black	Hispanic	non-Hispanic white and other
Number of consumer units (in 000s)	117,356	4,283	14,042	12,462	90,995
Average number of persons per consumer unit	2.5	2.9	2.6	3.4	2.3
Average before-tax income of consumer units	$58,712	$73,995	$39,385	$47,509	$63,203
Average annual spending of consumer units	46,409	52,054	32,849	40,123	49,331
FOOD	5,931	6,632	4,319	5,551	6,223
Food at home	3,297	3,580	2,663	3,344	3,384
Cereals and bakery products	445	492	363	400	463
Cereals and cereal products	143	216	132	147	144
Bakery products	302	276	231	253	319
Meats, poultry, fish, and eggs	764	892	787	876	746
Beef	228	196	193	285	225
Pork	153	164	170	160	150
Other meats	103	82	90	99	106
Poultry	134	147	177	177	122
Fish and seafood	113	259	121	109	113
Eggs	33	45	35	46	30
Dairy products	378	303	245	364	400
Fresh milk and cream	146	137	98	162	151
Other dairy products	232	166	147	202	249
Fruits and vegetables	552	814	428	640	558
Fresh fruits	182	284	122	219	185
Fresh vegetables	175	312	122	210	178
Processed fruits	106	125	99	119	105
Processed vegetables	89	93	85	92	89
Other food at home	1,158	1,078	840	1,064	1,217
Sugar and other sweets	119	102	82	90	128
Fats and oils	85	86	79	84	86
Miscellaneous foods	609	567	432	535	645
Nonalcoholic beverages	303	279	230	321	312
Food prepared by consumer unit on trips	41	45	17	33	46
Food away from home	2,634	3,052	1,657	2,207	2,838
ALCOHOLIC BEVERAGES	426	319	173	286	483
HOUSING	15,167	19,017	11,650	14,338	15,813
Shelter	8,805	12,659	6,524	8,937	9,134
Owned dwellings	5,958	8,623	3,188	4,886	6,527
Mortgage interest and charges	3,317	5,354	1,998	3,166	3,538
Property taxes	1,541	2,203	734	1,058	1,730
Maintenance, repair, insurance, other expenses	1,101	1,066	456	662	1,259
Rented dwellings	2,345	3,479	3,148	3,876	2,013
Other lodging	502	556	189	175	594
Utilities, fuels, and public services	3,183	3,018	3,253	2,986	3,201
Natural gas	473	454	549	378	475
Electricity	1,155	942	1,205	1,071	1,159
Fuel oil and other fuels	142	58	45	43	170
Telephone services	1,048	1,166	1,124	1,130	1,025
Water and other public services	366	398	330	365	371
Household services	801	948	530	605	868
Personal services	322	449	289	336	324
Other household services	479	499	241	268	544
Housekeeping supplies	611	439	352	508	663
Laundry and cleaning supplies	134	91	119	156	133
Other household products	320	233	160	252	352
Postage and stationery	157	115	74	100	178

	total consumer units	Asian	black	Hispanic	non-Hispanic white and other
Household furnishings and equipment	$1,767	$1,954	$991	$1,303	$1,947
Household textiles	132	172	93	95	143
Furniture	467	478	298	487	490
Floor coverings	56	97	16	20	67
Major appliances	223	377	143	171	242
Small appliances, miscellaneous housewares	105	94	46	85	117
Miscellaneous household equipment	782	737	393	445	887
APPAREL AND RELATED SERVICES	1,886	2,035	1,981	2,195	1,830
Men and boys	440	467	420	529	431
Men, aged 16 or older	349	366	297	416	347
Boys, aged 2 to 15	91	101	123	112	83
Women and girls	754	877	765	787	747
Women, aged 16 or older	633	715	635	597	637
Girls, aged 2 to 15	121	162	130	191	111
Children under age 2	82	97	77	149	74
Footwear	320	303	493	442	278
Other apparel products and services	290	291	226	288	300
TRANSPORTATION	8,344	8,899	5,850	7,900	8,791
Vehicle purchases	3,544	3,516	2,350	3,280	3,765
Cars and trucks, new	1,931	2,568	988	1,710	2,104
Cars and trucks, used	1,531	898	1,307	1,551	1,566
Other vehicles	82	50	55	20	95
Gasoline and motor oil	2,013	2,011	1,546	2,171	2,063
Other vehicle expenses	2,339	2,395	1,710	2,068	2,474
Vehicle finance charges	297	218	229	269	311
Maintenance and repairs	671	619	433	586	721
Vehicle insurance	913	914	747	837	949
Vehicle rentals, leases, licenses, other charges	458	643	301	376	493
Public transportation	448	978	245	380	489
HEALTH CARE	2,664	2,262	1,448	1,520	3,005
Health insurance	1,361	1,357	841	750	1,523
Medical services	677	499	321	444	763
Drugs	521	335	244	273	597
Medical supplies	105	72	43	54	122
ENTERTAINMENT	2,388	1,804	1,242	1,494	2,683
Fees and admissions	588	647	201	337	682
Audio and visual equipment and services	888	748	797	716	925
Pets, toys, hobbies, playground equipment	420	175	128	244	488
Other entertainment products and services	492	233	117	197	589
PERSONAL CARE PRODUCTS AND SERVICES	541	519	472	501	557
READING	126	117	52	55	148
EDUCATION	940	1,759	500	558	1,061
TOBACCO PRODUCTS AND SMOKING SUPPLIES	319	124	216	158	357
MISCELLANEOUS	808	794	416	665	887
CASH CONTRIBUTIONS	1,663	1,188	1,204	927	1,834
PERSONAL INSURANCE AND PENSIONS	5,204	6,584	3,325	3,974	5,659
Life and other personal insurance	381	465	292	140	428
Pensions and Social Security	4,823	6,119	3,033	3,834	5,232
PERSONAL TAXES	2,408	1,966	603	982	2,877
Federal income taxes	1,696	1,334	287	655	2,054
State and local income taxes	534	440	257	258	614
Other taxes	177	192	59	69	210
GIFTS FOR PEOPLE IN OTHER HOUSEHOLDS	1,091	1,185	587	636	1,229

Note: "Asian" and "black" include Hispanics and non-Hispanics who identify themselves as being of the respective race alone. "Hispanic" includes people of any race who identify themselves as Hispanic. "Other" includes people who identify themselves as non-Hispanic and as Alaska Native, American Indian, Asian (who are also included in the "Asian" column), Native Hawaiian or other Pacific Islander, as well as non-Hispanics reporting more than one race. Spending by category will not add to total spending because gift spending is also included in the preceding product and service categories and personal taxes are not included in the total.

Source: Bureau of Labor Statistics, 2005 Consumer Expenditure Survey, Internet site http://www.bls.gov/cex/

Table 45. Indexed spending by race and Hispanic origin of householder, 2005

(indexed average annual spending of consumer units by product and service category and by race and Hispanic origin of consumer unit reference person, 2005; index definition: an index of 100 is the average for all consumer units; an index of 132 means that spending by consumer units in that group is 32 percent above the average for all consumer units; an index of 68 indicates spending that is 32 percent below the average for all consumer units)

	total consumer units	Asian	black	Hispanic	non-Hispanic white and other
Average spending of consumer units, total	$46,409	$52,054	$32,849	$40,123	$49,331
Average spending of consumer units, index	100	112	71	86	106
FOOD	100	112	73	94	105
Food at home	100	109	81	101	103
Cereals and bakery products	100	111	82	90	104
Cereals and cereal products	100	151	92	103	101
Bakery products	100	91	76	84	106
Meats, poultry, fish, and eggs	100	117	103	115	98
Beef	100	86	85	125	99
Pork	100	107	111	105	98
Other meats	100	80	87	96	103
Poultry	100	110	132	132	91
Fish and seafood	100	229	107	96	100
Eggs	100	136	106	139	91
Dairy products	100	80	65	96	106
Fresh milk and cream	100	94	67	111	103
Other dairy products	100	72	63	87	107
Fruits and vegetables	100	147	78	116	101
Fresh fruits	100	156	67	120	102
Fresh vegetables	100	178	70	120	102
Processed fruits	100	118	93	112	99
Processed vegetables	100	104	96	103	100
Other food at home	100	93	73	92	105
Sugar and other sweets	100	86	69	76	108
Fats and oils	100	101	93	99	101
Miscellaneous foods	100	93	71	88	106
Nonalcoholic beverages	100	92	76	106	103
Food prepared by consumer unit on trips	100	110	41	80	112
Food away from home	100	116	63	84	108
ALCOHOLIC BEVERAGES	100	75	41	67	113
HOUSING	100	125	77	95	104
Shelter	100	144	74	101	104
Owned dwellings	100	145	54	82	110
Mortgage interest and charges	100	161	60	95	107
Property taxes	100	143	48	69	112
Maintenance, repair, insurance, other expenses	100	97	41	60	114
Rented dwellings	100	148	134	165	86
Other lodging	100	111	38	35	118
Utilities, fuels, and public services	100	95	102	94	101
Natural gas	100	96	116	80	100
Electricity	100	82	104	93	100
Fuel oil and other fuels	100	41	32	30	120
Telephone services	100	111	107	108	98
Water and other public services	100	109	90	100	101
Household services	100	118	66	76	108
Personal services	100	139	90	104	101
Other household services	100	104	50	56	114
Housekeeping supplies	100	72	58	83	109
Laundry and cleaning supplies	100	68	89	116	99
Other household products	100	73	50	79	110
Postage and stationery	100	73	47	64	113

	total consumer units	Asian	black	Hispanic	non-Hispanic white and other
Household furnishings and equipment	100	111	56	74	110
Household textiles	100	130	70	72	108
Furniture	100	102	64	104	105
Floor coverings	100	173	29	36	120
Major appliances	100	169	64	77	109
Small appliances, miscellaneous housewares	100	90	44	81	111
Miscellaneous household equipment	100	94	50	57	113
APPAREL AND RELATED SERVICES	100	108	105	116	97
Men and boys	100	106	95	120	98
Men, aged 16 or older	100	105	85	119	99
Boys, aged 2 to 15	100	111	135	123	91
Women and girls	100	116	101	104	99
Women, aged 16 or older	100	113	100	94	101
Girls, aged 2 to 15	100	134	107	158	92
Children under age 2	100	118	94	182	90
Footwear	100	95	154	138	87
Other apparel products and services	100	100	78	99	103
TRANSPORTATION	100	107	70	95	105
Vehicle purchases	100	99	66	93	106
Cars and trucks, new	100	133	51	89	109
Cars and trucks, used	100	59	85	101	102
Other vehicles	100	61	67	24	116
Gasoline and motor oil	100	100	77	108	102
Other vehicle expenses	100	102	73	88	106
Vehicle finance charges	100	73	77	91	105
Maintenance and repairs	100	92	65	87	107
Vehicle insurance	100	100	82	92	104
Vehicle rentals, leases, licenses, other charges	100	140	66	82	108
Public transportation	100	218	55	85	109
HEALTH CARE	100	85	54	57	113
Health insurance	100	100	62	55	112
Medical services	100	74	47	66	113
Drugs	100	64	47	52	115
Medical supplies	100	69	41	51	116
ENTERTAINMENT	100	76	52	63	112
Fees and admissions	100	110	34	57	116
Audio and visual equipment and services	100	84	90	81	104
Pets, toys, hobbies, playground equipment	100	42	30	58	116
Other entertainment products and services	100	47	24	40	120
PERSONAL CARE PRODUCTS AND SERVICES	100	96	87	93	103
READING	100	93	41	44	117
EDUCATION	100	187	53	59	113
TOBACCO PRODUCTS AND SMOKING SUPPLIES	100	39	68	50	112
MISCELLANEOUS	100	98	51	82	110
CASH CONTRIBUTIONS	100	71	72	56	110
PERSONAL INSURANCE AND PENSIONS	100	127	64	76	109
Life and other personal insurance	100	122	77	37	112
Pensions and Social Security	100	127	63	79	108
PERSONAL TAXES	100	82	25	41	119
Federal income taxes	100	79	17	39	121
State and local income taxes	100	82	48	48	115
Other taxes	100	108	33	39	119
GIFTS FOR PEOPLE IN OTHER HOUSEHOLDS	100	109	54	58	113

Note: "Asian" and "black" include Hispanics and non-Hispanics who identify themselves as being of the respective race alone. "Hispanic" includes people of any race who identify themselves as Hispanic. "Other" includes people who identify themselves as non-Hispanic and as Alaska Native, American Indian, Asian (who are also included in the "Asian" column), Native Hawaiian or other Pacific Islander, as well as non-Hispanics reporting more than one race.
Source: Calculations by New Strategist based on the Bureau of Labor Statistics' 2005 Consumer Expenditure Survey

Spending by Education, 2005

Because college graduates have the highest incomes, their spending is well above average. The average household headed by a college graduate spent $65,542 in 2005, or 41 percent more than the average household. In contrast, households headed by people who did not graduate from high school spent only $27,435, fully 41 percent less than the average household.

Households headed by the least educated—those without a high school diploma—spend more than average on only a few items. These include rent and tobacco.

High school graduates spent $38,162 in 2005, or 18 percent less than the average household. Their spending is also below average in most categories with some exceptions such as tobacco.

Householders with some college experience or an associate's degree make up the largest share of households (31 percent). Their spending is close to the average on most items.

College graduates, who account for 27 percent of householders, far outspend the average household on most items—particularly those favored by the affluent. These include food-away-from-home (41 percent above average) and alcoholic beverages (53 percent). They spend more than twice the average on other lodging (which includes college dorms, vacation homes and hotel and motel expenses) and nearly twice the average on public transportation (which includes airfares). They are also big spenders on education and fees and admissions to entertainment events.

Table 46. Average spending by education of householder, 2005

(average annual spending of consumer units by product and service category and educational attainment of consumer unit reference person, 2005)

	total consumer units	not a high school graduate	high school graduate	some college or associate's degree	college degree or more
Number of consumer units (in 000s)	117,356	18,028	30,389	36,877	32,062
Average number of persons per consumer unit	2.5	2.7	2.5	2.4	2.4
Average before-tax income of consumer units	$58,712	$30,643	$45,721	$54,806	$91,300
Average annual spending of consumer units	46,409	27,435	38,162	45,699	65,542
FOOD	**5,931**	**4,374**	**5,150**	**5,818**	**7,610**
Food at home	**3,297**	**2,912**	**3,040**	**3,161**	**3,891**
Cereals and bakery products	445	391	418	424	522
Cereals and cereal products	143	135	129	136	168
Bakery products	302	256	289	288	354
Meats, poultry, fish, and eggs	764	750	735	748	819
Beef	228	221	219	237	231
Pork	153	166	158	151	145
Other meats	103	94	104	97	113
Poultry	134	134	129	131	143
Fish and seafood	113	96	94	101	153
Eggs	33	38	30	31	34
Dairy products	378	330	343	359	459
Fresh milk and cream	146	148	139	140	159
Other dairy products	232	182	204	219	300
Fruits and vegetables	552	488	472	505	710
Fresh fruits	182	155	142	165	251
Fresh vegetables	175	156	146	157	231
Processed fruits	106	91	97	98	131
Processed vegetables	89	86	86	86	97
Other food at home	1,158	953	1,072	1,124	1,382
Sugar and other sweets	119	103	111	113	141
Fats and oils	85	79	83	79	96
Miscellaneous foods	609	474	556	590	750
Nonalcoholic beverages	303	277	292	304	327
Food prepared by consumer unit on trips	41	20	31	38	67
Food away from home	**2,634**	**1,462**	**2,110**	**2,658**	**3,719**
ALCOHOLIC BEVERAGES	**426**	**192**	**326**	**415**	**653**
HOUSING	**15,167**	**9,437**	**12,380**	**14,566**	**21,676**
Shelter	**8,805**	**5,361**	**6,958**	**8,309**	**13,062**
Owned dwellings	5,958	2,547	4,416	5,579	9,774
Mortgage interest and charges	3,317	1,308	2,362	3,231	5,450
Property taxes	1,541	732	1,256	1,342	2,494
Maintenance, repair, insurance, other expenses	1,101	507	798	1,007	1,830
Rented dwellings	2,345	2,728	2,304	2,303	2,216
Other lodging	502	86	238	427	1,071
Utilities, fuels, and public services	**3,183**	**2,613**	**3,066**	**3,169**	**3,633**
Natural gas	473	374	444	447	587
Electricity	1,155	1,013	1,154	1,149	1,243
Fuel oil and other fuels	142	114	169	134	139
Telephone services	1,048	826	977	1,069	1,215
Water and other public services	366	287	321	370	448
Household services	**801**	**287**	**520**	**769**	**1,391**
Personal services	322	134	200	324	540
Other household services	479	153	320	445	851
Housekeeping supplies	**611**	**386**	**533**	**588**	**822**
Laundry and cleaning supplies	134	126	131	132	144
Other household products	320	193	273	316	431
Postage and stationery	157	68	129	140	247

	total consumer units	not a high school graduate	high school graduate	some college or associate's degree	college degree or more
Household furnishings and equipment	$1,767	$790	$1,303	$1,731	$2,768
Household textiles	132	63	114	119	199
Furniture	467	247	312	503	697
Floor coverings	56	15	30	48	114
Major appliances	223	114	180	236	310
Small appliances, miscellaneous housewares	105	54	86	99	157
Miscellaneous household equipment	782	297	581	724	1,291
APPAREL AND RELATED SERVICES	1,886	1,237	1,464	1,847	2,670
Men and boys	440	268	362	435	608
Men, aged 16 or older	349	200	283	332	508
Boys, aged 2 to 15	91	68	79	104	100
Women and girls	754	459	580	732	1,088
Women, aged 16 or older	633	365	480	608	937
Girls, aged 2 to 15	121	94	100	125	151
Children under age 2	82	82	74	79	95
Footwear	320	282	268	320	391
Other apparel products and services	290	145	179	280	489
TRANSPORTATION	8,344	5,106	7,364	8,717	10,664
Vehicle purchases	3,544	2,131	3,112	3,845	4,402
Cars and trucks, new	1,931	916	1,585	1,944	2,815
Cars and trucks, used	1,531	1,192	1,456	1,772	1,514
Other vehicles	82	24	71	129	73
Gasoline and motor oil	2,013	1,471	1,941	2,119	2,265
Other vehicle expenses	2,339	1,316	2,078	2,384	3,109
Vehicle finance charges	297	168	281	333	342
Maintenance and repairs	671	387	564	647	961
Vehicle insurance	913	599	875	947	1,087
Vehicle rentals, leases, licenses, other charges	458	162	358	457	719
Public transportation	448	188	232	369	889
HEALTH CARE	2,664	1,835	2,457	2,528	3,480
Health insurance	1,361	980	1,346	1,259	1,706
Medical services	677	353	505	672	1,029
Drugs	521	447	519	495	593
Medical supplies	105	56	88	102	152
ENTERTAINMENT	2,388	1,152	1,877	2,531	3,402
Fees and admissions	588	123	331	513	1,179
Audio and visual equipment and services	888	553	777	935	1,127
Pets, toys, hobbies, playground equipment	420	261	314	448	577
Other entertainment products and services	492	215	455	635	518
PERSONAL CARE PRODUCTS AND SERVICES	541	301	432	512	805
READING	126	42	87	115	225
EDUCATION	940	131	457	958	1,831
TOBACCO PRODUCTS AND SMOKING SUPPLIES	319	379	425	351	148
MISCELLANEOUS	808	459	741	808	1,068
CASH CONTRIBUTIONS	1,663	659	1,148	1,601	2,787
PERSONAL INSURANCE AND PENSIONS	5,204	2,133	3,854	4,932	8,523
Life and other personal insurance	381	164	251	370	639
Pensions and Social Security	4,823	1,969	3,604	4,562	7,884
PERSONAL TAXES	2,408	396	1,194	2,272	4,845
Federal income taxes	1,696	166	772	1,583	3,562
State and local income taxes	534	142	288	531	993
Other taxes	177	87	134	158	290
GIFTS FOR PEOPLE IN OTHER HOUSEHOLDS	1,091	383	771	988	1,896

Note: Spending by category will not add to total spending because gift spending is also included in the preceding product and service categories and personal taxes are not included in the total.
Source: Bureau of Labor Statistics, 2005 Consumer Expenditure Survey, Internet site http://www.bls.gov/cex/

Table 47. Indexed spending by education of householder, 2005

(indexed average annual spending of consumer units by product and service category and educational attainment of consumer unit reference person, 2005; index definition: an index of 100 is the average for all consumer units; an index of 132 means that spending by consumer units in that group is 32 percent above the average for all consumer units; an index of 68 indicates spending that is 32 percent below the average for all consumer units)

	total consumer units	not a high school graduate	high school graduate	some college or associate's degree	college degree or more
Average spending of consumer units, total	$46,409	$27,435	$38,162	$45,699	$65,542
Average spending of consumer units, index	100	59	82	98	141
FOOD	100	74	87	98	128
Food at home	100	88	92	96	118
Cereals and bakery products	100	88	94	95	117
Cereals and cereal products	100	94	90	95	117
Bakery products	100	85	96	95	117
Meats, poultry, fish, and eggs	100	98	96	98	107
Beef	100	97	96	104	101
Pork	100	108	103	99	95
Other meats	100	91	101	94	110
Poultry	100	100	96	98	107
Fish and seafood	100	85	83	90	135
Eggs	100	115	91	95	103
Dairy products	100	87	91	95	121
Fresh milk and cream	100	101	95	96	109
Other dairy products	100	78	88	95	129
Fruits and vegetables	100	88	86	92	129
Fresh fruits	100	85	78	90	138
Fresh vegetables	100	89	83	90	132
Processed fruits	100	86	92	92	124
Processed vegetables	100	97	97	97	109
Other food at home	100	82	93	97	119
Sugar and other sweets	100	87	93	95	118
Fats and oils	100	93	98	93	113
Miscellaneous foods	100	78	91	97	123
Nonalcoholic beverages	100	91	96	100	108
Food prepared by consumer unit on trips	100	49	76	94	163
Food away from home	100	56	80	101	141
ALCOHOLIC BEVERAGES	100	45	77	97	153
HOUSING	100	62	82	96	143
Shelter	100	61	79	94	148
Owned dwellings	100	43	74	94	164
Mortgage interest and charges	100	39	71	97	164
Property taxes	100	48	82	87	162
Maintenance, repair, insurance, other expenses	100	46	72	91	166
Rented dwellings	100	116	98	98	94
Other lodging	100	17	47	85	213
Utilities, fuels, and public services	100	82	96	100	114
Natural gas	100	79	94	94	124
Electricity	100	88	100	100	108
Fuel oil and other fuels	100	80	119	94	98
Telephone services	100	79	93	102	116
Water and other public services	100	78	88	101	122
Household services	100	36	65	96	174
Personal services	100	42	62	101	168
Other household services	100	32	67	93	178
Housekeeping supplies	100	63	87	96	135
Laundry and cleaning supplies	100	94	98	98	107
Other household products	100	60	85	99	135
Postage and stationery	100	43	82	89	157

	total consumer units	not a high school graduate	high school graduate	some college or associate's degree	college degree or more
Household furnishings and equipment	100	45	74	98	157
Household textiles	100	48	86	90	151
Furniture	100	53	67	108	149
Floor coverings	100	27	54	86	204
Major appliances	100	51	81	106	139
Small appliances, miscellaneous housewares	100	51	82	94	150
Miscellaneous household equipment	100	38	74	93	165
APPAREL AND RELATED SERVICES	100	66	78	98	142
Men and boys	100	61	82	99	138
Men, aged 16 or older	100	57	81	95	146
Boys, aged 2 to 15	100	75	87	115	110
Women and girls	100	61	77	97	144
Women, aged 16 or older	100	58	76	96	148
Girls, aged 2 to 15	100	78	83	103	125
Children under age 2	100	100	90	96	116
Footwear	100	88	84	100	122
Other apparel products and services	100	50	62	97	169
TRANSPORTATION	100	61	88	104	128
Vehicle purchases	100	60	88	108	124
Cars and trucks, new	100	47	82	101	146
Cars and trucks, used	100	78	95	116	99
Other vehicles	100	29	87	157	89
Gasoline and motor oil	100	73	96	105	113
Other vehicle expenses	100	56	89	102	133
Vehicle finance charges	100	57	95	112	115
Maintenance and repairs	100	58	84	96	143
Vehicle insurance	100	66	96	104	119
Vehicle rentals, leases, licenses, other charges	100	35	78	100	157
Public transportation	100	42	52	82	198
HEALTH CARE	100	69	92	95	131
Health insurance	100	72	99	93	125
Medical services	100	52	75	99	152
Drugs	100	86	100	95	114
Medical supplies	100	53	84	97	145
ENTERTAINMENT	100	48	79	106	142
Fees and admissions	100	21	56	87	201
Audio and visual equipment and services	100	62	88	105	127
Pets, toys, hobbies, playground equipment	100	62	75	107	137
Other entertainment products and services	100	44	92	129	105
PERSONAL CARE PRODUCTS AND SERVICES	100	56	80	95	149
READING	100	33	69	91	179
EDUCATION	100	14	49	102	195
TOBACCO PRODUCTS AND SMOKING SUPPLIES	100	119	133	110	46
MISCELLANEOUS	100	57	92	100	132
CASH CONTRIBUTIONS	100	40	69	96	168
PERSONAL INSURANCE AND PENSIONS	100	41	74	95	164
Life and other personal insurance	100	43	66	97	168
Pensions and Social Security	100	41	75	95	163
PERSONAL TAXES	100	16	50	94	201
Federal income taxes	100	10	46	93	210
State and local income taxes	100	27	54	99	186
Other taxes	100	49	76	89	164
GIFTS FOR PEOPLE IN OTHER HOUSEHOLDS	100	35	71	91	174

Source: Calculations by New Strategist based on the Bureau of Labor Statistics' 2005 Consumer Expenditure Survey

Spending by Household Size, 2005

Spending tends to increase with household size because larger households usually have more earners. Incomes peak for households with five people, at $81,275 in 2005. Spending is highest for this household size as well, at $62,618—35 percent above average. Less than 10 percent of the nation's households are home to five or more people, however.

Two-person households are most common, accounting for 32 percent of the total. They spent an average of $48,492 in 2005—or 4 percent more than the average household. Households with two people (many of them empty-nesters) spend more than other households on alcoholic beverages, other lodging (primarily hotel and motel expenses on trips), and reading material.

Households with five or more people have slightly higher incomes and spending than those with just four people. They spend more than other households on many nondiscretionary items such as food-at-home, laundry and cleaning supplies, utilities, and clothing.

Single-person households are almost as numerous as two-person households, accounting for 29 percent of the total in 2005. Single-person households spend less than the average household on almost every item.

Table 48. Average spending by size of household, 2005

(average annual spending of consumer units by product and service category, by number of people in consumer unit, 2005)

	total consumer units	one person	two or more people				
			total	two people	three people	four people	five or more people
Number of consumer units (in 000s)	117,356	34,339	83,017	37,489	18,451	15,807	11,270
Average number of persons per consumer unit	2.5	1.0	3.1	2.0	3.0	4.0	5.7
Average before-tax income of consumer units	$58,712	$30,290	$70,468	$62,195	$74,069	$78,183	$81,275
Average annual spending of consumer units	46,409	26,773	54,483	48,492	55,096	62,215	62,618
FOOD	**5,931**	**3,073**	**7,085**	**5,851**	**7,088**	**8,622**	**9,078**
Food at home	**3,297**	**1,638**	**3,965**	**3,142**	**3,925**	**4,846**	**5,583**
Cereals and bakery products	445	227	533	411	513	666	793
Cereals and cereal products	143	69	173	124	165	223	277
Bakery products	302	158	360	286	347	442	516
Meats, poultry, fish, and eggs	764	332	938	738	941	1,140	1,332
Beef	228	90	283	212	304	344	408
Pork	153	67	188	156	182	228	253
Other meats	103	45	127	102	115	155	188
Poultry	134	61	164	119	170	204	253
Fish and seafood	113	52	138	117	133	164	178
Eggs	33	18	39	32	38	46	53
Dairy products	378	193	453	350	448	556	668
Fresh milk and cream	146	74	175	126	182	216	270
Other dairy products	232	118	278	223	265	340	398
Fruits and vegetables	552	290	657	543	645	780	889
Fresh fruits	182	100	214	178	209	254	290
Fresh vegetables	175	91	209	177	210	245	261
Processed fruits	106	58	126	102	118	155	176
Processed vegetables	89	42	108	86	108	126	161
Other food at home	1,158	597	1,384	1,100	1,378	1,704	1,901
Sugar and other sweets	119	61	142	121	131	170	191
Fats and oils	85	44	101	84	100	119	140
Miscellaneous foods	609	312	729	562	732	910	1,037
Nonalcoholic beverages	303	161	360	282	366	459	477
Food prepared by consumer unit on trips	41	19	50	51	49	45	57
Food away from home	**2,634**	**1,435**	**3,120**	**2,709**	**3,163**	**3,776**	**3,495**
ALCOHOLIC BEVERAGES	**426**	**327**	**466**	**507**	**485**	**412**	**377**
HOUSING	**15,167**	**9,835**	**17,366**	**15,273**	**17,466**	**20,076**	**20,342**
Shelter	**8,805**	**6,179**	**9,891**	**8,704**	**10,006**	**11,333**	**11,626**
Owned dwellings	5,958	3,055	7,159	6,052	7,086	8,702	8,795
Mortgage interest and charges	3,317	1,429	4,098	2,994	4,146	5,535	5,673
Property taxes	1,541	907	1,803	1,741	1,699	2,003	1,899
Maintenance, repair, insurance, other expenses	1,101	720	1,258	1,317	1,241	1,163	1,222
Rented dwellings	2,345	2,889	2,120	1,966	2,341	2,066	2,344
Other lodging	502	235	612	686	579	566	487
Utilities, fuels, and public services	**3,183**	**2,024**	**3,663**	**3,270**	**3,725**	**4,059**	**4,313**
Natural gas	473	312	540	482	514	628	654
Electricity	1,155	719	1,335	1,196	1,360	1,473	1,565
Fuel oil and other fuels	142	99	159	161	160	151	163
Telephone services	1,048	664	1,206	1,054	1,275	1,340	1,412
Water and other public services	366	230	422	377	417	467	520
Household services	**801**	**383**	**973**	**675**	**1,064**	**1,434**	**1,169**
Personal services	322	42	437	107	553	901	697
Other household services	479	341	536	568	511	533	473
Housekeeping supplies	**611**	**321**	**728**	**673**	**682**	**843**	**824**
Laundry and cleaning supplies	134	66	162	130	168	195	214
Other household products	320	159	384	353	356	462	422
Postage and stationery	157	96	182	190	157	186	188

	total consumer units	one person	two or more people			
			total	two people	three people	four people	five or more people
Household furnishings and equipment	$1,767	$928	$2,111	$1,951	$1,988	$2,406	$2,410
Household textiles	132	65	160	145	167	189	153
Furniture	467	218	570	519	566	593	717
Floor coverings	56	25	69	65	62	61	105
Major appliances	223	104	273	260	222	315	333
Small appliances, miscellaneous housewares	105	62	123	118	132	117	135
Miscellaneous household equipment	782	454	917	843	840	1,132	967
APPAREL AND RELATED SERVICES	1,886	980	2,253	1,657	2,441	2,850	3,123
Men and boys	440	223	528	389	572	649	756
Men, aged 16 or older	349	212	404	355	463	415	464
Boys, aged 2 to 15	91	11	124	34	110	235	292
Women and girls	754	386	902	656	998	1,183	1,178
Women, aged 16 or older	633	370	739	614	854	867	790
Girls, aged 2 to 15	121	16	163	42	144	315	387
Children under age 2	82	16	109	43	158	149	202
Footwear	320	172	380	240	401	542	587
Other apparel products and services	290	183	334	328	311	327	401
TRANSPORTATION	8,344	4,030	10,128	9,124	10,438	11,553	10,963
Vehicle purchases	3,544	1,395	4,433	4,043	4,639	5,044	4,536
Cars and trucks, new	1,931	673	2,452	2,452	2,372	2,697	2,238
Cars and trucks, used	1,531	669	1,887	1,514	2,163	2,209	2,226
Other vehicles	82	54	94	77	105	138	72
Gasoline and motor oil	2,013	1,032	2,419	2,043	2,524	2,802	2,964
Other vehicle expenses	2,339	1,336	2,753	2,489	2,796	3,160	2,992
Vehicle finance charges	297	121	369	301	405	459	413
Maintenance and repairs	671	437	768	728	769	841	799
Vehicle insurance	913	521	1,076	944	1,118	1,261	1,186
Vehicle rentals, leases, licenses, other charges	458	258	540	517	505	599	593
Public transportation	448	267	523	549	479	548	471
HEALTH CARE	2,664	1,750	3,042	3,359	2,815	2,786	2,718
Health insurance	1,361	893	1,554	1,731	1,442	1,453	1,291
Medical services	677	424	782	777	727	771	904
Drugs	521	368	584	722	525	451	409
Medical supplies	105	65	121	129	121	111	114
ENTERTAINMENT	2,388	1,335	2,822	2,622	2,615	3,152	3,364
Fees and admissions	588	336	692	605	634	876	821
Audio and visual equipment and services	888	591	1,011	897	1,051	1,110	1,182
Pets, toys, hobbies, playground equipment	420	233	496	495	454	545	501
Other entertainment products and services	492	175	622	625	476	621	860
PERSONAL CARE PRODUCTS AND SERVICES	541	328	628	583	626	732	631
READING	126	103	136	149	123	136	117
EDUCATION	940	500	1,122	766	1,265	1,491	1,559
TOBACCO PRODUCTS AND SMOKING SUPPLIES	319	227	357	338	391	361	361
MISCELLANEOUS	808	563	909	947	852	887	908
CASH CONTRIBUTIONS	1,663	1,313	1,808	1,900	1,683	1,648	1,932
PERSONAL INSURANCE AND PENSIONS	5,204	2,409	6,360	5,418	6,809	7,510	7,145
Life and other personal insurance	381	162	472	407	452	515	657
Pensions and Social Security	4,823	2,247	5,888	5,010	6,358	6,995	6,488
PERSONAL TAXES	2,408	1,425	2,814	2,868	3,001	2,855	2,270
Federal income taxes	1,696	1,016	1,978	2,094	2,071	1,910	1,533
State and local income taxes	534	286	637	557	760	735	566
Other taxes	177	124	199	217	170	210	171
GIFTS FOR PEOPLE IN OTHER HOUSEHOLDS	1,091	769	1,224	1,541	1,253	888	583

Note: Spending by category will not add to total spending because gift spending is also included in the preceding product and service categories and personal taxes are not included in the total.
Source: Bureau of Labor Statistics, 2005 Consumer Expenditure Survey, Internet site http://www.bls.gov/cex/

Table 49. Indexed spending by size of household, 2005

(indexed annual spending of consumer units by product and service category and by number of people in consumer unit, 2005; index definition: an index of 100 is the average for all consumer units; an index of 132 means that spending by consumer units in that group is 32 percent above the average for all consumer units; an index of 68 indicates spending that is 32 percent below the average for all consumer units)

	total consumer units	one person	two or more people total	two people	three people	four people	five or more people
Average spending of consumer unit, total	$46,409	$26,773	$54,483	$48,492	$55,096	$62,215	$62,618
Average spending of consumer unit, index	100	58	117	104	119	134	135
FOOD	100	52	119	99	120	145	153
Food at home	100	50	120	95	119	147	169
Cereals and bakery products	100	51	120	92	115	150	178
Cereals and cereal products	100	48	121	87	115	156	194
Bakery products	100	52	119	95	115	146	171
Meats, poultry, fish, and eggs	100	43	123	97	123	149	174
Beef	100	39	124	93	133	151	179
Pork	100	44	123	102	119	149	165
Other meats	100	44	123	99	112	150	183
Poultry	100	46	122	89	127	152	189
Fish and seafood	100	46	122	104	118	145	158
Eggs	100	55	118	97	115	139	161
Dairy products	100	51	120	93	119	147	177
Fresh milk and cream	100	51	120	86	125	148	185
Other dairy products	100	51	120	96	114	147	172
Fruits and vegetables	100	53	119	98	117	141	161
Fresh fruits	100	55	118	98	115	140	159
Fresh vegetables	100	52	119	101	120	140	149
Processed fruits	100	55	119	96	111	146	166
Processed vegetables	100	47	121	97	121	142	181
Other food at home	100	52	120	95	119	147	164
Sugar and other sweets	100	51	119	102	110	143	161
Fats and oils	100	52	119	99	118	140	165
Miscellaneous foods	100	51	120	92	120	149	170
Nonalcoholic beverages	100	53	119	93	121	151	157
Food prepared by consumer unit on trips	100	46	122	124	120	110	139
Food away from home	100	54	118	103	120	143	133
ALCOHOLIC BEVERAGES	100	77	109	119	114	97	88
HOUSING	100	65	114	101	115	132	134
Shelter	100	70	112	99	114	129	132
Owned dwellings	100	51	120	102	119	146	148
Mortgage interest and charges	100	43	124	90	125	167	171
Property taxes	100	59	117	113	110	130	123
Maintenance, repair, insurance, other expenses	100	65	114	120	113	106	111
Rented dwellings	100	123	90	84	100	88	100
Other lodging	100	47	122	137	115	113	97
Utilities, fuels, and public services	100	64	115	103	117	128	136
Natural gas	100	66	114	102	109	133	138
Electricity	100	62	116	104	118	128	135
Fuel oil and other fuels	100	70	112	113	113	106	115
Telephone services	100	63	115	101	122	128	135
Water and other public services	100	63	115	103	114	128	142
Household services	100	48	121	84	133	179	146
Personal services	100	13	136	33	172	280	216
Other household services	100	71	112	119	107	111	99
Housekeeping supplies	100	53	119	110	112	138	135
Laundry and cleaning supplies	100	49	121	97	125	146	160
Other household products	100	50	120	110	111	144	132
Postage and stationery	100	61	116	121	100	118	120

	total consumer units	one person	two or more people				
			total	two people	three people	four people	five or more people
Household furnishings and equipment	100	53	119	110	113	136	136
Household textiles	100	49	121	110	127	143	116
Furniture	100	47	122	111	121	127	154
Floor coverings	100	45	123	116	111	109	188
Major appliances	100	47	122	117	100	141	149
Small appliances, miscellaneous housewares	100	59	117	112	126	111	129
Miscellaneous household equipment	100	58	117	108	107	145	124
APPAREL AND RELATED SERVICES	100	52	119	88	129	151	166
Men and boys	100	51	120	88	130	148	172
Men, aged 16 or older	100	61	116	102	133	119	133
Boys, aged 2 to 15	100	12	136	37	121	258	321
Women and girls	100	51	120	87	132	157	156
Women, aged 16 or older	100	58	117	97	135	137	125
Girls, aged 2 to 15	100	13	135	35	119	260	320
Children under age 2	100	20	133	52	193	182	246
Footwear	100	54	119	75	125	169	183
Other apparel products and services	100	63	115	113	107	113	138
TRANSPORTATION	100	48	121	109	125	138	131
Vehicle purchases	100	39	125	114	131	142	128
Cars and trucks, new	100	35	127	127	123	140	116
Cars and trucks, used	100	44	123	99	141	144	145
Other vehicles	100	66	115	94	128	168	88
Gasoline and motor oil	100	51	120	101	125	139	147
Other vehicle expenses	100	57	118	106	120	135	128
Vehicle finance charges	100	41	124	101	136	155	139
Maintenance and repairs	100	65	114	108	115	125	119
Vehicle insurance	100	57	118	103	122	138	130
Vehicle rentals, leases, licenses, other charges	100	56	118	113	110	131	129
Public transportation	100	60	117	123	107	122	105
HEALTH CARE	100	66	114	126	106	105	102
Health insurance	100	66	114	127	106	107	95
Medical services	100	63	116	115	107	114	134
Drugs	100	71	112	139	101	87	79
Medical supplies	100	62	115	123	115	106	109
ENTERTAINMENT	100	56	118	110	110	132	141
Fees and admissions	100	57	118	103	108	149	140
Audio and visual equipment and services	100	67	114	101	118	125	133
Pets, toys, hobbies, playground equipment	100	55	118	118	108	130	119
Other entertainment products and services	100	36	126	127	97	126	175
PERSONAL CARE PRODUCTS AND SERVICES	100	61	116	108	116	135	117
READING	100	82	108	118	98	108	93
EDUCATION	100	53	119	81	135	159	166
TOBACCO PRODUCTS AND SMOKING SUPPLIES	100	71	112	106	123	113	113
MISCELLANEOUS	100	70	113	117	105	110	112
CASH CONTRIBUTIONS	100	79	109	114	101	99	116
PERSONAL INSURANCE AND PENSIONS	100	46	122	104	131	144	137
Life and other personal insurance	100	43	124	107	119	135	172
Pensions and Social Security	100	47	122	104	132	145	135
PERSONAL TAXES	100	59	117	119	125	119	94
Federal income taxes	100	60	117	123	122	113	90
State and local income taxes	100	54	119	104	142	138	106
Other taxes	100	70	112	123	96	119	97
GIFTS FOR PEOPLE IN OTHER HOUSEHOLDS	100	70	112	141	115	81	53

Source: Calculations by New Strategist based on the Bureau of Labor Statistics' 2005 Consumer Expenditure Survey

Spending by Homeowners and Renters, 2005

Homeowners spend far more than renters because their incomes are higher. Homeowners had an average income of $70,791 in 2005, and they spent $54,126—17 percent more than the average household. In contrast, the average income of renters was just $33,765 and they spent $30,462—34 percent less than the average household.

Renters spend less than homeowners on nearly every product and service category. They spend 18 percent more than the average household on tobacco.

Table 50. Average spending by homeowners and renters, 2005

(average annual spending of consumer units (CUs) by product and service category and by homeownership status, 2005)

	total consumer units	homeowners	renters
Number of consumer units (in 000s)	117,356	79,072	38,284
Average number of persons per CU	2.5	2.6	2.2
Average before-tax income of CUs	$58,712	$70,791	$33,765
Average annual spending of CUs	46,409	54,126	30,462
FOOD	5,931	6,712	4,314
Food at home	3,297	3,693	2,475
Cereals and bakery products	445	500	330
Cereals and cereal products	143	156	117
Bakery products	302	345	214
Meats, poultry, fish, and eggs	764	845	597
Beef	228	251	179
Pork	153	170	119
Other meats	103	115	79
Poultry	134	146	111
Fish and seafood	113	129	81
Eggs	33	35	29
Dairy products	378	428	274
Fresh milk and cream	146	161	115
Other dairy products	232	268	159
Fruits and vegetables	552	617	416
Fresh fruits	182	205	133
Fresh vegetables	175	196	130
Processed fruits	106	117	83
Processed vegetables	89	99	70
Other food at home	1,158	1,302	858
Sugar and other sweets	119	136	82
Fats and oils	85	94	66
Miscellaneous foods	609	685	452
Nonalcoholic beverages	303	335	238
Food prepared by consumer unit on trips	41	52	19
Food away from home	2,634	3,019	1,839
ALCOHOLIC BEVERAGES	426	463	351
HOUSING	15,167	17,262	10,838
Shelter	8,805	9,535	7,296
Owned dwellings	5,958	8,800	89
Mortgage interest and charges	3,317	4,901	44
Property taxes	1,541	2,275	24
Maintenance, repair, insurance, other expenses	1,101	1,624	21
Rented dwellings	2,345	60	7,065
Other lodging	502	676	142
Utilities, fuels, and public services	3,183	3,751	2,011
Natural gas	473	586	242
Electricity	$1,155	$1,353	$745
Fuel oil and other fuels	142	192	38
Telephone services	1,048	1,145	847
Water and other public services	366	475	139
Household services	801	996	397
Personal services	322	379	203
Other household services	479	617	194
Housekeeping supplies	611	746	331
Laundry and cleaning supplies	134	154	94
Other household products	320	400	152
Postage and stationery	157	192	85

	total consumer units	homeowners	renters
Household furnishings and equipment	$1,767	$2,234	$803
Household textiles	132	161	73
Furniture	467	576	243
Floor coverings	56	78	11
Major appliances	223	296	74
Small appliances, miscellaneous housewares	105	130	55
Miscellaneous household equipment	782	993	347
APPAREL AND RELATED SERVICES	1,886	2,065	1,516
Men and boys	440	484	348
Men, aged 16 or older	349	384	275
Boys, aged 2 to 15	91	100	73
Women and girls	754	853	547
Women, aged 16 or older	633	716	460
Girls, aged 2 to 15	121	137	87
Children under age 2	82	86	75
Footwear	320	325	309
Other apparel products and services	290	316	236
TRANSPORTATION	8,344	9,778	5,382
Vehicle purchases	3,544	4,188	2,213
Cars and trucks, new	1,931	2,496	765
Cars and trucks, used	1,531	1,603	1,381
Other vehicles	82	89	67
Gasoline and motor oil	2,013	2,316	1,388
Other vehicle expenses	2,339	2,748	1,493
Vehicle finance charges	297	354	179
Maintenance and repairs	671	784	439
Vehicle insurance	913	1,061	607
Vehicle rentals, leases, licenses, other charges	458	549	268
Public transportation	448	525	288
HEALTH CARE	2,664	3,318	1,314
Health insurance	1,361	1,696	667
Medical services	677	845	330
Drugs	521	644	267
Medical supplies	105	132	49
ENTERTAINMENT	2,388	2,921	1,286
Fees and admissions	588	750	253
Audio and visual equipment and services	888	1,000	656
Pets, toys, hobbies, playground equipment	$420	$524	$205
Other entertainment products and services	492	647	172
PERSONAL CARE PRODUCTS AND SERVICES	541	625	367
READING	126	152	73
EDUCATION	940	1,078	654
TOBACCO PRODUCTS AND SMOKING SUPPLIES	319	292	375
MISCELLANEOUS	808	957	501
CASH CONTRIBUTIONS	1,663	2,061	841
PERSONAL INSURANCE AND PENSIONS	5,204	6,441	2,649
Life and other personal insurance	381	511	112
Pensions and Social Security	4,823	5,930	2,537
PERSONAL TAXES	2,408	3,162	848
Federal income taxes	1,696	2,241	570
State and local income taxes	534	667	259
Other taxes	177	254	19
GIFTS FOR PEOPLE IN OTHER HOUSEHOLDS	1,091	1,386	483

Note: Spending by category will not add to total spending because gift spending is also included in the preceding product and service categories and personal taxes are not included in the total.
Source: Bureau of Labor Statistics, 2005 Consumer Expenditure Survey, Internet site http://www.bls.gov/cex/

Table 51. Indexed spending by homeowners and renters, 2005

(indexed annual spending of consumer units by product and service category and by homeownership status, 2005; index definition: an index of 100 is the average for all consumer units; an index of 132 means that spending by consumer units in that group is 32 percent above the average for all consumer units; an index of 68 indicates spending that is 32 percent below the average for all consumer units)

	total consumer units	homeowners	renters
Average spending of CUs, total	$46,409	$54,126	$30,462
Average spending of CUs, index	100	117	66
FOOD	100	113	73
Food at home	100	112	75
Cereals and bakery products	100	112	74
Cereals and cereal products	100	109	82
Bakery products	100	114	71
Meats, poultry, fish, and eggs	100	111	78
Beef	100	110	79
Pork	100	111	78
Other meats	100	112	77
Poultry	100	109	83
Fish and seafood	100	114	72
Eggs	100	106	88
Dairy products	100	113	72
Fresh milk and cream	100	110	79
Other dairy products	100	116	69
Fruits and vegetables	100	112	75
Fresh fruits	100	113	73
Fresh vegetables	100	112	74
Processed fruits	100	110	78
Processed vegetables	100	111	79
Other food at home	100	112	74
Sugar and other sweets	100	114	69
Fats and oils	100	111	78
Miscellaneous foods	100	112	74
Nonalcoholic beverages	100	111	79
Food prepared by consumer unit on trips	100	127	46
Food away from home	100	115	70
ALCOHOLIC BEVERAGES	100	109	82
HOUSING	100	114	71
Shelter	100	108	83
Owned dwellings	100	148	1
Mortgage interest and charges	100	148	1
Property taxes	100	148	2
Maintenance, repair, insurance, other expenses	100	148	2
Rented dwellings	100	3	301
Other lodging	100	135	28
Utilities, fuels, and public services	100	118	63
Natural gas	100	124	51
Electricity	100	117	65
Fuel oil and other fuels	100	135	27
Telephone services	100	109	81
Water and other public services	100	130	38
Household services	100	124	50
Personal services	100	118	63
Other household services	100	129	41
Housekeeping supplies	100	122	54
Laundry and cleaning supplies	100	115	70
Other household products	100	125	48
Postage and stationery	100	122	54

	total consumer units	homeowners	renters
Household furnishings and equipment	100	126	45
Household textiles	100	122	55
Furniture	100	123	52
Floor coverings	100	139	20
Major appliances	100	133	33
Small appliances, miscellaneous housewares	100	124	52
Miscellaneous household equipment	100	127	44
APPAREL AND RELATED SERVICES	100	109	80
Men and boys	100	110	79
Men, aged 16 or older	100	110	79
Boys, aged 2 to 15	100	110	80
Women and girls	100	113	73
Women, aged 16 or older	100	113	73
Girls, aged 2 to 15	100	113	72
Children under age 2	100	105	91
Footwear	100	102	97
Other apparel products and services	100	109	81
TRANSPORTATION	100	117	65
Vehicle purchases	100	118	62
Cars and trucks, new	100	129	40
Cars and trucks, used	100	105	90
Other vehicles	100	109	82
Gasoline and motor oil	100	115	69
Other vehicle expenses	100	117	64
Vehicle finance charges	100	119	60
Maintenance and repairs	100	117	65
Vehicle insurance	100	116	66
Vehicle rentals, leases, licenses, other charges	100	120	59
Public transportation	100	117	64
HEALTH CARE	100	125	49
Health insurance	100	125	49
Medical services	100	125	49
Drugs	100	124	51
Medical supplies	100	126	47
ENTERTAINMENT	100	122	54
Fees and admissions	100	128	43
Audio and visual equipment and services	100	113	74
Pets, toys, hobbies, playground equipment	100	125	49
Other entertainment products and services	100	132	35
PERSONAL CARE PRODUCTS AND SERVICES	100	116	68
READING	100	121	58
EDUCATION	100	115	70
TOBACCO PRODUCTS AND SMOKING SUPPLIES	100	92	118
MISCELLANEOUS	100	118	62
CASH CONTRIBUTIONS	100	124	51
PERSONAL INSURANCE AND PENSIONS	100	124	51
Life and other personal insurance	100	134	29
Pensions and Social Security	100	123	53
PERSONAL TAXES	100	131	35
Federal income taxes	100	132	34
State and local income taxes	100	125	49
Other taxes	100	144	11
GIFTS FOR PEOPLE IN OTHER HOUSEHOLDS	100	127	44

Source: Calculations by New Strategist based on the Bureau of Labor Statistics' 2005 Consumer Expenditure Survey

Spending by Number of Earners, 2005

Dual-earners account for 33 percent of the nation's households, and they outspend the average household by 30 percent. In 2005, the average dual-income household spent $60,197. Households with three or more earners spend even more ($69,805), but they account for a much smaller share of households—just 9 percent in 2005.

By category, spending does not always rise with the number of earners in a household. Single-person households with one earner (many of them young adults) spend more than other households on rent. Two-or-more-person households with no earners (many of them elderly) spend more than twice the average on drugs. In general, however, three-earner households out-spend the others on many products and services because they are the largest households, averaging 4.4 people.

The needs of two-earner households are readily apparent in these tables. This household type spends 33 percent more than the average household on food away from home, 95 percent more than average on personal household services (primarily day care), and 36 percent more on new cars and trucks.

Table 52. Average spending by number of earners in household, 2005

(average annual spending of consumer units (CU) by product and service category, by consumer unit size and number of earners in consumer unit, 2005)

	total consumer units	single-person CUs		CUs with two or more people			
		no earner	one earner	no earner	one earner	two earners	three+ earners
Number of consumer units (in 000s)	117,356	13,087	21,252	10,051	23,925	39,014	10,027
Average number of persons per CU	2.5	1.0	1.0	2.3	3.0	3.0	4.4
Average before-tax income of CUs	$58,712	$16,261	$38,929	$27,954	$56,331	$82,521	$99,921
Average annual spending of CUs	46,409	19,865	31,017	33,796	47,594	60,197	69,805
FOOD	5,931	2,304	3,543	5,180	6,296	7,471	9,577
Food at home	3,297	1,542	1,697	3,328	3,714	3,956	5,361
Cereals and bakery products	445	230	225	471	494	534	699
Cereals and cereal products	143	66	71	141	160	176	226
Bakery products	302	164	154	330	333	359	473
Meats, poultry, fish, and eggs	764	321	339	808	869	912	1,380
Beef	228	81	95	236	258	275	436
Pork	153	69	66	185	176	177	272
Other meats	103	45	44	110	119	124	178
Poultry	134	61	61	125	151	161	253
Fish and seafood	113	45	56	116	126	138	193
Eggs	33	19	17	37	38	37	48
Dairy products	378	192	193	385	416	461	592
Fresh milk and cream	146	80	71	151	168	173	224
Other dairy products	232	112	122	234	248	287	368
Fruits and vegetables	552	283	294	588	640	637	863
Fresh fruits	182	94	103	197	216	204	276
Fresh vegetables	175	84	94	178	201	205	279
Processed fruits	106	63	55	115	120	124	156
Processed vegetables	89	42	42	97	102	105	151
Other food at home	1,158	516	646	1,077	1,296	1,412	1,828
Sugar and other sweets	119	61	61	144	129	139	186
Fats and oils	85	44	44	96	99	95	141
Miscellaneous foods	609	264	341	537	684	755	945
Nonalcoholic beverages	303	136	177	256	336	372	491
Food prepared by consumer unit on trips	41	12	24	44	48	50	65
Food away from home	2,634	762	1,845	1,852	2,581	3,516	4,216
ALCOHOLIC BEVERAGES	426	125	450	318	342	541	638
HOUSING	15,167	8,156	10,868	11,342	16,037	19,076	19,945
Shelter	8,805	4,872	6,985	5,724	9,093	11,073	11,370
Owned dwellings	5,958	2,271	3,538	3,679	6,133	8,270	8,772
Mortgage interest and charges	3,317	488	2,008	1,112	3,402	4,975	5,337
Property taxes	1,541	901	910	1,443	1,593	1,973	2,003
Maintenance, repair, insurance, other expenses	1,101	883	620	1,124	1,138	1,322	1,431
Rented dwellings	2,345	2,427	3,173	1,564	2,434	2,120	1,926
Other lodging	502	173	273	482	526	683	672
Utilities, fuels, and public services	3,183	1,952	2,068	3,038	3,462	3,743	4,459
Natural gas	473	340	295	485	526	533	657
Electricity	1,155	700	731	1,174	1,309	1,345	1,520
Fuel oil and other fuels	142	133	77	179	137	163	179
Telephone services	1,048	533	745	832	1,089	1,271	1,611
Water and other public services	366	247	219	369	401	430	492
Household services	801	423	358	609	826	1,204	791
Personal services	322	82	18	120	327	628	278
Other household services	479	341	341	488	499	577	513
Housekeeping supplies	611	295	336	615	662	782	793
Laundry and cleaning supplies	134	67	65	140	155	162	202
Other household products	320	132	175	304	352	415	424
Postage and stationery	157	96	96	171	156	205	167

	total consumer units	single-person CUs		CUs with two or more people			
		no earner	one earner	no earner	one earner	two earners	three+ earners
Household furnishings and equipment	$1,767	$614	$1,121	$1,357	$1,992	$2,274	$2,533
Household textiles	132	43	78	136	144	162	216
Furniture	467	155	257	358	541	624	647
Floor coverings	56	30	22	35	90	68	56
Major appliances	223	74	122	199	225	283	427
Small appliances, miscellaneous housewares	105	63	62	107	92	134	175
Miscellaneous household equipment	782	249	579	522	902	1,002	1,013
APPAREL AND RELATED SERVICES	1,886	566	1,233	1,318	2,012	2,421	3,191
Men and boys	440	104	295	310	454	577	750
Men, aged 16 or older	349	97	283	258	292	453	646
Boys, aged 2 to 15	91	7	13	52	162	124	105
Women and girls	754	223	486	564	802	934	1,402
Women, aged 16 or older	633	213	466	513	615	757	1,233
Girls, aged 2 to 15	121	10	20	51	187	177	168
Children under age 2	82	10	19	40	125	116	116
Footwear	320	134	196	269	340	393	548
Other apparel products and services	290	95	238	135	292	401	376
TRANSPORTATION	8,344	2,639	4,886	6,001	8,662	11,228	13,491
Vehicle purchases	3,544	925	1,684	2,603	3,945	4,891	5,650
Cars and trucks, new	1,931	653	685	1,702	2,258	2,624	2,997
Cars and trucks, used	1,531	246	929	886	1,638	2,147	2,473
Other vehicles	82	26	70	15	49	120	180
Gasoline and motor oil	2,013	633	1,277	1,373	2,050	2,660	3,413
Other vehicle expenses	2,339	881	1,617	1,640	2,269	3,069	3,801
Vehicle finance charges	297	40	171	117	284	449	514
Maintenance and repairs	671	301	521	550	659	826	1,023
Vehicle insurance	913	403	593	689	848	1,170	1,640
Vehicle rentals, leases, licenses, other charges	458	137	332	283	477	624	624
Public transportation	448	200	308	385	398	608	627
HEALTH CARE	2,664	2,397	1,351	4,087	2,911	2,810	3,212
Health insurance	1,361	1,262	665	2,253	1,469	1,427	1,554
Medical services	677	482	388	643	753	789	965
Drugs	521	565	246	1,054	584	475	540
Medical supplies	105	88	51	137	106	119	153
ENTERTAINMENT	2,388	883	1,612	1,722	2,423	3,234	3,289
Fees and admissions	588	184	429	443	569	799	821
Audio and visual equipment and services	888	443	682	697	948	1,092	1,156
Pets, toys, hobbies, playground equipment	420	149	285	286	463	572	494
Other entertainment products and services	492	107	217	297	442	771	818
PERSONAL CARE PRODUCTS, SERVICES	541	285	355	447	543	673	851
READING	126	94	108	122	115	150	146
EDUCATION	940	332	602	214	887	1,266	2,035
TOBACCO PRODUCTS AND SMOKING SUPPLIES	319	180	255	256	318	380	464
MISCELLANEOUS	808	399	664	942	799	883	1,256
CASH CONTRIBUTIONS	1,663	1,289	1,328	1,467	1,659	1,896	2,164
PERSONAL INSURANCE AND PENSIONS	5,204	214	3,762	378	4,591	8,167	9,544
Life and other personal insurance	381	136	178	275	477	498	552
Pensions and Social Security	4,823	77	3,584	103	4,114	7,669	8,993
PERSONAL TAXES	2,408	231	2,161	612	1,818	3,907	3,146
Federal income taxes	1,696	82	1,591	356	1,213	2,815	2,169
State and local income taxes	534	3	460	54	441	885	725
Other taxes	177	146	110	202	164	206	252
GIFTS FOR PEOPLE IN OTHER HOUSEHOLDS	1,091	578	886	753	1,032	1,401	1,465

Note: Spending by category will not add to total spending because gift spending is also included in the preceding product and service categories and personal taxes are not included in the total.
Source: Bureau of Labor Statistics, 2005 Consumer Expenditure Surveys, Internet site http://www.bls.gov/cex/

Table 53. Indexed spending by number of earners in household, 2005

(indexed average annual spending of consumer units by product and service category, consumer unit size, and number of earners in consumer unit, 2005; index definition: an index of 100 is the average for all consumer units; an index of 132 means that spending by consumer units in that group is 32 percent above the average for all consumer units; an index of 68 indicates spending that is 32 percent below the average for all consumer units)

	total consumer units	single-person CUs		CUs with two or more people			
		no earner	one earner	no earner	one earner	two earners	three+ earners
Average spending of consumer units, total	$46,409	$19,865	$31,017	$33,796	$47,594	$60,197	$69,805
Average spending of consumer units, index	100	43	67	73	103	130	150
FOOD	100	39	60	87	106	126	161
Food at home	100	47	51	101	113	120	163
Cereals and bakery products	100	52	51	106	111	120	157
Cereals and cereal products	100	46	50	99	112	123	158
Bakery products	100	54	51	109	110	119	157
Meats, poultry, fish, and eggs	100	42	44	106	114	119	181
Beef	100	36	42	104	113	121	191
Pork	100	45	43	121	115	116	178
Other meats	100	44	43	107	116	120	173
Poultry	100	46	46	93	113	120	189
Fish and seafood	100	40	50	103	112	122	171
Eggs	100	58	52	112	115	112	145
Dairy products	100	51	51	102	110	122	157
Fresh milk and cream	100	55	49	103	115	118	153
Other dairy products	100	48	53	101	107	124	159
Fruits and vegetables	100	51	53	107	116	115	156
Fresh fruits	100	52	57	108	119	112	152
Fresh vegetables	100	48	54	102	115	117	159
Processed fruits	100	59	52	108	113	117	147
Processed vegetables	100	47	47	109	115	118	170
Other food at home	100	45	56	93	112	122	158
Sugar and other sweets	100	51	51	121	108	117	156
Fats and oils	100	52	52	113	116	112	166
Miscellaneous foods	100	43	56	88	112	124	155
Nonalcoholic beverages	100	45	58	84	111	123	162
Food prepared by consumer unit on trips	100	29	59	107	117	122	159
Food away from home	100	29	70	70	98	133	160
ALCOHOLIC BEVERAGES	100	29	106	75	80	127	150
HOUSING	100	54	72	75	106	126	132
Shelter	100	55	79	65	103	126	129
Owned dwellings	100	38	59	62	103	139	147
Mortgage interest and charges	100	15	61	34	103	150	161
Property taxes	100	58	59	94	103	128	130
Maintenance, repair, insurance, other expenses	100	80	56	102	103	120	130
Rented dwellings	100	103	135	67	104	90	82
Other lodging	100	34	54	96	105	136	134
Utilities, fuels, and public services	100	61	65	95	109	118	140
Natural gas	100	72	62	103	111	113	139
Electricity	100	61	63	102	113	116	132
Fuel oil and other fuels	100	94	54	126	96	115	126
Telephone services	100	51	71	79	104	121	154
Water and other public services	100	67	60	101	110	117	134
Household services	100	53	45	76	103	150	99
Personal services	100	25	6	37	102	195	86
Other household services	100	71	71	102	104	120	107
Housekeeping supplies	100	48	55	101	108	128	130
Laundry and cleaning supplies	100	50	49	104	116	121	151
Other household products	100	41	55	95	110	130	133
Postage and stationery	100	61	61	109	99	131	106

	total consumer units	single-person CUs		CUs with two or more people			
		no earner	one earner	no earner	one earner	two earners	three+ earners
Household furnishings and equipment	100	35	63	77	113	129	143
Household textiles	100	33	59	103	109	123	164
Furniture	100	33	55	77	116	134	139
Floor coverings	100	54	39	63	161	121	100
Major appliances	100	33	55	89	101	127	191
Small appliances, miscellaneous housewares	100	60	59	102	88	128	167
Miscellaneous household equipment	100	32	74	67	115	128	130
APPAREL AND RELATED SERVICES	100	30	65	70	107	128	169
Men and boys	100	24	67	70	103	131	170
Men, aged 16 or older	100	28	81	74	84	130	185
Boys, aged 2 to 15	100	8	14	57	178	136	115
Women and girls	100	30	64	75	106	124	186
Women, aged 16 or older	100	34	74	81	97	120	195
Girls, aged 2 to 15	100	8	17	42	155	146	139
Children under age 2	100	12	23	49	152	141	141
Footwear	100	42	61	84	106	123	171
Other apparel products and services	100	33	82	47	101	138	130
TRANSPORTATION	100	32	59	72	104	135	162
Vehicle purchases	100	26	48	73	111	138	159
Cars and trucks, new	100	34	35	88	117	136	155
Cars and trucks, used	100	16	61	58	107	140	162
Other vehicles	100	32	85	18	60	146	220
Gasoline and motor oil	100	31	63	68	102	132	170
Other vehicle expenses	100	38	69	70	97	131	163
Vehicle finance charges	100	13	58	39	96	151	173
Maintenance and repairs	100	45	78	82	98	123	152
Vehicle insurance	100	44	65	75	93	128	180
Vehicle rentals, leases, licenses, other charges	100	30	72	62	104	136	136
Public transportation	100	45	69	86	89	136	140
HEALTH CARE	100	90	51	153	109	105	121
Health insurance	100	93	49	166	108	105	114
Medical services	100	71	57	95	111	117	143
Drugs	100	108	47	202	112	91	104
Medical supplies	100	84	49	130	101	113	146
ENTERTAINMENT	100	37	68	72	101	135	138
Fees and admissions	100	31	73	75	97	136	140
Audio and visual equipment and services	100	50	77	78	107	123	130
Pets, toys, hobbies, playground equipment	100	35	68	68	110	136	118
Other entertainment products and services	100	22	44	60	90	157	166
PERSONAL CARE PRODUCTS AND SERVICES	100	53	66	83	100	124	157
READING	100	75	86	97	91	119	116
EDUCATION	100	35	64	23	94	135	216
TOBACCO PRODUCTS AND SMOKING SUPPLIES	100	56	80	80	100	119	145
MISCELLANEOUS	100	49	82	117	99	109	155
CASH CONTRIBUTIONS	100	78	80	88	100	114	130
PERSONAL INSURANCE AND PENSIONS	100	4	72	7	88	157	183
Life and other personal insurance	100	36	47	72	125	131	145
Pensions and Social Security	100	2	74	2	85	159	186
PERSONAL TAXES	100	10	90	25	75	162	131
Federal income taxes	100	5	94	21	72	166	128
State and local income taxes	100	1	86	10	83	166	136
Other taxes	100	82	62	114	93	116	142
GIFTS FOR PEOPLE IN OTHER HOUSEHOLDS	100	53	81	69	95	128	134

Source: Calculations by New Strategist based on the Bureau of Labor Statistics' 2005 Consumer Expenditure Survey

Spending by Occupation, 2005

Households headed by managers and professionals spent $64,559 in 2005, 39 percent more than the average household. Behind the higher level of spending are their higher incomes, averaging $94,060 in 2005. Among all wage-and-salary workers, average household income was $67,478 and their spending was only 9 percent above average. Households headed by retirees spend 29 percent less than the average household, while the self-employed spend 21 percent more than average.

Households headed by managers and professionals spend more than average on many of the products and services associated with the income elite. They spend 43 percent more than the average household on food away from home; 46 percent more on alcoholic beverages; 80 percent more on other lodging (which includes vacation homes and hotel and motel expenses); 42 to 46 percent more on men's and women's clothes; 45 percent more on new cars and trucks; 77 percent more on fees and admissions to entertainment events, and 62 percent more on gifts for people in other households.

The self-employed are big spenders on products and services needed by people who are likely to work at home. They spend more than average on electricity and out-of-pocket health insurance expenses. Their spending is below average on household personal services (mostly day care).

The retired spend more than the average household on reading material, maintenance and repairs for owned homes, fuel oil, and health care.

Table 54. Average spending by occupation of householder, 2005

(average annual spending of consumer units (CUs) by product and service category and by selected occupation of consumer unit reference person, 2005)

	total consumer units	self-employed	wage and salary workers						retired
			total	managers and professionals	technical, sales, admin. support	service workers	construction workers, mechanics	operators, fabricators, laborers	
Number of consumer units (in 000s)	117,356	5,759	76,718	27,894	22,305	12,424	4,392	9,703	20,514
Average number of persons per CU	2.5	2.7	2.6	2.6	2.5	2.7	2.7	2.7	1.7
Average before-tax income of CU	$58,712	$80,272	$67,478	$94,060	$59,200	$43,165	$56,697	$46,104	$31,353
Average annual spending of CU	46,409	56,215	50,759	64,559	48,103	36,932	44,952	37,221	32,903
FOOD	**5,931**	**6,796**	**6,393**	**7,581**	**6,037**	**5,117**	**6,573**	**5,196**	**4,335**
Food at home	**3,297**	**3,816**	**3,406**	**3,817**	**3,219**	**3,073**	**3,327**	**3,041**	**2,689**
Cereals and bakery products	445	502	456	528	421	409	417	391	379
Cereals and cereal products	143	153	150	168	145	142	138	127	106
Bakery products	302	349	305	360	277	267	279	264	273
Meats, poultry, fish, and eggs	764	864	793	825	763	774	812	779	606
Beef	228	263	238	240	239	216	255	249	169
Pork	153	179	156	156	145	165	171	159	132
Other meats	103	108	107	109	101	107	122	109	81
Poultry	134	134	143	153	138	138	136	131	93
Fish and seafood	113	143	117	134	110	114	95	97	101
Eggs	33	38	33	33	30	34	34	34	29
Dairy products	378	443	388	443	367	331	367	346	311
Fresh milk and cream	146	179	147	157	137	139	147	145	117
Other dairy products	232	264	241	286	230	192	221	201	194
Fruits and vegetables	552	667	560	648	505	511	515	499	495
Fresh fruits	182	215	184	218	159	177	157	156	170
Fresh vegetables	175	219	178	205	167	151	171	158	149
Processed fruits	106	127	108	126	98	98	101	95	98
Processed vegetables	89	106	90	100	81	86	87	90	78
Other food at home	1,158	1,339	1,209	1,373	1,163	1,048	1,214	1,026	898
Sugar and other sweets	119	157	118	138	110	101	121	98	109
Fats and oils	85	94	87	94	86	82	86	76	74
Miscellaneous foods	609	668	643	744	622	537	621	531	463
Nonalcoholic beverages	303	367	319	334	308	307	349	299	211
Food prepared by consumer unit on trips	41	52	42	64	37	21	38	22	41
Food away from home	**2,634**	**2,981**	**2,987**	**3,764**	**2,818**	**2,044**	**3,246**	**2,155**	**1,646**
ALCOHOLIC BEVERAGES	**426**	**553**	**495**	**622**	**429**	**323**	**568**	**439**	**257**
HOUSING	**15,167**	**17,341**	**16,398**	**20,790**	**15,413**	**12,865**	**13,853**	**11,668**	**11,334**
Shelter	**8,805**	**10,156**	**9,686**	**12,538**	**8,946**	**7,536**	**8,346**	**6,547**	**5,857**
Owned dwellings	5,958	7,333	6,639	9,437	5,967	4,131	5,491	3,874	3,915
Mortgage interest and charges	3,317	4,127	3,966	5,550	3,616	2,540	3,470	2,269	1,079
Property taxes	1,541	1,951	1,582	2,259	1,409	977	1,258	957	1,487
Maintenance, repair, insurance, other expenses	1,101	1,256	1,091	1,628	942	615	763	648	1,349
Rented dwellings	2,345	2,043	2,533	2,197	2,586	3,206	2,578	2,497	1,478
Other lodging	502	779	513	904	393	199	277	176	464
Utilities, fuels, and public services	**3,183**	**3,494**	**3,292**	**3,678**	**3,211**	**2,897**	**3,108**	**2,956**	**2,812**
Natural gas	473	530	478	566	448	390	446	424	478
Electricity	1,155	1,297	1,173	1,276	1,159	1,067	1,101	1,077	1,030
Fuel oil and other fuels	142	198	129	134	109	123	166	153	186
Telephone services	1,048	1,089	1,141	1,256	1,142	1,019	1,069	994	750
Water and other public services	366	379	371	445	354	299	325	308	368
Household services	**801**	**829**	**893**	**1,313**	**843**	**538**	**476**	**439**	**639**
Personal services	322	232	417	584	424	269	211	202	109
Other household services	479	597	476	729	420	269	265	238	530
Housekeeping supplies	**611**	**629**	**642**	**781**	**609**	**509**	**516**	**518**	**548**
Laundry and cleaning supplies	134	138	137	141	136	134	118	144	114
Other household products	320	325	339	412	324	267	294	265	275
Postage and stationery	157	165	165	228	149	108	105	109	159

	total consumer units	self-employed	wage and salary workers						retired
			total	managers and professionals	technical, sales, admin. support	service workers	construction workers, mechanics	operators, fabricators, laborers	
Household furnishings and equipment	$1,767	$2,235	$1,886	$2,479	$1,804	$1,386	$1,407	$1,207	$1,477
Household textiles	132	166	140	185	135	103	87	92	107
Furniture	467	494	506	676	496	345	334	326	364
Floor coverings	56	81	52	68	56	30	30	34	47
Major appliances	223	286	241	312	215	190	211	172	188
Small appliances, miscellaneous housewares	105	81	116	155	105	89	85	72	100
Miscellaneous household equipment	782	1,127	830	1,082	796	629	660	510	671
APPAREL AND RELATED SERVICES	1,886	2,001	2,143	2,703	2,003	1,768	1,608	1,536	1,047
Men and boys	440	455	510	612	482	429	545	365	214
Men, aged 16 or older	349	369	408	496	376	342	453	283	189
Boys, aged 2 to 15	91	85	103	116	106	87	92	83	25
Women and girls	754	899	843	1,103	791	661	469	584	479
Women, aged 16 or older	633	768	701	926	655	560	322	485	447
Girls, aged 2 to 15	121	131	142	177	136	101	147	99	32
Children under age 2	82	52	91	93	94	92	83	81	31
Footwear	320	282	356	377	347	376	307	313	186
Other apparel products and services	290	314	342	517	288	210	205	193	137
TRANSPORTATION	8,344	8,449	9,294	10,963	9,572	6,758	9,105	7,184	5,527
Vehicle purchases	3,544	3,010	3,958	4,584	4,495	2,643	3,777	2,695	2,255
Cars and trucks, new	1,931	1,621	2,034	2,809	2,157	1,128	1,484	931	1,572
Cars and trucks, used	1,531	1,253	1,819	1,684	2,177	1,462	2,136	1,696	663
Other vehicles	82	137	106	90	160	53	158	68	20
Gasoline and motor oil	2,013	2,286	2,247	2,452	2,195	1,900	2,493	2,109	1,269
Other vehicle expenses	2,339	2,676	2,607	3,142	2,536	1,950	2,444	2,145	1,642
Vehicle finance charges	297	288	360	414	376	276	335	289	115
Maintenance and repairs	671	859	722	857	700	552	790	567	542
Vehicle insurance	913	1,043	1,004	1,145	993	778	966	930	692
Vehicle rentals, leases, licenses, other charges	458	487	521	725	467	344	353	360	294
Public transportation	448	477	482	786	347	265	391	234	361
HEALTH CARE	2,664	3,209	2,347	2,880	2,341	1,672	1,900	1,893	4,057
Health insurance	1,361	1,703	1,172	1,439	1,163	850	999	918	2,216
Medical services	677	802	668	832	675	428	530	551	745
Drugs	521	588	406	477	405	330	289	350	961
Medical supplies	105	116	101	132	98	64	81	74	135
ENTERTAINMENT	2,388	2,989	2,621	3,402	2,515	1,626	2,401	1,952	1,637
Fees and admissions	588	751	650	1,040	570	292	339	308	422
Audio and visual equipment and services	888	1,025	946	1,130	921	759	831	766	641
Pets, toys, hobbies, playground equipment	420	577	461	594	425	306	461	350	240
Other entertainment products and services	492	637	564	638	600	268	769	528	335
PERSONAL CARE PRODUCTS AND SERVICES	541	614	586	753	562	453	433	391	451
READING	126	149	129	198	113	69	76	73	141
EDUCATION	940	1,035	1,095	1,724	944	563	625	525	236
TOBACCO PRODUCTS AND SMOKING SUPPLIES	319	384	339	233	358	371	526	471	187
MISCELLANEOUS	808	1,123	845	1,076	816	576	802	623	796
CASH CONTRIBUTIONS	1,663	2,263	1,664	2,475	1,425	923	1,271	1,007	1,801
PERSONAL INSURANCE AND PENSIONS	5,204	9,309	6,412	9,159	5,575	3,848	5,212	4,263	1,094
Life and other personal insurance	381	504	403	580	384	239	201	237	344
Pensions and Social Security	4,823	8,805	6,009	8,580	5,191	3,608	5,010	4,027	750
PERSONAL TAXES	2,408	2,485	3,046	5,089	2,353	1,246	2,543	1,298	632
Federal income taxes	1,696	1,834	2,166	3,746	1,609	807	1,787	817	343
State and local income taxes	534	395	712	1,106	590	327	635	385	57
Other taxes	177	256	168	237	154	111	122	96	233
GIFTS FOR PEOPLE IN OTHER HOUSEHOLDS	1,091	1,140	1,202	1,763	1,017	751	823	752	888

Note: Spending by category will not add to total spending because gift spending is also included in the preceding product and service categories and personal taxes are not included in the total.
Source: Bureau of Labor Statistics, 2005 Consumer Expenditure Surveys, Internet site http://www.bls.gov/cex/

Table 55. Indexed spending by occupation of householder, 2005

(indexed average annual spending of consumer units by product and service category and selected occupation of consumer unit reference person, 2005; index definition: an index of 100 is the average for all consumer units; an index of 132 means that spending by consumer units in that group is 32 percent above the average for all consumer units; an index of 68 indicates spending that is 32 percent below the average for all consumer units)

	total consumer units	self- employed	wage and salary workers						retired
			total	managers and professionals	technical, sales, admin. support	service workers	construction workers, mechanics	operators, fabricators, laborers	
Average spending of consumer units, total	$46,409	$56,215	$50,759	$64,559	$48,103	$36,932	$44,952	$37,221	$32,903
Average spending of consumer units, index	100	121	109	139	104	80	97	80	71
FOOD	100	115	108	128	102	86	111	88	73
Food at home	100	116	103	116	98	93	101	92	82
Cereals and bakery products	100	113	102	119	95	92	94	88	85
Cereals and cereal products	100	107	105	117	101	99	97	89	74
Bakery products	100	116	101	119	92	88	92	87	90
Meats, poultry, fish, and eggs	100	113	104	108	100	101	106	102	79
Beef	100	115	104	105	105	95	112	109	74
Pork	100	117	102	102	95	108	112	104	86
Other meats	100	105	104	106	98	104	118	106	79
Poultry	100	100	107	114	103	103	101	98	69
Fish and seafood	100	127	104	119	97	101	84	86	89
Eggs	100	115	100	100	91	103	103	103	88
Dairy products	100	117	103	117	97	88	97	92	82
Fresh milk and cream	100	123	101	108	94	95	101	99	80
Other dairy products	100	114	104	123	99	83	95	87	84
Fruits and vegetables	100	121	101	117	91	93	93	90	90
Fresh fruits	100	118	101	120	87	97	86	86	93
Fresh vegetables	100	125	102	117	95	86	98	90	85
Processed fruits	100	120	102	119	92	92	95	90	92
Processed vegetables	100	119	101	112	91	97	98	101	88
Other food at home	100	116	104	119	100	91	105	89	78
Sugar and other sweets	100	132	99	116	92	85	102	82	92
Fats and oils	100	111	102	111	101	96	101	89	87
Miscellaneous foods	100	110	106	122	102	88	102	87	76
Nonalcoholic beverages	100	121	105	110	102	101	115	99	70
Food prepared by consumer unit on trips	100	127	102	156	90	51	93	54	100
Food away from home	100	113	113	143	107	78	123	82	62
ALCOHOLIC BEVERAGES	100	130	116	146	101	76	133	103	60
HOUSING	100	114	108	137	102	85	91	77	75
Shelter	100	115	110	142	102	86	95	74	67
Owned dwellings	100	123	111	158	100	69	92	65	66
Mortgage interest and charges	100	124	120	167	109	77	105	68	33
Property taxes	100	127	103	147	91	63	82	62	96
Maintenance, repair, insurance, other expenses	100	114	99	148	86	56	69	59	123
Rented dwellings	100	87	108	94	110	137	110	106	63
Other lodging	100	155	102	180	78	40	55	35	92
Utilities, fuels, and public services	100	110	103	116	101	91	98	93	88
Natural gas	100	112	101	120	95	82	94	90	101
Electricity	100	112	102	110	100	92	95	93	89
Fuel oil and other fuels	100	139	91	94	77	87	117	108	131
Telephone services	100	104	109	120	109	97	102	95	72
Water and other public services	100	104	101	122	97	82	89	84	101
Household services	100	103	111	164	105	67	59	55	80
Personal services	100	72	130	181	132	84	66	63	34
Other household services	100	125	99	152	88	56	55	50	111
Housekeeping supplies	100	103	105	128	100	83	84	85	90
Laundry and cleaning supplies	100	103	102	105	101	100	88	107	85
Other household products	100	102	106	129	101	83	92	83	86
Postage and stationery	100	105	105	145	95	69	67	69	101

	total consumer units	self-employed	wage and salary workers						retired
			total	managers and professionals	technical, sales, admin. support	service workers	construction workers, mechanics	operators, fabricators, laborers	
Household furnishings and equipment	100	126	107	140	102	78	80	68	84
Household textiles	100	126	106	140	102	78	66	70	81
Furniture	100	106	108	145	106	74	72	70	78
Floor coverings	100	145	93	121	100	54	54	61	84
Major appliances	100	128	108	140	96	85	95	77	84
Small appliances, miscellaneous housewares	100	77	110	148	100	85	81	69	95
Miscellaneous household equipment	100	144	106	138	102	80	84	65	86
APPAREL AND RELATED SERVICES	100	106	114	143	106	94	85	81	56
Men and boys	100	103	116	139	110	98	124	83	49
Men, aged 16 or older	100	106	117	142	108	98	130	81	54
Boys, aged 2 to 15	100	93	113	127	116	96	101	91	27
Women and girls	100	119	112	146	105	88	62	77	64
Women, aged 16 or older	100	121	111	146	103	88	51	77	71
Girls, aged 2 to 15	100	108	117	146	112	83	121	82	26
Children under age 2	100	63	111	113	115	112	101	99	38
Footwear	100	88	111	118	108	118	96	98	58
Other apparel products and services	100	108	118	178	99	72	71	67	47
TRANSPORTATION	100	101	111	131	115	81	109	86	66
Vehicle purchases	100	85	112	129	127	75	107	76	64
Cars and trucks, new	100	84	105	145	112	58	77	48	81
Cars and trucks, used	100	82	119	110	142	95	140	111	43
Other vehicles	100	167	129	110	195	65	193	83	24
Gasoline and motor oil	100	114	112	122	109	94	124	105	63
Other vehicle expenses	100	114	111	134	108	83	104	92	70
Vehicle finance charges	100	97	121	139	127	93	113	97	39
Maintenance and repairs	100	128	108	128	104	82	118	85	81
Vehicle insurance	100	114	110	125	109	85	106	102	76
Vehicle rentals, leases, licenses, other charges	100	106	114	158	102	75	77	79	64
Public transportation	100	106	108	175	77	59	87	52	81
HEALTH CARE	100	120	88	108	88	63	71	71	152
Health insurance	100	125	86	106	85	62	73	67	163
Medical services	100	118	99	123	100	63	78	81	110
Drugs	100	113	78	92	78	63	55	67	184
Medical supplies	100	110	96	126	93	61	77	70	129
ENTERTAINMENT	100	125	110	142	105	68	101	82	69
Fees and admissions	100	128	111	177	97	50	58	52	72
Audio and visual equipment and services	100	115	107	127	104	85	94	86	72
Pets, toys, hobbies, playground equipment	100	137	110	141	101	73	110	83	57
Other entertainment products and services	100	129	115	130	122	54	156	107	68
PERSONAL CARE PRODUCTS AND SERVICES	100	113	108	139	104	84	80	72	83
READING	100	118	102	157	90	55	60	58	112
EDUCATION	100	110	116	183	100	60	66	56	25
TOBACCO PRODUCTS AND SMOKING SUPPLIES	100	120	106	73	112	116	165	148	59
MISCELLANEOUS	100	139	105	133	101	71	99	77	99
CASH CONTRIBUTIONS	100	136	100	149	86	56	76	61	108
PERSONAL INSURANCE AND PENSIONS	100	179	123	176	107	74	100	82	21
Life and other personal insurance	100	132	106	152	101	63	53	62	90
Pensions and Social Security	100	183	125	178	108	75	104	83	16
PERSONAL TAXES	100	103	126	211	98	52	106	54	26
Federal income taxes	100	108	128	221	95	48	105	48	20
State and local income taxes	100	74	133	207	110	61	119	72	11
Other taxes	100	145	95	134	87	63	69	54	132
GIFTS FOR PEOPLE IN OTHER HOUSEHOLDS	100	104	110	162	93	69	75	69	81

Source: Calculations by New Strategist based on the Bureau of Labor Statistics' 2005 Consumer Expenditure Survey

About the Consumer Expenditure Survey

History

The Consumer Expenditure Survey (CEX) is an ongoing study of the day-to-day spending of American households. In taking the survey, government interviewers collect spending data on products and services as well as the amount and sources of household income, changes in saving and debt, and demographic and economic characteristics of household members. Data collection for the CEX is done by the Bureau of the Census, under contract with the Bureau of Labor Statistics (BLS). The BLS is responsible for analysis and release of the survey data.

Since the late 19th century, the federal government has conducted expenditure surveys about every ten years. Although the results have been used for a variety of purposes, their primary application is to track consumer prices. Beginning in 1980, the CEX became a continuous survey with annual release of data (with a lag time of about two years between data collection and release). The survey is used to update prices for the market basket of products and services used in calculating the Consumer Price Index.

Description of the Consumer Expenditure Survey

The CEX is two surveys: an interview survey and a diary survey. In the interview portion of the survey, respondents are asked each quarter for five consecutive quarters to report their expenditures for the previous three months. The purchase of big-ticket items such as houses, cars, and major appliances, or recurring expenses such as insurance premiums, utility payments, and rent are recorded by the interview survey. About 95 percent of all expenditures are covered by the interview component.

Expenditures on small, frequently purchased items are recorded during a two-week period by the diary survey. These detailed records include expenses for food and beverages purchased in grocery stores and at restaurants, as well as other items such as tobacco, housekeeping supplies, nonprescription drugs, and personal care products and services. The diary survey is intended to capture expenditures respondents are likely to forget or recall incorrectly over longer periods of time.

The average spending figures shown in this report are the integrated data from both the diary and interview components of the survey. Integrated data provide a more complete accounting of consumer expenditures than either component of the survey is designed to do alone.

Data collection and processing

Two separate, nationally representative samples are used for the interview and diary surveys. For the interview survey, about 7,500 consumer units are interviewed on a rotating panel basis each quarter for five consecutive quarters. Another 7,500 consumer units keep weekly diaries of spending for two consecutive weeks. Data collection is carried out in 105 areas of the country.

The data are reviewed, audited, and cleaned by the BLS, and then weighted to reflect the number and characteristics of all U.S. consumer units. As with any sample survey, the CEX is subject to two major types of error. Nonsampling error occurs when respondents misinterpret questions or interviewers are inconsistent in the way they ask questions or record answers. Respondents may forget items, recall expenses incorrectly, or deliberately give wrong answers. A respondent may remember how much he or she spent at the grocery store but forget the items picked up at a local convenience store. Most surveys of alcohol consumption or spending on alcohol suffer from this type of underreporting, for example. Nonsampling error can also be caused by mistakes during the various stages of data processing and refinement.

Sampling error occurs when a sample does not accurately represent the population it is supposed to represent. This kind of error is present in every sample-based survey and is minimized by using a proper sampling procedure. Standard error tables documenting the extent of sampling error in the CEX are available from the BLS at http://www.bls.gov/cex/csxstnderror.htm.

Although the CEX is the best source of information about the spending behavior of American households, it should be treated with caution because of the above problems. Comparisons with consumption data from other sources show that CEX data tend to underestimate expenditures except for rent, fuel, telephone service, furniture, transportation, and personal care services. Despite these problems, the data reveal important spending patterns by demographic segment that can be used to better understand consumer behavior.

The definition of consumer units

The CEX uses consumer units as its sampling unit instead of households, which are the sampling units used by the Census Bureau. The term "household" is used interchangeably with the term "consumer unit" in this book for convenience, although they are not exactly the same. Some households contain more than one consumer unit.

Consumer units are defined by the BLS as either: 1) members of a household who are related by blood, marriage, adoption, or other legal arrangements; 2) a person living alone or sharing a household with others or living as a roomer in a private home or lodging house or in permanent living quarters in a hotel or motel, but who is financially independent; or 3) two persons or more living together who pool their income to make joint expenditure decisions. The BLS defines financial independence in terms of "the three major expenses categories: housing, food, and other living expenses. To be considered financially independent, at least two of the three major expense categories have to be provided by the respondent."

The Census Bureau uses households as its sampling unit in the decennial census and in the monthly Current Population Survey. The Census Bureau's household "consists of all persons who occupy a housing unit. A house, an apartment or other groups of rooms, or a single room is regarded as a housing unit when it is occupied or intended for occupancy as separate living quarters; that is, when the occupants do not live and eat with any other persons in the structure and there is direct access from the outside or through a common hall."

The definition goes on to specify that "a household includes the related family members and all the unrelated persons, if any, such as lodgers, foster children, wards, or employees who share the housing unit. A person living alone in a housing unit or a group of unrelated persons sharing a housing unit as partners is also counted as a household. The count of households excludes group quarters."

Because there can be more than one consumer unit in a household, consumer units outnumber households by several million. Most of the excess consumer units are headed by young adults, under age 25.

For more information

If you want to know more about the Consumer Expenditure Survey, contact the CEX specialists at the Bureau of Labor Statistics at (202) 691-6900, or visit the Consumer Expenditure Survey home page at http://www.bls.gov/cex/. The CEX web site includes news releases, technical documentation, and current and historical CEX data.

Glossary

alcoholic beverages Includes beer and ale, wine, whiskey, gin, vodka, rum, and other alcoholic beverages.

annual spending The annual amount spent per household. The Bureau of Labor Statistics calculates the annual average for all households in a segment, not just for those purchasing an item. The averages are calculated by integrating the results of the diary (weekly) and interview (quarterly) portions of the Consumer Expenditure Survey. For items purchased by most households—such as bread—average annual spending figures are a fairly accurate account of actual spending. For products and services purchased by few households during a year's time—such as cars—the average annual amount spent is much less than what purchasers spend. See the weekly and quarterly spending tables in each chapter for the percentage of consumer units reporting an expenditure during an average week or quarter and the amount spent by purchasers during the week or quarter. For more about the methodology of the Consumer Expenditure Survey, see Appendix A.

apparel, accessories, and related services Includes the following:

- *men's and boys' apparel* Includes coats, jackets, sweaters, vests, sport coats, tailored jackets, slacks, shorts and short sets, sportswear, shirts, underwear, nightwear, hosiery, uniforms, and other accessories.

- *women's and girls' apparel* Includes coats, jackets, furs, sport coats, tailored jackets, sweaters, vests, blouses, shirts, dresses, dungarees, culottes, slacks, shorts, sportswear, underwear, nightwear, uniforms, hosiery, and other accessories.

- *infants' apparel* Includes coats, jackets, snowsuits, underwear, diapers, dresses, crawlers, sleeping garments, hosiery, footwear, and other accessories for children.

- *footwear* Includes articles such as shoes, slippers, boots, and other similar items. It excludes footwear for babies and footwear used for sports such as bowling or golf shoes.

- *other apparel products and services* Includes material for making clothes, shoe repair, alterations and sewing patterns and notions, clothing rental, clothing storage, dry cleaning, sent-out laundry, watches, jewelry, and repairs to watches and jewelry.

cash contributions Includes cash contributed to persons or organizations outside the consumer unit including court-ordered alimony, child support payments, and support for college students, and contributions to religious, educational, charitable, or political organizations.

consumer unit Defined as follows:

- All members of a household who are related by blood, marriage, adoption, or other legal arrangements.

- A person living alone or sharing a household with others or living as a roomer in a private home or lodging house or in permanent living quarters in a hotel or motel, but who is financially independent.

- Two persons or more living together who pool their income to make joint expenditure decisions. Financial independence is determined by the three major expense categories: housing, food, and other living expenses. To be considered financially independent, at least two of the three major expense categories have to be provided by the respondent. For convenience, called households in the text of this report.

education Includes tuition, fees, books, supplies, and equipment for public and private nursery schools, elementary and high schools, colleges and universities, and other schools.

entertainment Includes the following:

- *fees and admissions* Includes fees for participant sports; admissions to sporting events, movies, concerts, plays; health, swimming, tennis, and country club memberships, and other social recreational and fraternal organizations; recreational lessons or instructions; and recreational expenses on trips.

- *audio and visual equipment and services* Includes televisions; radios; cable TV; tape recorders and players; video cassettes, tapes, and discs; VCRs and video disc players; video game hardware and software; personal digital audio players; streaming and downloading audio and video; sound components; CDs, records, and tapes; musical instruments; and rental and repair of TV and sound equipment.

- *pets, toys, hobbies, and playground equipment* Includes pet food, pet services, veterinary expenses, toys, games, hobbies, and playground equipment.

- *other entertainment equipment and services* Includes indoor exercise equipment, athletic shoes, bicycles, trailers, campers, camping equipment, rental of cameras and trailers, hunting and fishing equipment, sports equipment, winter sports equipment, water sports equipment, boats, boat motors and boat trailers, rental of boat, landing and docking fees, rental and repair of sports equipment, photographic equipment, film, photo processing, photographer fees, repair and rental of photo equipment, fireworks, pinball and electronic video games.

expenditure The transaction cost including excise and sales taxes of goods and services acquired during the survey period. The full cost of each purchase is recorded even though full payment may not have been made at the date of purchase. Expenditure estimates include gifts. Excluded from expenditures are purchases or portions of purchases directly assignable to business purposes and periodic credit or installment payments on goods and services already acquired.

federal income tax Includes federal income tax withheld in the survey year to pay for income earned in survey year plus additional tax paid in survey year to cover any underpayment or under withholding of tax in the year prior to the survey.

financial products and services Includes accounting fees, legal fees, union dues, professional dues and fees, other occupational expenses, funerals, cemetery lots, dating services, shopping club memberships, and unclassified fees and personal services.

food Includes the following:

• *food at home* Refers to the total expenditures for food at grocery stores or other food stores during the interview period. It is calculated by multiplying the number of visits to a grocery or other food store by the average amount spent per visit. It excludes the purchase of nonfood items.

• *food away from home* Includes all meals (breakfast, lunch, brunch, and dinner) at restaurants, carry-outs, and vending machines, including tips, plus meals as pay, special catered affairs such as weddings, bar mitzvahs, and confirmations, and meals away from home on trips.

gifts for people in other households Includes gift expenditures for people living in other consumer units. The amount spent on gifts is also included in individual product and service categories.

health care Includes the following:

• *health insurance* Includes health maintenance plans (HMOs), Blue Cross/Blue Shield, commercial health insurance, Medicare, Medicare supplemental insurance, long-term care insurance, and other health insurance.

• *medical services* Includes hospital room and services, physicians' services, services of a practitioner other than a physician, eye and dental care, lab tests, X-rays, nursing, therapy services, care in convalescent or nursing home, and other medical care.

• *drugs* Includes prescription and non-prescription drugs, internal and respiratory over-the-counter drugs.

• *medical supplies* Includes eyeglasses and contact lenses, topicals and dressings, antiseptics, bandages, cotton, first aid kits, contraceptives; medical equipment for general use such as syringes, ice bags, thermometers, vaporizers, heating pads; supportive or convalescent medical equipment such as hearing aids, braces, canes, crutches, and walkers.

household According to the Census Bureau, all the people who occupy a household. A group of unrelated people who share a housing unit as roommates or unmarried partners is also counted as a household. Households do not include group quarters such as college dormitories, prisons, or nursing homes. A household may contain more than one consumer unit. The terms "household" and "consumer unit" are used interchangeably in this report.

household furnishings and equipment Includes the following:

• *household textiles* Includes bathroom, kitchen, dining room, and other linens, curtains and drapes, slipcovers and decorative pillows, and sewing materials.

• *furniture* Includes living room, dining room, kitchen, bedroom, nursery, porch, lawn, and other outdoor furniture.

• *carpet, rugs, and other floor coverings* Includes installation and replacement of wall-to-wall carpets, room-size rugs, and other soft floor coverings.

• *major appliances* Includes refrigerators, freezers, dishwashers, stoves, ovens, garbage disposals, vacuum cleaners, microwaves, air-conditioners, sewing machines, washing machines and dryers, and floor cleaning equipment.

• *small appliances and miscellaneous housewares* Includes small electrical kitchen appliances, portable heating and cooling equipment, china and other dinnerware, flatware, glassware, silver and other serving pieces, nonelectric cookware, and plastic dinnerware. Excludes personal care appliances.

• *miscellaneous household equipment* Includes computer hardware and software, luggage, lamps and other lighting fixtures, window coverings, clocks, lawn mowers and gardening equipment, hand and power tools, telephone answering devices, personal digital assistants, Internet services away from home, office equipment for home use, fresh flowers and house plants, rental of furniture, closet and storage items, household decorative items, infants' equipment, outdoor equipment, smoke alarms, other household appliances and small miscellaneous furnishing.

household services Includes the following:

• *personal services* Includes baby sitting, day care, and care of elderly and handicapped persons.

• *other household services* Includes computer information services; housekeeping services; gardening and lawn care services; coin-operated laundry and dry-cleaning of household textiles; termite and pest control products; moving, storage, and freight expenses;

repair of household appliances and other household equipment; reupholstering and furniture repair; rental and repair of lawn and gardening tools; and rental of other household equipment.

housekeeping supplies Includes soaps, detergents, other laundry cleaning products, cleansing and toilet tissue, paper towels, napkins, and miscellaneous household products; lawn and garden supplies, postage, stationery, stationery supplies, and gift wrap.

income before taxes The total money earnings and selected money receipts accruing to a consumer unit during the 12 months prior to the interview date. Income includes the following components:

• *wages and salaries* Includes total money earnings for all members of the consumer unit aged 14 or older from all jobs, including civilian wages and salaries, Armed Forces pay and allowances, piece-rate payments, commissions, tips, National Guard or Reserve pay (received for training periods), and cash bonuses before deductions for taxes, pensions, union dues, etc.

• *self-employment income* Includes net business and farm income, which consists of net income (gross receipts minus operating expenses) from a profession or unincorporated business or from the operation of a farm by an owner, tenant, or sharecropper. If the business or farm is a partnership, only an appropriate share of net income is recorded. Losses are also recorded.

• *Social Security, private and government retirement* Includes the following: payments by the federal government made under retirement, survivor, and disability insurance programs to retired persons, dependents of deceased insured workers, or to disabled workers; and private pensions or retirement benefits received by retired persons or their survivors, either directly or through an insurance company.

• *interest, dividends, rental income, and other property income* Includes interest income on savings or bonds; payments made by a corporation to its stockholders, periodic receipts from estates or trust funds; net income or loss from the rental of property, real estate, or farms, and net income or loss from roomers or boarders.

• *unemployment and workers' compensation and veterans' benefits* Includes income from unemployment compensation and workers' compensation, and veterans' payments including educational benefits, but excluding military retirement.

• *public assistance, supplemental security income, and food stamps* Includes public assistance or welfare, including money received from job training grants; supplemental security income paid by federal, state, and local welfare agencies to low-income persons who are aged 65 or older, blind, or disabled; and the value of food stamps obtained.

• *regular contributions for support* Includes alimony and child support as well as any regular contributions from persons outside the consumer unit.

• *other income* Includes money income from care of foster children, cash scholarships, fellowships, or stipends not based on working; and meals and rent as pay.

indexed spending The indexed spending figures compare the spending of each demographic segment with that of the average household. To compute an index, the amount spent on an item by a demographic segment is divided by the amount spent on the item by the average household. That figure is then multiplied by 100. An index of 100 is the average for all households. An index of 132 means average spending by households in a segment is 32 percent above average (100 plus 32). An index of 75 means average spending by households in a segment is 25 percent below average (100 minus 25). Indexed spending figures identify the consumer units that spend the most on a product or service.

life and other personal insurance Includes premiums from whole life and term insurance; endowments; income and other life insurance; mortgage guarantee insurance; mortgage life insurance; premiums for personal life liability, accident and disability; and other non-health insurance other than homes and vehicles.

market share The market share is the percentage of total household spending on an item that is accounted for by a demographic segment. Market shares are calculated by dividing a demographic segment's total spending on an item by the total spending of all households on the item. Total spending on an item for all households is calculated by multiplying average spending by the total number of households. Total spending on an item for each demographic segment is calculated by multiplying the segment's average spending by the number of households in the segment. Market shares reveal the demographic segments that account for the largest share of spending on a product or service.

pensions and Social Security Includes all Social Security contributions paid by employees; employees' contributions to railroad retirement, government retirement and private pensions programs; retirement programs for self-employed.

personal care Includes products for the hair, oral hygiene products, shaving needs, cosmetics and bath products, suntan lotions and hand creams, electric personal care appliances, incontinence products, other personal care products, personal care services such as hair care services (haircuts, bleaching, tinting, coloring, conditioning treatments, permanents, press, and curls), styling and other services for wigs and hairpieces, body massages or slenderizing treatments, facials, manicures, pedicures, shaves, electrolysis.

quarterly spending Quarterly spending data are collected in the interview portion of the Consumer Expenditure Survey. The quarterly spending tables show the percentage of households purchasing an item during an average quarter, and the amount spent during the quarter on the item by purchasers. Not all items are included in the interview portion of the Consumer Expenditure Survey. For more about the methodology of the Consumer Expenditure Survey, see Appendix A.

reading Includes subscriptions for newspapers, magazines, and books through book clubs; purchase of single-copy newspapers and magazines, books, and encyclopedias and other reference books.

reference person The first member mentioned by the respondent when asked to "Start with the name of the person or one of the persons who owns or rents the home." It is with respect to this person that the relationship of other consumer unit members is determined. Also called the householder or head of household.

shelter Includes the following:

• *owned dwellings* Includes interest on mortgages, property taxes and insurance, refinancing and pre-payment charges, ground rent, expenses for property management/security, homeowners' insurance, fire insurance and extended coverage, landscaping expenses for repairs and maintenance contracted out (including periodic maintenance and service contracts), and expenses of materials for owner-performed repairs and maintenance for dwellings used or maintained by the consumer unit, but not dwellings maintained for business or rent.

• *rented dwellings* Includes rent paid for dwellings, rent received as pay, parking fees, maintenance, and other expenses.

• *other lodging* Includes all expenses for vacation homes, school, college, hotels, motels, cottages, trailer camps, and other lodging while out of town.

• *utilities, fuels, and public services* Includes natural gas, electricity, fuel oil, coal, bottled gas, wood, and other fuels; residential telephone service; cell phone service; phone cards; water, garbage and trash collection; sewerage maintenance; septic tank cleaning; and other public services.

state and local income taxes Includes state and local income taxes withheld in the survey year to pay for income earned in survey year plus additional taxes paid in the survey year to cover any underpayment or under withholding of taxes in the year prior to the survey.

tobacco and smoking supplies Includes cigarettes, cigars, snuff, loose smoking tobacco, chewing tobacco, and smoking accessories such as cigarette or cigar holders, pipes, flints, lighters, pipe cleaners, and other smoking products and accessories.

transportation Includes the following:

• *vehicle purchases (net outlay)* Includes the net outlay (purchase price minus trade-in value) on new and used domestic and imported cars and trucks and other vehicles, including motorcycles and private planes.

• *gasoline and motor oil* Includes gasoline, diesel fuel, and motor oil.

• *other vehicle expenses* Includes vehicle finance charges, maintenance and repairs, vehicle insurance, and vehicle rental licenses and other charges.

• *vehicle finance charges* Includes the dollar amount of interest paid for a loan contracted for the purchase of vehicles described above.

• *maintenance and repairs* Includes tires, batteries, tubes, lubrication, filters, coolant, additives, brake and transmission fluids, oil change, brake adjustment and repair, front-end alignment, wheel balancing, steering repair, shock absorber replacement, clutch and transmission repair, electrical system repair, repair to cooling system, drive train repair, drive shaft and rear-end repair, tire repair, vehicle video equipment, other maintenance and services, and auto repair policies.

• *vehicle insurance* Includes the premium paid for insuring cars, trucks, and other vehicles.

• *vehicle rental, licenses, and other charges* Includes leased and rented cars, trucks, motorcycles, and aircraft, inspection fees, state and local registration, drivers' license fees, parking fees, towing charges, tolls on trips, and global positioning services.

• *public transportation* Includes fares for mass transit, buses, trains, airlines, taxis, private school buses, and fares paid on trips for trains, boats, taxis, buses, and trains.

weekly spending Weekly spending data are collected in the diary portion of the Consumer Expenditure Survey. The data show the percentage of households purchasing an item during an average week, and the amount spent per week on the item by purchasers. Not all items are included in the diary portion of the Consumer Expenditure Survey. For more about the methodology of the Consumer Expenditure Survey, see Appendix A.